EXPLORING THE ARTS WITH CHILDREN

EXPLORING THE ARTS WITH CHILDREN

Geraldine Dimondstein
California State University, Los Angeles

Macmillan Publishing Co., Inc.
New York

Collier Macmillan Publishers
London

Copyright © 1974, Geraldine Dimondstein

Printed in the United States of America

A portion of this material has been reprinted from *Children Dance in the
Classroom,* copyright © 1971 by Geraldine Dimondstein.

Macmillan Publishing Co., Inc.
866 Third Avenue, New York, New York 10022

Collier-Macmillan Canada, Ltd.

Library of Congress Cataloging in Publication Data

Dimondstein, Geraldine.
Exploring the arts with children.

Bibliography: p.

1. Art—Study and teaching (Elementary) 2. Perceptual learning. I. Title.
N350.D55   372.5'044   73-8488
ISBN 0-02-329910-X

Printing: 1 2 3 4 5 6 7 8   Year: 4 5 6 7 8 9 0

PREFACE

This book has taken form in the passionate belief that the arts have a necessary and vital function in educating children. Since the days of Dewey, American educators have insisted that there is some value in learning for its own sake, for self-realization in developing expressive, creative human beings. In reality, attention has been directed toward a very limited view of what constitutes knowledge within an educational experience.

The underlying premise here is that the arts are a way of knowing about the self as well as about the external world. Ideally, then, the arts in education should be an ongoing experience, beginning in early school and continuing through high school and college. The lack of priority reflects an approach to education in terms of disciplines (subject matter) rather than in terms of perception. But the creative force in children is not a neutral element in the classroom. If we as teachers are to seek it out and invite it in, we can no longer remain passive; we must be actively engaged in the art process. Our expectation is that children from their youngest years be encouraged to believe that their creative ideas and efforts have value and are worth exploring.

This book deals with painting, sculpture, dance, and poetry, to provide to teachers—and therefore to children—a variety of forms, for each one speaks through its own image. It is designed to help teachers free their own sensory perceptions—to give expression to their eyes, hands, bodies, voices, minds—so that they may enter freely into the teaching process as an energetic exchange between teacher and student. It is also intended to help a child explore the unlimited horizons of his imagination as student artist, sculptor, dancer, poet.

If the arts cannot be "taught," we can create the conditions under which they come into being by providing an appropriate atmosphere and by taking the arts seriously. All we are trying to do is to put a child in closer touch with his own feelings, to find an expressive language for those feelings through the forms of art, and to respect his efforts. Our concern for the education of feelings through the arts encompasses children of all ethnic groups, from inner city to suburbia, in the belief that meaningful art experiences should be effective in any classroom. What will vary will be the expressive content reflecting the cultural impact of any particular community. The conceptual approach offered here, it is hoped, both allows for and encourages diversity of responses.

The subject matter of art itself does not provide any clues to what might be deemed proper sequencing. Yet we do not want to perpetuate teaching in the arts as a series of fragmented "activities" having no continuity within themselves and no relationship to each other. For this reason, we have presented the arts within a conceptual framework of space–time–force, which act as both subjective and objective elements. Within this broad frame of reference, each art form is discussed in relation to four aspects: (1) definition and description, (2) distinguishing characteristics, (3) experiential approach, (4) art elements. This structure enables us to view the arts in terms of how they are unified and what makes them special.

Because the thrust of this approach is conceptual rather than prescriptive, each chapter devoted to a particular art form is meant to inform the teacher that the basic concepts within it are the generating sources from which learning experiences are developed. Out of these concepts, the book focuses on certain prototype learning experiences which characterize the essential qualities of each form. All the dialogue and notations are transcriptions of observed responses of children in different classroom situations and are intended to serve a dual purpose: to acquaint teachers with the diversity and variability of children's responses and to formulate a vocabulary emanating directly from the art experience itself. They are designed in terms of creative problem solving, which permits children to understand concepts, explore media, evoke images, and create expressive forms.

The exploration also demonstrates alternative modes of teaching, but the common denominator is conceptual. Because each art form has its own internal structure, there is no uniformity in relation to children's verbal responses or in the amount of time allotted to an experience. Nor is there any delineation of age levels, because we assume that each child copes with a problem in relation to his own experience and level of consciousness. Respecting the diversity of teaching styles and recognizing that no two groups of children are alike, the specifics of "how to do it" are not spelled out. Rather, each experience is defined by the initial statement of the problem so that a teacher may communicate both the context and the selected elements to be explored. The intent is not to reduce these suggested procedures to techniques that teachers and children must follow mechanically, but to present ideas that yield to adaptation and improvisation as each session unfolds.

The prototype lessons on painting and sculpture suggest certain references, but other books may be used in working with a particular concept. The purpose is not to conduct a historical survey or to make judgments as to which are "masterpieces." Much can be learned from viewing historical and contemporary work if we understand that we are dealing with adult sensibilities in relation to possibilities and standards. Our concern, however, is to present materials that relate to the expressive content of children's forms. The author's experience in introducing this procedure to college students and teachers not sophisticated in the arts is that they produce work of artistic merit with children.

The type of material described here is not a "method" or a system; it is an attitude, an approach, a construct which attaches great importance to teaching in the arts but is also concerned with developing children's aesthetic sensibility. It is the organization of ideas and the sensitivity of a teacher which make such growth possible. The book makes no attempt to be comprehensive in the sense of including all current philosophical outlooks or all possible forms or media, such as photography, assemblage, or graphics in the visual arts—or music, drama, or prose. The import of the conceptual design presented here is that it may serve as a model and be flexible enough to incorporate new media, new forms, and new perceptions that are constantly coming into being.

G. D.

ACKNOWLEDGMENTS

To those who have shared my interest in the importance of the arts in education and who in various ways have supported my efforts in writing this book, my gratitude and acknowledgments:

The teachers across the country whose innovative work with children from nursery school through sixth grade provides some of the rich material recorded here; particularly Janet Kroll, for her inspired poetry making, and Selma Moskowitz, for generously permitting me to observe and photograph her classes in the visual arts.

Cleo Trumbo, photographer, who brings a sensitive and perceptive eye in capturing children's behavior and the products of their artistic expression.

Freda Maddow, dancer and musician, who read the chapter on dance, as well as other chapters, and provided helpful criticism.

Ben Maddow, poet and writer, whose suggestions, both poetic and literary, gave clarity to the chapter on poetry.

Professor Ronald Silverman, colleague in the Art Department at California State University, Los Angeles, for his careful, constructive, and aesthetic criticism in reading the manuscript.

My husband, Morton Dimondstein, painter and sculptor, whose continued encouragement and intellectual stimulation helped this book come to fruition.

G. D.

CONTENTS

LEARNING
THROUGH
THE ARTS

1
KNOWING AND FEELING

The contemporary child lives in an environment of uncomprehended facts, imposed meanings, and prejudged values. In both school and society, his world is a confusion of seemingly unrelated events far removed from himself as the center. Of all the social forces to which he is subject, education is perhaps the most compelling; its unique function is to help him to know how to select, evaluate, and relate what he considers essential to a feeling of wholeness. To do this he needs experience in forming synthesized ideas and patterns.

We are concerned here with those meanings that enhance a child's self-awareness which are expressed through his potential for image making. The focus is on the ways in which a child organizes and expresses his responses to his experiences through involvement in the arts. The school can provide this focus because it can present artistic experiences in a context that is not otherwise available.

The arts can help a child look inward, in the sense that he is put in closer touch with his own feelings; and they can help him look outward, in the sense that they open new windows on the world and enable him to perceive his world more richly. Thus, the arts have a twofold purpose: communion with self and communication with others. They communicate through forms which are not expressed in conventional language but each speaks through its own image. The experience is one of subjective attitudes directed toward and affected by real objects or events. The result of this "inward–outward" relationship is that it allows a child to grasp those aspects of experience that he feels are significant and to re-create them in visual, aural, tactile, and kinesthetic forms.

3

Such experience can be open to children only if teachers understand the arts as having values inherent in themselves and not as a means of achieving other educational or social goals. Nor can they be regarded as tools or techniques that mechanically open the windows of perception. Although they may affect learning in other areas, there is no guarantee, for example, that awareness of left–right relationships in dance will enhance reading, or that creating shapes on a surface will assure a better understanding of mathematical concepts of measurement. Any such transference, however, is to be observed and eagerly accepted. Learning in the arts does affect a child's openness to experience—to an exciting anticipation of possibilities he can make come into being. It is conceivable, therefore, that this may affect his learning in other areas.

CONTRIBUTION OF THE ARTS TO EDUCATION

The contribution that the arts make is found in two of their most important functions—the way they enhance knowing and the way they give form to feelings. For young children in the early and elementary phase of schooling, the arts are defined as those modes of expression in which perception and feeling are interrelated to create selected experiences in tangible, symbolic forms. They are the means through which children give order to qualities of sense and form by coalescing feelings, moods, and ideas with sensory perceptions. What is unique to the arts is that they permit a child not only to perceive and experience feelings, but to gain an understanding of those perceptions as they are expressed in concrete forms. This means that a child involved in the arts not only must feel the inward meaning of things, but must find a way to express or document his feelings. The *process* is a transformation of each child's personal imagination; therefore the forms he creates go beyond mere representational images or imitations of what already exists. The *product* is the material reflection of this symbolic transformation.

A definition embracing process and product makes it possible to go beyond the question of what art is and ask what the characteristics and conditions are under which it comes into being. Within the context of the classroom, it enables us to describe those conditions where children acquire new attitudes and feelings. It is hoped that the results will be to help them enjoy their own creative efforts and to find deeper meanings about themselves through the arts.

Meanings come to a child through two main sources—knowledge, as cognition, conveyed through discursive, conventional language (logical, deductive modes of thought), and emotion, expressed through nondiscursive language (intuitive, inductive thinking). This does not imply a dichotomy, for a sound approach to learning must include not only intellectual and rational but sensory and emotional aspects as well.

Unfortunately, it is not uncommon in education for areas of learning designated as "subject matter" to be arbitrarily assigned to one domain or the other. Math, science, reading, for example, are assumed to be indisputably cognitive. The arts, viewed as "activities," are deemed purely affective and are used to fill time not given to more "serious" pursuits. An approach to knowledge which draws a dichotomy between intuition and reason, emotion and intellect, sensing and doing, tends to separate a child from himself and from his immediate environment. What seems necessary is a more comprehensive view of the way cognition and affect function in the learning process, particularly in relation to the arts.

Although rigid designations of knowledge as subject matter are not always desirable (e.g., do we learn to read or read to learn?), the arts have a seriousness of purpose and mode of inquiry which have an important place in the educational process. As such, they must not be regarded as activities in terms of projects or disconnected units, but as experiences in the sense of encountering, undergoing, "living-through." Lacking this recognition, there is a wide gap between the way teachers perceive the "doing" of art and the "knowing" of art as a conceptual body of material. There are basic concepts about the arts, just as there are fundamental ideas about math and science which help to make subject matter comprehensible. The difference is that the arts are not conventional subject matter. Taken singly or together, they do not present one mass of material to be "covered" in a given amount of time; learning cannot be divided into units, for it does not follow a logical, sequential progression, and evaluations of what has been learned demand different criteria. But there is "knowledge" to be learned. The end product of that knowledge is not more facts about the objective world, but deeper feelings about the self. The "subject" is the individual; the "matter" is the education of feelings and the development of sensibility.

The Arts as Knowing

To separate the arts from other spheres of experience which produce knowledge reflects a misunderstanding of the nature of cognition and denies that artistic knowing differs significantly from other areas of learning. As a function of the whole child, knowledge is considered here as a process that begins in the senses, involves intelligence, and is charged with emotion.

Traditional educational practice equates cognition with "knowing about" a subject rather than with how it may relate to a child's perceptions and needs. When no recognition is given to the affects as well as to the effects of learning, cognition becomes the end product. Yet we know from observing children in all their complexity that this is an unproductive goal, for knowing something "in the head" does not guarantee commensurate action. We also know from psychology that cognition which functions as intelligence, learning, or memory cannot be dealt with apart from the affective elements of wishes, needs, and attitudes.

Cognition alone cannot wholly influence behavior, because behavior includes both objective and subjective elements. In any learning situation it is these elements that make the difference between *knowing about* something and *knowing* it through the senses. It is the difference, for example, between *knowing about* a snowstorm—the objective conditions of how snow is produced, the degree of temperature, warm and cold air currents, condensations, and so on, and *experiencing* a snowstorm—the weight, texture, wetness, shapes. Both experiences produce knowledge but they differ qualitatively. It is in the perception of qualities that the arts reveal their unique mode of knowing.

Cognition in the arts differs from intelligence, which is commonly accepted as logical, rational thinking; it is a mode of thought concerned with the qualitative and sensuous aspects of experience. By qualities we do not mean media such as paint, clay, words, movements, sounds, for these are the "raw materials." We are referring to sensuous elements produced by a particular medium, such as shape, line, color, texture. Using sensory data in any art form is much more than the recording of simple facts. The challenge is not one of accurately reproducing what has been seen, felt, touched, experienced, but of creating a new reality by transforming sensory impressions into sensuous forms. Such transformation can only come about through a child's perceptual awareness of what actually "touches" or "moves" him through the senses. To recall an earlier metaphor, it is like looking through a window framed by one's prior and current perceptions rather than just looking into a mirror.

Thus, knowing in the arts is not concerned with the facts of the matter—that is, sky is blue, grass is green, sun is yellow—but with how qualities of "blueness," "greenness," "yellowness," can be used to express and communicate feelings which may relate to facts. The difference in response to the question, "what do you see in the spring?" may be seen in a logical statement, "Spring is one of the seasons of the year when there are many changes in color," and in the poetic images of two nine-year-olds:

> White bells have fallen
> They sunk way down
> Into earth
> Leafy fingers drop
>
> Purple flowered hills
> Nature spilled
> Her paint can

Just as we accept thinking in terms of mathematical symbols or scientific constructs, so must we understand thinking as an expression of relations of qualities. It calls forth a qualitative kind of intelligence, a concept first formulated by Dewey, who wrote,

> Any idea that ignores the necessary role of intelligence in production of art works is based upon identification of thinking with use of one special kind of material, verbal signs or words. To think effectively in terms of relations of qualities is as severe a demand upon thought as to think in terms of symbols, verbal, and mathematical. . . .[1]

We may describe the art process as creative problem solving. This is not to be confused with merely "manipulating media" (although it is a necessary beginning), and departs from the notion of arts as crafts. The distinction, simply stated, is that in crafts, message is the massage, whereas in the arts, the medium is neither message nor massage. A crafts approach has been outmoded by what we know of the functions of art. Art is involved with ideas; it is a creation of the

[1] John Dewey, *Art as Experience* (New York: Minton, Balch, 1934), p. 46.

mind as well as the hand. The art experience requires that a child respond to problems with a kind of intelligence that guides him in searching for qualities that give expressive force to whatever form he is engaged in—in music or dance, the dynamics of tempo; in sculpture, the plasticity of a shape; in poetry, the vividness of a word picture. In "playing with qualities," a child is combining his emotional, expressive needs with sensuous elements to produce forms that hold some artistic meaning for him.

In the process of "doing," a child's thoughts are continuously directed toward the reordering of further qualities, which is perhaps a more appropriate description of terms such as "refinement of skills" or "more sophisticated" solutions. To view "thinking" and "doing" in relation to qualities raises another frequently misunderstood notion that knowledge in the arts can be equated with skills. Even in the early years of schooling, where the approach to learning is usually more flexible, the arts are referred to as skills by academicians and teachers alike. This misconception is twofold: that once certain skills are achieved, knowledge is automatically enhanced, and that one skill must be mastered before another is learned. (An outgrowth of the latter is that certain experiences should be delayed until the appropriate skills are learned.)

Both assumptions rest on the false idea that there is a sharp division between learning necessary skills and using them in creative activities. To adopt this approach in teaching is to separate method from content—the "how to do it" from the "what to do." The effects often appear in other areas, such as reading, where we may teach a child to acquire certain reading skills, although he may not understand what he has read. We must find a conceptual way to overcome the drift toward reducing the arts to a system of measurable skills.

An approach more in keeping with what we know of how children learn is that their creative potentialities need to be developed simultaneously with their skill in the medium. Skill in the arts requires a control of the senses differing from that required for task-oriented activities. The body in dance is not used in the same way as it is in sports or gymnastics; a line in painting does not have to "work" as in a blueprint; the expressiveness of a poem does not depend upon correct spelling or proper grammar. Moreover, the ability to execute a movement, draw a straight line, shape clay, or make words rhyme does not indicate knowledge of an art form. In the making or teaching of the arts, skills have validity only when they grow out of the expressive needs of a child. They function when there is a gap between the intellectual or emotional grasp of a problem and its intended solution. Needs differ according to each child's perception and sensibility as weighed against his intent and capacity. Skills, then, become the means through which he grapples subjectively with the qualitative elements of an art form to shape a personal statement.

Creative problem solving calls upon a child to bring something into being that for him did not formerly exist, and for which there is no predetermined end. It can best be understood as an open-ended process of problem–solution–problem. The intial problem may be "given" by a teacher to illuminate a concept, such as how space changes its function when used in dance, painting, or sculpture. Or it may be formulated by a child himself, but in either case the search for solutions evokes new problems. Whether a child is shaping pictorial space in painting, displacing actual space in sculpture, or creating kinesthetic space in dance, he is using qualitative means for achieving qualitative ends.

The path toward solutions, however, is not a neat progression of steps but follows a zigzag pattern of starting and stopping, hesitating and pursuing, reflecting and refining. Nor are the sources for becoming initially involved always clearly evident. A child may begin with a particular quality, such as the tension of one volume against another, the vividness of a "warm" color against a cool, or the sensation of one body pushing or pulling against another. Or he may begin with a specific idea and select those qualities which most forcefully project or symbolize that idea.

Qualitative intelligence ultimately involves decision making—solving given problems, setting new ones, seeking alternative solutions, selecting and rejecting qualities on the basis of what feels "right" to him according to the direction he is taking at that moment. It serves him in becoming creator–performer–critic of his own work, and in making qualitative rather than moral judgments about the creative efforts of others. But knowing in the arts does not exist without feeling. The entire process not only depends upon a child's ability to reorganize his perceptions in formal relationships, but includes continuous reintegration and refinement of emotions.

The Arts as Feeling

It is only through a direct encounter with the arts that children grasp the importance of emotions in the organized expression of feelings that might otherwise remain dormant. The arts are central in meeting a child's needs to organize and interpret his experiences, to control his emotional responses, and to help him toward *self-discovery* rather than the familiar self-expression. The means of such discovery are through intelligence that is qualitative and through emotions that are controlled. The ends lie in the development of sensibility toward the objects and events in one's experience, and in a greater consciousness of one's self.

Although not a newly professed goal in education, an emphasis upon knowing oneself is central to the arts. It is knowledge that reveals to a child his inner feelings, not only about himself but about people and phenomena around him. Such feelings become known to him through a growing awareness of his attitudes and emotions, which speak to him through forms he alone symbolizes and conceives. It is because the arts reveal the unique and very particular nature of each child that the focus is not on *what* he is as one of many, but on *who* he is as one of a kind. Although the arts exist within the social environment of the classroom, and forms such as dance and poetry may be group endeavors, we must recognize that it is always an individual child who is engaged in the experience and that experience is ultimately personal.

The arts touch children at various levels of understanding and involvement, just as different media hold special appeal for different children. In any instance, children deal with some kind of content as the subject of their creative efforts.

but the point of reference is always the self. Whether the content derives from real or imagined sources, we find an attitude revealed. The apparent subject may be the force of the wind in dance, a figure of "mother earth" in painting, a nameless creature in sculpture, the evanescence of a cloud in poetry, but the ultimate subject is the individual. It is his perceptions and responses expressed not in terms of a "story line" or "telling it like it really is," but as a symbolic composition of his own feelings. The intrinsic nature of the art experience is that in the process of creating images, he is creating his own world. In transforming his feelings into tangible forms, he is grappling with his emotional self.

CONCEPT OF SELF

Modern psychological theory treats the self as having two meanings: *self as object*—as an individual's feelings and awareness of himself as the focal point of identification in the external world; and *self as process*—as an acting, experiencing self dealing with his immediate world in time–space. Seen as a unity, the self functions as a kind of screening process for the whole perceiving, learning, remembering, responding behavior of the individual. Everything we know about the dynamics of growth shows that action or expression is the means by which a child conceptualizes and gains control of himself and his environment. Everything we have observed about children indicates that expressiveness is central to their being. Thus, the arts are the language of human experience.

Whether or not we believe that children have a conscious need to document themselves, it is clear that without some type of structure their energies and emotions become diffuse and uncontrolled. The self provides a frame of reference through which selected aspects of the external world are perceived, judged, and acted upon. Although this applies to behavior generally, it is even more characteristic of involvement in the arts, where the self acts as both subject and object.

The arts, then, may be considered as a mode of action as well as one of inquiry. And it is the emotions initiating the flow of energy that gives vitality to creative expression. We suggest that art "happens" when the "right" amount of vitality blends with the "right" amount of formality. Through artistic experience children use their energies to gain control of their feelings (subject), which are, in effect, the essence of the aesthetic meanings of that experience (object). Involvement in the various arts presents a child with different ways of using his senses to perceive his immediate world and to clarify his own position within it. At the same time, it opens to him new ways of feeling and responding which nurture and enrich his concept of self.

SELF-EXPRESSION VERSUS CREATIVE EXPRESSION

When we speak of emotional expression as leading to a greater consciousness of self, we need to examine the conditions of this expression in relation to the arts. Although emotions are the generating force, the function of the arts in education is not emotional adjustment, nor is it therapy or catharsis. Confusion as to the role of emotions has led to a kind of mystique about creativity which equates self-expression with creative effort. As a consequence, the arts have been viewed as an "outlet" for self-expression, with little recognition of their aesthetic values. To draw a distinction suggests that the emotions function in two ways: as *self-expression,* which is giving *vent* to feelings that may be random or uncontrolled and reflect the way a child feels at the moment; and *artistic expression,* which is giving *form* to feelings that are either evoked or controlled in relation to the sensuous qualities of a medium, the organization of materials, and response to the subject.

For example, a child in a flush of exuberance who pounds clay for the sake of the sound or the sense of his own strength is giving vent to feelings, but if he pounds as a means of exploring shapes and feeling the tactility of the clay, he is giving form to feelings by producing an object that reflects his explorations. Seen in another medium, a child in a fit of rage who flails his arms and legs in striking, slashing gestures is giving vent to his emotions; but if he uses these gestures of anger in exploring percussive movement in a dance problem, he is not only giving expression to feelings but to the experience of those feelings.

In venting feelings, a child's behavior expresses his immediate emotional state, whether he is distressed, angry, sad, or happy. Although these are important to a teacher in making diagnoses about a child's personality, they are of little aesthetic interest. An amusing but very apt example is offered by Suzanne Langer, "Self-expression does not require composition or lucidity; a screaming baby gives his feelings more release than any musician, but we don't go into a concert hall to hear a baby scream; in fact, if that baby is brought in, we are likely to go out." [2] The inference is that human expression may be completely devoid of formal arrangement, and it is this lack of coherence which takes it out of the realm of art.

If self-expression is seen as the aim, we are equating art with therapy and the focus is totally *child-centered.* In this case, only the child can judge the value of his products. But the relation of the arts to feeling is subtler than sheer catharsis. It is possible to consider the emotional aspects of artistic work as something integral to it, as objective as the physical forms of color, line, rhythm, patterns, and so on. Thus, although feelings are subjective, in the arts they become objective in that they not only are aroused and emitted, but are transformed into images.

Although the arts are expressive, they cannot be expressed without being formed, and each medium has its own formative process. In any artistic effort emotions are abstracted from a whole range of feelings and are conceived and created as forms which take on a life of their own. It is in this sense that the arts may also be considered as *content-centered.* This means that we can find values in a piece of artwork apart from the child who produces it. With this approach we have two sources for making judgments: what we know about a child in terms of his own expectations and values and what we perceive of the relations of qualities within the work itself.

Those who look upon the arts as a vehicle for the release of emotions tend to regard self-expression as a passive, projective outpouring of what is felt inside. On the contrary, artistic expression requires an active, disciplined concentration

[2] Suzanne K. Langer, *Problems of Art* (New York: Scribner, 1957), p. 25.

of a child's organizing powers which he brings to bear upon the expression that he embodies in a given form. The difference can be seen not only in process but in results. The results of self-expression are symptoms or feeling states; the results of artistic expression are symbols of feelings, or feeling-images. Langer expresses this eloquently when she writes, "a work of art expresses a concept of life, emotion, inward reality. But it is neither a confessional nor a frozen tantrum; it is a developed metaphor, a non-discursive symbol that articulates what is verbally ineffable, the logic of consciousness itself." [3]

Although children express their emotions directly and honestly, artistic expression does not emerge from actual emotional states. It draws upon remembered or imagined feelings. This is because the forms of a particular feeling in everyday life are never expressed completely except as a memory, for it never fully exists at one time. That feelings are abstracted and transformed in the reporting and recording of experiences may be observed not only in the arts but in common occurrences.

If, for example, a child has an accident on the playground such as falling off a piece of equipment or being hit by an object, he responds immediately and explosively. He may wail and scream or cry silently, but at that moment he will let all his feelings out. Later, in relating that experience to a teacher or a parent, he will not recount every nuance of feeling any more than he can give a minute-by-minute description of what happened. In the process of translating events, he selects only those aspects that have emotional or factual import. In this sense he is acting as a poet, for to make that experience coherent in the telling, he must objectify and give some order to his feelings. It is in examining feelings that they become objectified. They are then no longer random or subjective but are expressed in a new form. Perceiving, feeling, expressing are ingredients of all behavior. The arts, however, require not only self-expression but self-control. This does not mean that the arts involve only purposefully controlled action, for many artistic efforts emerge as "happy accidents" in the process of exploration. What is required is an inner discipline which each child, according to his level of awareness and experience, brings to his emotions as well as his intellect.

The conditions unique to the arts through which feelings are given form point to a further distinction between self-expression and artistic expression. It is the difference between *having* a feeling such as being lonely and *giving expression* to a feeling called loneliness. If a child wishes to convey a feeling of loneliness or solitude and he actually feels that way, he may find it difficult to rise above that feeling to give it objective expression. On the other hand, a teacher setting a mood situation for poetry might suggest that he *imagine* feeling all alone, even though someone else is near. Under these conditions, he may recall an emotion he has experienced before and respond to that emotion through the mood quality of his words, as in the poem on p. 12 by a ten-year-old child.

Emphasizing the expressiveness of a particular art form rather than a literal idea also reveals the nature of feeling. In the poem on p. 12, for example, we are not concerned with the truthfulness of the idea but with the emotional content

[3] Ibid., p. 26.

Marie

alone

Empty.

in darkness,

No feeling

standing in one

corner, afraid.

alone

a world of

your own.

expanded by two images seemingly so unrelated. In the process of composing an image, it is unnecessary that the child feel isolated or that he stand in a corner. What is important is that in forming the poem he is able to examine his feelings, and in this case the very meagerness of language gives the poem impact.

IMAGINING VERSUS PRETENDING

The importance of the arts is that they call forth a child's imaginable feelings and emotions from his most personal, inner life. But imagination is neither pretending nor daydreaming. Pretending implies simulating an experience. Requiring make-believe removes both the experience and the emotion from the child who is really the subject. The difference in approach between pretending and imagining may be reflected simply in the way a problem is stated, such as, "Pretend you are a pussycat," or, "How does a pussycat move?" Children do not respond in depth when called upon to pretend to be or make something. On the other hand, imagination is the capacity to think in terms of the possible—that is, to entertain incongruous possibilities of what may be. Thus, it is not pretending which inspires expression; it is sense of being. Daydreaming, which is different from pretending, is an imagined experience eliciting emotions a child would have in a similar situation in real life. In daydreams or fantasy, feelings are evoked; in the arts, they are transformed, shaped, and take on added meanings.

We may speak of emotion as the way an experience feels. Although it is possible to identify certain specific emotions such as anger, love, joy, or fear, children experience and express in their work many feelings too fleeting or ephemeral to be given names. Feelings range from *sensations,* which are physical responses to sensory elements such as "feeling" colors, sounds, movements, to *sensibility,* which is a disposition toward an awareness and responsiveness to the senuous qualities of experience. Children have experiences which are "knowable" but do not lend themselves to verbal description. It is these nameless feelings as well as emotions, attitudes, and moods that we have referred to as the subjective or inner life. All these elements act as a compelling force in pushing a child to grasp an idea that moves him toward the solution of a problem, whether it be designing a movement in dance, creating a color relationship in painting, shaping a space in sculpture, or finding emotionally toned words in poetry.

Although the arts speak through the language of feelings, naming a feeling does not necessarily give a piece of work its validity. Artistic meaning does not derive from literal interpretations, nor is it communicated through conventional language. It is abstracted from everyday experience and presented symbolically. For example, in exploring the problem, "How round is round?" whether as a body shape in dance, the direction of a line in painting, or curved planes in sculpture, a child would abstract all the experiences he has had with roundness, using himself as the center of reference. As he can never show all of his experiences at once, however, he must choose and simplify significant aspects of those experiences and find ways of objectifying them.

Thus, knowing and feeling in the arts is a mutually affecting and integrative process, for it is difficult to see how feelings and emotions could exist independently of thoughts. The art process involves not simply part of a child, but a total pattern of behavior which we may call "imaging behavior." It is through this kind of expression that a child's world becomes filled with images and symbols. If, however, his world does not open possibilities for him to stretch his imagination, he lacks the means of expressing his thoughts and feelings. Although each art form speaks through its own image, all contribute to the creation of a child's expressive self. Imaging, then, serves a double purpose: by constructing images in media and mixtures of media through color, shape, line, movement, sounds, words, a child *shapes his unique world;* by becoming sensitive and responding to sensory experiences he *discovers an image of himself.* Children generate their own images by becoming involved in the learnings inherent in the creative process. As a departure from the traditional view that learning is being told what happened or what should happen, engagement in the creative process reveals that learning is a happening in itself.

2
CREATING AND EXPRESSING

In its broadest sense creativity involves the capacity to be open to experience, to welcome novelty, to be intrigued by discovery, and to exercise new dimensions of imaginative thought. In the arts it is a means by which children externalize their ideas, emotions, and feelings not only through utilizing physical media but through creating shaped, expressive forms. It is a subtle and complex process of feeling and knowing which evolves from the constant flow of experience with sensuous qualities. Out of such an encounter, new knowledge is combined with energy and emotions to bring forth new forms of expression.

The Creative Process

The creative process begins with individual discovery. Children use both conscious and unconscious efforts in dealing with feelings and ideas which need to come to realization in producing desired forms of expression. Whether a particular act has been done before is of no consequence. For each child it is a completely personalized process beginning with his own perceptions, the nature of the experience, and his level of awareness at any given time. It is personal in the sense that realizing one's experience in a qualitative way means that a vital confrontation has occurred between a child, his perceptions, and his understanding of what his senses communicate to him. It is more than being casually aware

15

of the sense data of everyday living. It is an active "flashing on" to a range and nuance of meanings in a particular situation, whether it is observations made on a walk around the school, sensing the "heavy" elements of a suffocating smog, a graying rain, a scintillating sunlight, or such detailed perceptions as a child may make. It is also objective in the sense that a child expresses his experience, transformed through media, in imaginatively new ways in a form he has created.

LEVELS OF FEELING

In the arts children "know" and "feel" mainly through the senses. They are the organs through which children participate directly in the ongoingness of the world around them. As used here, *sense* embraces a wide range of responses, including *sensory, sensitive, sensible,* and ultimately *sensuous.* A *sensory response* is the initial physical and emotional awareness of material qualities—that is, colors, sounds, shapes, rhythms, lines. Each child receives sensory impressions from the outside world and seeks his own expression through meanings he reconstructs from objects and events to which he relates. Children develop *sensitivity* by responding to the meaning of things presented in an immediate experience, such as the "purpleness" of a sunset, the stridency of a sound, the cadence of words, the sharpness of a movement, or the shapefulness of a hole.

It seems obvious that a child could not begin to be imaginative if he were not capable of being stimulated or excited by sensory qualities around him. In attending to the immediate qualities of an experience, sensitivity is enhanced because children are presented not only with the appearance of things, but with possibilities for discovering new meanings embodied within them. By *sensibility* we are referring to a more intense response to the aesthetic and emotional qualities of experience. In poetry making, for example, children become aware of fundamental sensations such as rhythm, cadence, inflection, intonation, sound; in dance, dynamics, tensions, flow of different combinations of movement; in painting and sculpture, the qualitative effects of shapes, volumes, planes, textures, lines. All of these may be termed *sensuous characteristics* because they induce or depend upon sensations. Involvement in the various arts encourages a child to turn his attention to sensations and to become *consciously aware* of the perceptual responses that he makes to those sensations.

In exploring the sensory data around him a child begins to build an individually ordered conception of his world. The importance of the art encounter is that it offers an openness to sensuous experience. That is, a child who charges his own senses with the expressive force of dance, the visual impact of painting and sculpture, the sounds and rhythms of poetry, is moving beyond the conventional bounds of experience. He is, in both a practical and symbolic sense, extending the horizons of his perceptions and enlarging his capacity for more experience. Is in cultivating an awareness of his feelings that he gradually moves toward becoming a *sensuously responsive* human being.

Philosophers and psychologists have attempted to define discrete steps in the process of a creative act, but children's performance shows little evidence of a consistent progression. In keeping with their general pattern of growth and development, the path is zig-zag, with crests and plateaus, rather than sequential.

Dewey's observation that "creativity involves continuous reintegration of experiences with alternating periods of fallowness or incubation and expression" [1] is pertinent here. The whole picture of a child, his growth process and his expression, is larger and more complex than the summation of a series of steps or parts. As children go through overlapping phases of development, so may the creative process be viewed as a continuum, ranging from routine associations through the beginning of reorganization or innovation, to a highly creative effort resulting in deeper meanings or experience. Yet we may consider three general phases which appear to be characteristic of artistic action.

ARTISTIC EXPRESSION

First, as has been suggested, there must be a receptiveness to sense data—something that piques or excites a child's emotional being, sometimes even producing indefinable physical or psychological reactions; second, the perceptions of such material qualities must be charged with some feeling or emotion that stimulates the organization of these perceptions into shapes and patterns—that is, something must affect him strongly enough so that he feels he has something to say (metaphorically); third, the organization of his perceptions must correspond with his underlying state of emotion or feeling to produce an externalized symbolic form—that is, he must find the means to relate how he feels with what he feels through forms which best express it. In this process emotion or feeling is both the connective tissue and the motive force. What finally results depends upon everything that has happened in integrating sensuous responses with objective forms.

CONDITIONS FOR ARTISTIC EXPRESSION

Although we cannot identify steps in a creative act, we can, within an educational context, describe certain conditions which may enhance or inhibit its production. We must understand, however, that the search to relate internal responses to external phenomena is very much a trial and error process. In the production of any art form, therefore, anything must be entertained as a possibility. A child is not fully engaged in the creative process unless he can take advantage of the many accidental happenings that occur as he explores solutions. He must feel free to experiment, to pursue seemingly unproductive ends to discover for himself that certain directions are unproductive, and, in general, to function in an atmosphere giving play to his intuitive impulses.

Children who feel constrained, either because of rigid impositions by a teacher or by society's precast images of what is "art," find it difficult to cope with their own shifting ideas and responses. If they cannot adapt to the ever-changing experience of the creative process, they tend to resort to stereotyped patterns. We see this in children who repeat the same forms over and over regardless of how a problem is defined, or who attempt to imitate conventional images projected through TV, movies, magazines, or commercial slogans.

It is not a question of suppressing a child when his initial responses reflect

[1] John Dewey, *Art as Experience* (New York: Minton, Balch, 1934), p. 72.

stereotyped images—for example, the familiar blue skyline, green baseline, lolly-pop trees in painting; the snakes, Easter baskets, handprints in sculpture; the fluttery "ballet" gestures in dance; the stultified rhyming in poetry. We begin from where a child is and we can only know that by taking an attentive attitude and making thoughtful observations. In the early phases of the process children must be permitted to explore and have open experiences. At the same time, a teacher's educated judgment can open children's perceptions to the richer more expansive qualities of their own creative efforts. This is the most delicate and sensitive role of the teacher in the arts. It is she who can present, progressively but not necessarily sequentially, interesting problems which excite children to push beyond their immediate responses.

We are dealing with a seemingly "touch and go" process, and if the development of sensibility is faltering and hesistant, this is to be expected. What is not acceptable over long periods of time are stereotypes that simply reinforce a child's notion of what is "safe" to make, or what will be acknowledged by adults as "real." John Holt's premise of why children fail has relevance for the arts when he comments that children learn what teachers want them to learn instead of learning that is inherently for themselves.

Openness to the Unpredictable. An essential condition of the creative process, then, is an openness to modes of exploration that depart from the provable and predictable. Given this condition, we must be sensitive in judging the handling of materials as merely physical skills or manipulatory steps. Although a child must continuously adapt his expression to the medium he is using, he must also be flexible in dealing with inchoate ideas which emerge as the process unfolds. As he becomes more deeply involved in searching out the qualitative aspects of a particular art form, he is better able to "feel" or "sense" relationships. The challenge lies in actually transforming his newly felt sensory perceptions into symbolic images. "Knowing" comes to him not by logically analyzing "how he did it," but by experiencing a feeling of having shaped something to completion, even if it brings him only momentary satisfaction.

The conditions that release children from stereotyped responses are the very ones that foster spontaneity, which is intrinsic to creative effort. Children show spontaneous behavior without instruction. They chant, gallop, draw, paint, use words in their own way, and these are useful beginnings in developing a feeling for creative expression. But as unlearned as these responses appear to be, we must recognize that all expression has its base in experience. Although there is not always a direct relationship to an existing situation, spontaneity cannot be explained in terms of unlearned or unformed responses. There is an immediacy about spontaneous action that is part of its expressiveness, but it is expressive to the extent that it draws from past experience and connects with something in the present.

Spontaneity Based on Knowing. Spontaneity does not occur in a vacuum, but emerges from a heightened awareness of sensory data which provides sources of feelings and ideas. Yet children do not automatically respond to such data unless their own senses are attuned and sharpened. They clarify what they perceive by responding in some physical way to what they see, hear, touch, or feel.

And it is through the arts that they are able to give tangible form to such perceptions. Young children do experience freshly and produce spontaneously derived symbols. Such efforts are not as readily forthcoming, however, as some educators hope when they take the position, "just give children materials and they will create." Translated to classroom procedure, this implies that it is a reasonable if not rewarding expectation for teachers simply to play a record and let children "dance," dole out clay and allow them to "sculpt," or put out pigments and presume they will paint.

Spontaneity is not merely a random outpouring of creative energy, for children have to search beyond the impulse of the moment. It is shaped by involvement in the art experience, in the nature of the problems through which it is generated and released. In order for spontaneity to be educative, children must be offered a structure. From the teacher it means providing a motivating environment and a comprehensible vocabulary so that children have a frame of reference within which they can sort out their ideas and feelings and find their own sense of order. From the child it requires a willingness to commit himself to an unpredictable process of transforming feelings into forms. Only under these conditions can he create symbols and images which adequately express his thoughts and emotions.

Experience, then, is the objective condition, yet there are also subjective factors which allow for one child to be spontaneous while another is not. It is generally agreed that each child reflects his own unique inherited characteristics and his own particular set of experiences which together shape his personality. But if experience is the source of expression, it is also the basis of an individual's understanding and interpretation. We may assume, therefore, that all children may benefit from a broad scope of experiences in the various arts which call upon their "imaging" powers and allows them to put together new combinations of ideas.

Diversity of Experience. Within the domain of the classroom we can offer children rich and diverse experiences which open possibilities for creative expression. The conditions of the creative process are such that each child must evolve his work in terms of a special quality that is not part of any other person. His choice of movements, colors, lines, shapes, words cannot always be articulated or "explained." For example, leaping in the air produces a feeling of exhilaration but it may not be identifiable beyond that sensation. Such choices depend on qualities having a feeling of "rightness" or "completeness" which come from within the child and are projected to the forms with which he is working. Whatever aesthetic judgments he makes must be seen as responses developed through the experience he brings to the moment of decision making. The process, of which he is not consciously aware, is one of inspiration–creation–contemplation–judgment and is repeated again and again. It is this continuous choosing–judging–interpreting that makes a child both a performer and a critic.

Terms such as *creative* or *aesthetic* in relation to young children are meant to convey the processes of "doing" or "making" integrated with those of perceiving, appreciating, enjoying. A child's creative efforts hold little meaning for him other than another "doing" activity unless recognition comes by means of aesthetic perception, which is in itself a creative act. In order for an aesthetic experience to become internalized into the life of a child, therefore, he must become *consciously aware* of his own efforts in forming his new perceptions.

OBSERVABLE BEHAVIORS

Because this process is complex and illusory, the difficulty arises in observing and making children aware of how their creative efforts become manifest. In the most obvious way, they take on tangible forms through the products created; in a more subtle way, they are expressed through certain observable behaviors.

Emotional Involvement.   The underlying condition is *emotional involvement,* which is the extent to which a child is engaged or immersed in what he is doing. To the outside eye, children are "enjoying" themselves when they are "busy." To a conscious teacher, a child is enjoying what he is doing when he is captured by a problem. The intensity of his involvement is an indicator to her, for a high level is reflected by behavior directed toward the creative demands of a problem. Although intense involvement does not always guarantee artistic results, creative behavior is always accompanied by deep emotional involvement. In attending to a problem, the imagination, in the sense of its capacity to evoke images, comes into play. Exactly how a child releases his imagination is unknown, but we know that identification with an artistic experience is a prerequisite for a child's desire to give of himself creatively. The reverse may also be true in that a lack of involvement in a particular problem may mean that it holds no personal meaning for him.

Whether we call such behavior emotional involvement or commitment, it is a child's way of showing that he has the necessary impetus for creative work. Just as energy begets energy, so creativity begets creativity. This implies that only sustained involvement will reinforce this impetus or creative energy so that it becomes a part of a child's consciousness. It does not mean that it reaches an end with the making of a given product, but at that moment it reaches an intensity or presence which becomes *known* to him. In order to insure continuous growth and extension of this energy, it must be fed and expanded by continuous artistic experiences.

Focus on a Problem.   With this type of engagement, a child begins to *focus on a problem* through the particular way he concentrates on reorganizing and refining sensory impressions (absorbed consciously or otherwise). It is a complicated process of selection and abstraction (what to "put in," what to "take out") and is subject to its own time. Given the same problem of drawing an outdoor landscape, for example, one child may sit quietly for half an hour carefully absorbing the scene before deciding on how broad or narrow a vision he wishes to capture; another may draw some exploratory lines to define a general shape; and another may focus on the qualities of one tree and begin working immediately. However he begins, this is his initial move to make a form out of the formless in the sense of beginning to structure. In relating new sensory data to existing information, he is attempting to create or work out a focus to produce a product.

Although there is a common behavioral pattern within the creative process, each child's efforts that result in a work of art generate their own direction and momentum. Once he chooses an element, which may be any sort of thing—a shape, a gesture, an object, a simile—it sets up its own artistic demands, both opening alternatives and presenting limitations. For example, a simple line on a paper, a movement of an arm, a "pulled-out" volume in clay create a space that did not exist before, just as a sequence of events expressed poetically creates a new sense of time. A child's unique controlling power in giving focus to a yet-undefined problem lies in his perception of the particular stage or condition of the unfinished work itself, the possibilities it presents, and the development it permits.

Development of an Idea Into a Form. These two behavioral conditions in combination should eventually lead to the *development of an idea into an objective form.* We observe this as a kind of directed control by a child who is sufficiently inspired or motivated to give form to an idea or emotion. Whatever the source, whether a concept suggested by the teacher, an object directly perceived in nature, or an experience taken from memory, it can never be presented as an idea apart from the mode of expression which gives it form. Just as an idea in the arts finds its expression in sensuous materials, so sensuous expression becomes the vehicle through which ideas are articulated.

When we speak of "giving form" to an experience or of an object "having form," we mean that the elements are related in such a way that we are able to perceive the form relatively simply. When we say that something has an "interesting" form, we may be perceiving that it has a sense of being organic within itself. Thus, in observing the relationship of space–time–force in a movement study, the way lines define a child's features in a self-portrait, how volumes convey the "weightiness" of an animal in sculpture, or the connectedness of words in poetry, we become aware that there is a certain organic unity which gives a form its vitality. It is because of this quality that a piece of artwork, once conceived and shaped, is not reducible to a collection or enumeration of its elements, any more than the pieces of a jigsaw puzzle have meaning unless put together into a coherent whole.

On an artistic level, developing an idea into an objective form is a search for "wholeness." On a behavioral level, it calls forth a persistent probing which we observe in a child's attitude as well as in his performance. After he has experienced the initial spontaneous impulses and the commitment to "stay with it," his creative energies become transformed into a newly controlled direction. What he must necessarily bring to bear is an inner discipline that may be observed as a calmer, more reflective demeanor. It is this self-discipline that sustains his efforts, for what he is grappling with at this point is a more considered judgment of the relationships he has put together and a self-critical examination of whether the form works in terms of "does it say what I feel?" Whether he is alone at an easel, surrounded by others at a table, or actively involved with a group, he is ultimately working out his own problem.

If, during this phase of the process, feeling–thinking–doing are brought into an organic relationship, a child finds his fruition in some tangible, formal expression. It is not the product that is of sole importance, but rather the excitement of realizing that in the process of creating, something personally meaningful has come into being. Involvement in the creative process permits a child not only to perceive and express his feelings, but to gain a knowledge about those perceptions and feelings. In forming an image of himself, he must be able to look at his emotions and accept the idea not only that emotions have a "right'" to be expressed, but that he can discover forms for such expression. Thus, self-knowledge is not simply a subject of curiosity, it is a fundamental search for oneself, and within the arts, the creative process is the vehicle.

Yet the arts are not merely an expression from the "inside out," and we do not view them as a precious or exclusive experience. Nor do we see them as "enrichment" in the sense of a cultural frill. As such, they are not something to be added or cut out according to the exigencies of scheduling. Because the experience is also one of perceiving and relating to the outside world, it is not separate from a child's total being. The search for an organized expression of feeling is part of every child's consciousness and therefore must be an integral part of his education.

3
TEACHING AND LEARNING

Although children speak through forms of art before they are able to express themselves in words, the arts are the most neglected area of the curriculum. Even in nursery school, where there is more flexibility for experimentation, the arts are rarely separated from the recreational or manipulative crafts, either in concept or in practice. For classroom teachers with limited background and little opportunity to share observations with specialists, the need is for an approach providing structure and yet permitting spontaneity from the children. The question is one of how to create categories for identifying and communicating the arts to children of all ages with varying abilities and interests. For teachers already involved in one form or another, the question is one of extending their perceptions to a coherent approach that embraces all the arts.

Because of the complex nature of process and product, the arts require an open system, for the qualities of individual work are unpredictable and unforeseeable. Without some kind of conceptual approach that accounts for the qualities found in various artistic makings and doings, each encounter tends to be reduced to a fragmented activity. If learning is to be an integrative process, it must exist within a context that helps us to understand not only how the elements are related, but how they may be distinguished from each other.

23

Prevailing Misconceptions

Teaching in the arts has been limited by two prevailing misconceptions in education: First, that the arts are really one art and that differences exist only in the use of materials. It is this emphasis upon materials as both means and ends that largely accounts for the confusion between arts and crafts. For example, a frequently heard reference to the "clay table" implies that the objective is to play with clay, rather than to explore through a plastic medium those unique qualities that give it its potential shapes and forms.

The making of forms in crafts requires fairly specific skills (cutting, pasting, joining, steps in folk dancing) directed toward particular materials. They may be designed for some use, but in any case, the purpose is to produce an object. The result is viewed as an end in itself. Thus, the ability to manipulate and control materials becomes a primary concern.

The making of forms in the arts also requires an ability to handle materials (whether a paintbrush or one's own body) but is directed toward a different purpose. Materials here become the vehicles for transforming personal ideas and feelings through an array of qualities to form an objective image. That is, they become the means of organizing forms which, at any given time, reflect a child's intention and sensibility. In his exploration of media he begins to discover the properties and potential qualities that "work" for him in expressing a particular form. The result is an experience for contemplation and is viewed as an aspect of a process that continues to evolve.

To this end, it is important that teachers recognize and help children become aware that each material has its own visual, tactile, kinesthetic, and auditory characteristics through which expressive forms are produced. In experiencing how they function the children also come to understand their limitations. They learn that what may be formed in one material cannot be formed in another, because each makes its own inherent demands. In sculpture, as in dance, for example, the form comes out of the material itself and therefore the relationship between form and materials is closer than in other arts. A child's choice of materials may affect the successful execution of an idea, just as he may be stimulated by the nature of the material. Again, using sculpture as an example, different possibilities are opened to a child in knowing that "hard" materials such as wood or stone do not have the same qualities as "soft" materials such as clay or paper.

This does not imply that knowing how to handle materials technically guarantees artistic results. By materials we are referring to the matter or external appearance of an object or phenomenon, not to its internal organization. All materials have the same value—that of merely being vehicles for making expressive forms. In painting or sculpture, for example, we may conceive of the hand as the dancer, following the rhythm and dynamics of the imagination. If the imagination is closed, the hand knows nothing. Thinking in this way, we can replace the notion of art as technique with art as process, and shift the focus to the "how" of making, rather than the "with what."

The significance of materials is that they can be conceived and used as media of artistic expression and not as ends in themselves. Thus, an art form is not defined by its material but by the way it appeals to our senses. Paints alone do not make a painting, but through lines, colors, patterns they create a visual image; clay alone does not make a sculpture, but through shapes, volumes, planes it forms a visual–kinesthetic image; dance is not arrived at by disconnected gestures, but through movements combining space, time, and force to produce a kinesthetic–visual image; and poetry is not simply talking words, but composing word pictures through visual–auditory images. The materials of art—pigments, clay, movements, sounds—already exist in the environment and may be found and used. But an image is not something found; it must be brought into being.

A second misconception in education is that all the arts can be adequately described by the general term *art*. Because this usually refers only to the visual arts, it denies an understanding of the autonomous nature of forms such as poetry and dance in terms of the alternative ways they provide children for perceiving their worlds. If we accept the position that all the arts are essentially the same, we learn neither about that sameness nor about the differences between them. This view is reflected by teachers whose mode of inquiry is limited to pointing out or focusing only on subject matter. Questions such as, "What are you going to 'make' or 'do'?" before a child has even begun to explore a problem, followed by, "What is it?" emphasize the story-telling aspects, which may be the least important, because children create essentially what they feel, not what they see. We need to bear in mind that whatever the form, children's intentions are expressive, not depictive. For example, once a child has identified the objects in his painting, named the figure he has sculptured, explained what he was "supposed to be" in dance, how do we help him to perceive those particular qualities that make his work special? Several children may paint the same house or still life or landscape, but what is it that makes each one distinctive?

Each art form speaks uniquely through its own image. If children are to appreciate their efforts in artistic terms, they must understand that they create these images out of the internal sensory qualities of a given form—for example, that qualities such as the energy of a line, the intensity of color, the spatial relationships of shapes create the pictorial image; that the repetition of volumes, the smooth or jagged edge of a plane, the design of a texture give form to sculpture; that direction, level, and range carry the kinesthetic power of dance—just as rhythm, cadence, meter give emotional energy to a word picture. When meanings come from sources within the arts themselves, a child can be engaged beyond the initial statements of, "I like it," "I don't like it," "It's no good," to those qualities which, in combination and relationship, give expression to meaning.

Without commonly understood concepts, both teachers and children are reduced to seeking only the superficial aspects of creative efforts and to appraising these efforts in simple generalities. We can, we hope, help children acquire insight and sensibility so that they will move from simple statements of preference to more thoughtful judgments. This implies a willingness from both teachers and children to defer judgments until they relate to a perception of qualities. For example, a teacher's observations, such as, "That was a strong movement; try to make it even stronger," or, "I like the way this bright color works with the dark to form the pattern," or, "Those words give me a picture in my mind, can you develop the rest of your idea?" reflect a concern with qualities rather than statements of preference. Comments upon particular qualities do not have to refer to the entire work. It is frequently more supportive to focus upon a specific area, which may, in turn, open up a whole new perception.

Reconsiderations for Teaching

Teaching in the arts, as in any other important study in the curriculum, bears certain considerations. We do not know, for example, how children will respond to particular art forms or exactly how they will participate. For this reason, it is important to stimulate and involve them in an understanding of the potentials of each art form as well as of how they are related. It is equally important to offer them opportunities to select the form that may best express a particular idea, feeling, or mood. For a child, choices geared toward his expressive needs inevitably involve him in exploring the similarities and differences among the various arts. For a teacher, such choices offer rich observations as to the differences in children's preferred modes of expression and perhaps even as to why some children work successfully in one medium and unproductively in another.

The arts involve many levels of understanding and a variety of ways of experiencing and valuing creative work. What has been lacking is a frame of reference making the arts comprehensible in terms of their basic characteristics and also encompassing a child's personal attributes—his self-expression, perception, style. An approach is desirable that combines considerations for the development of his artistic sensibility with an organization of ideas that makes such growth possible.

One of the important functions of the educational process is to provide children with a structure that enables them to give form to their experience. In order to teach within the broad context of the arts and yet to communicate the essential nature of each one, we need to understand how they speak through different images. Only in knowing how they are different do we come to their similarities, and only then can we use them meaningfully in interrelationship. Is it conceivable, for example, that some kinds of feelings may be better expressed in sculpture than in painting? Or, if we "dance" a poem, should the movements follow the exact meaning of the words? To consider these ideas in some organized way is to present them within a conceptual framework that describes, through a carefully selected vocabulary, the underlying concepts of each art form and their relationship to the expressive, symbolic nature of the art experience.

Generally, a conceptual framework is a means of organizing experiences that might otherwise appear separate and unrelated. In the arts it is a way of relating the inherent elements of each form (what is painting? sculpture? dance? poetry?) to the unique experience producing them (how is each created?). It is not a syllabus or a manual of instruction because it is not based on preconceived ideas of what to teach, nor is it geared toward a series of anticipated responses. Such an approach is limiting and inflexible, for it assumes that both teachers and children should behave in predictable ways.

How, then, can we function effectively in a system that is open-ended and still bring to it a sense of structure? What we are suggesting is not a "method" but an approach to knowledge which presents somewhat familiar but unconnected ideas in newly defined relationships. It is a structure which sees relationships among the arts not only in terms of their sameness but in terms of their differences. The function of a framework is that it identifies the context in which learning takes place. In this case contexts are formulated as basic concepts and learning is expressed through the problem-solving process. Reflecting on our earlier considerations of the unpredictability of children's behavior, a framework makes it possible for teachers to make qualitative judgments as to the variety of ways children respond within these contexts, given the same problems. At the same time it allows for differing levels of creative effort in response to problems of varying sophistication. As teachers become more attuned to the direction of these creative efforts, they can suggest new problems to meet individual needs.

The learning experiences presented here are not designed in terms of grade levels. As there is no external sequential pattern to the art process, other than a child's maturation at any given time, the arts, perhaps more than other fields of study, lend themselves to a nongraded structure. Thus, the problems of exploring a body shape, creating a volume in space, defining a shape through color, or inventing a metaphor are equally challenging to first-, third-, or sixth-grade children, all of whom will produce wholly individualized solutions. In view of this, conventional notions of what is "typical" for a particular age level, ranging from learning capacity to performance, have little relevance. What is relevant is that each child establishes his own continuity as he develops his idiosyncratic pattern.

A Conceptual Approach

The function of a conceptual approach is that it provides a frame of reference for continuously reformulating ideas and teaching practices. The atmosphere for learning must be a consistent search to extend and expand expressive meanings in the arts. Therefore, teachers must not be tied to static, conventional procedures which largely call forth stereotyped responses or commonplace images from children. One of the elements that renders a teaching–learning situation most ineffective is a closing off of ideas. This occurs when children's perceptions are limited by restricted experiences or by an overemphasis on systematic, rigorous "methods." A feeling of closure develops when a child's intellectual or emotional curiosity is narrowed rather than released; when his insights are so confined that he seems unwilling or unable to make judgments of new experiences. When children's thinking is blocked or limited by stereotypes, it may also be that their own frames of reference need to be extended. Extending a child's thinking, feeling, perceiving at his stage of development comes about by opening up concepts, that is, by exposure to larger, fundamental ideas.

Engagement in the art experience requires that it be filled with the action of discovery. It is far more important in the classroom that a child regard himself as a creative painter, sculptor, dancer, poet (in the same way as he would a scientist, mathematician, historian) by experimenting, interpreting, and discovering the concepts and potentials of the arts, than that he follow any prescribed pattern. But the teacher must provide a structure dealing with the inherent concepts in such a way that a child can directly experience the effects of putting qualities together to express feelings. The essence of any art form becomes most clear to a child when he discovers for himself the relationship of the elements as he becomes involved in a personal search for meanings. To do this, he must participate in all aspects of the creative process—creating, performing, composing, listening and looking with critical awareness, judging his own work and that of others.

The value of a conceptual approach is that it opens possibilities for a teacher to function in two important ways: to understand what she observes so that judgments are based on the inherent qualities of the work itself; and to understand a child in still another dimension, for the focus of the arts is ultimately on the individual rather than on subject matter. A conceptual approach provides an open system for teaching and learning because it does not depend upon pre-existing "proofs." For teachers it affords the freedom to select a broad range of content for any particular group drawn from other areas of the curriculum as well as from elements related to various art forms. For children it offers a source of limitless ideas that they can project and explore. Perhaps most important, it offers children alternatives wherein they cannot be "wrong," because meanings are clarified in relation to what they are seeking to express.

Thus, within a structure of commonly shared concepts a child may be stimulated both to discover and to discipline his creative responses. For the teacher, it offers a conceptual rather than a technical basis for identifying certain kinds of responses that encourage a child to produce personally meaningful work. For the child, it allows an investigation of sensuous forms derived from his own developing perceptions and gives him a vocabulary so that he may share perceptions of emerging or completed work.

Sharing concepts requires a shared vocabulary, and therefore we need an appropriate mode of communicating about the arts to children. For example, if a child is to relate *what* is to be learned with *how* it is to be learned, he must be able to think in the medium in which he is involved. This means that he must have a conceptual grasp of the form and understand the language of its imagery. Because each individual sees the world through his own concepts, language becomes an extension of those concepts. Consequently, the type of language that he learns both causes and reflects an awareness of certain kinds of experiences more than others. Language is frequently presented to children as a tool, but this tends to reduce communication to a technique—to a way of thinking separated from what is thought. The effects are especially evident in the arts; because they lack any kind of consistent vocabulary, language is directed toward developing techniques rather than toward broadening a child's perceptions. We are suggesting that language be regarded as a vehicle through which something is affected or accomplished. A nondiscursive, symbolic language of the arts helps us to organize feelings, emotions, and ideas. What is necessary, then, is a language that illuminates and defines operationally those qualities inherent in a particular form as well as those that act as connective tissue.

A Language for the Arts

Thinking is expressed on two levels. On a discursive level, such as in math or science, language is communicated through logical, conventionally accepted meanings that translate experience in relatively definite, precise terms. On a nondiscursive level the arts express experience involving impressions and associations that stem not only from words, but from shapes, movements, colors, sounds, and other sense data. In discursive language thought follows thought in a sequential order according to generally understood rules. Nondiscursive language is subjective in that it evokes a particular but not precise set of meanings. It is the difference between a written paragraph, in which each sentence must logically flow from the other to formulate an idea, and a poem, in which words may be used in any combination to create a word picture. Thus, understanding an "idea" in any art form lies not in analyzing or classifying its components, but in experiencing it in its totality. This is not to imply that nondiscursive thought is so subjective that it cannot communicate from one human being to another. On the contrary, it is a mode of communicating meanings that can be perceived and understood by people of all cultures and classes. For this reason, we must recognize that nondiscursive communication is as significant a way of thinking, feeling, and expressing as discursive language.

The arts, both in the way they are formed and in the way they are presented are not conventionally verbal, for even poetry does not use the language of everyday speech. The arts have their own inner logic which departs from conventional descriptions and explanations. They speak through their own symbolic language and they speak for themselves. The special qualities a child invests in his creative work are found in the experience itself and do not need reduplication in language. This means that each quality, whether a particular color relationship, a thrust of a sculptural shape, a lyrical flow of movement, or a fanciful use of words, is a concrete experience and varies with each individual, reflecting his uniqueness. Although words cannot duplicate the infinite variety of individualized responses, we need to find a means of internal description so that the focus is not on peripheral issues, such as subject matter or technique, but on the expressive aspects. In sculpting a self-portrait or figure, for example, children frequently design hair by various arrangements of lines. A teacher may respond that a child has shown *texture* because he has made eyebrows, or eyelashes, or hair on the head; or, that by indicating hair in contrast to the smoothness of skin, he has shown a difference in textures in the material he has used. The difference in use of language is between literal translation and concepts directed toward the observation of qualities. It is perhaps through the latter we can help children better understand art as "a quality of doing and what is done." [1]

[1] John Dewey, *Art as Experience* (New York: Minton, Balch, 1934), p. 214.

We cannot "talk" the arts, but we can communicate concepts. In the teaching–learning process the problem arises as to how ideas can be communicated so that each child can relate to them in developing his own responses. If these concepts are to become integral to the art experience, teachers need to develop a language flexible in permitting variability of expression, yet definite enough so that children understand the sources of their creative efforts. A conceptualized language serves this purpose as a practical means by which we can express the diversity of feelings and responses, because it emanates from the arts themselves. As seen in the preceding brief discussion of texture, it summons and evokes in a functional way the vital responses from children which help them to experience more fully the qualities they have brought into being. Within the vagaries of the creative process, it offers children a means of understanding how the elements they select and with which they are directly involved take on subjective, artistic forms.

It is neither unrealistic nor an imposition to expect that children can learn linguistic concepts related to the formal aspects of the arts. Just as in painting, the process of transforming "real" round objects on a flat picture plane requires learning a vocabulary of pictorial forms, so in all arts formal qualities have a language that can be learned. What is created in a painting is an arrangement of colors, lines, shapes, patterns to combine forms that produce responses different from those produced by spoken language. Thus, the language of art is not a vocabulary in a discursive sense, but in the sense of evoking a broad range of responses shaped by qualities internal to the form itself. Terms such as *shape, rhythm, line, color* can be understood even by very young children if we begin with them as the point of reference—their eyes, ears, voices, hands, bodies. As children reach the middle elementary years, they discover that "free" expression without a related vocabulary becomes an inarticulate circle of "It looks like . . ." or "What's it supposed to be?" We want to encourage children to move beyond descriptions of the purely literal aspects of an art form, whether a dance study or a poem, expressed in whatever representational forms it displays or in conventional worn-out ideas. It may be assuring to children to know that in any object or event in the arts, they may see or feel different things, and that each child's imagination is his own source of subject matter. As a child begins to extend his vocabulary, broaden his perceptual frame, and explore further the elements of art, he finds that his ideas and emotions need a structure to contain them and give them coherence. When inquiry can go no further, the problem is usually conceptual. What is required then is a stretching of concepts, which means a new, basic vocabulary.

A Conceptual Framework in the Arts

Each art form has its own distinguishing characteristics, provides a unique image, and uses particular media. How, then, can we give the arts a sense of unity as well as recognize their distinctiveness? To do so is to consider them in their broadest context, as parameters of space–time–force through which the functions of the arts are expressed. As parameters, they may have various values, yet each in its own way is necessary in creating and determining the aesthetic effects of any particular form. They cannot, then, be conceived as technical elements, but as the connective tissue underlying the expression of ideas and feelings.

SPACE–TIME–FORCE

Space–time–force enter our lives on both a conceptual and perceptual level, and each plays an important role in determining ways in which an individual responds to his environment. In our daily lives they exist as physical properties of which we are hardly aware—as units of time, dimensions of space, amounts of energy—whereas in the arts they become tangible as aesthetic qualities. In everyday life the outcome of any interaction between an individual and his environment is experience. In the arts the experience is one of participation and communication by means of the senses. This kind of encounter, however, does not take place in a generalized, amorphous environment, but rather, in a space–time environment which becomes defined by the way a child organizes his perceptions and concepts. Although not generally included in this context, force, too, becomes a component of space–time, in the manner in which energy or tension is conceived. Energy itself is a basic concept, yet we can observe its effects in a child's extension of effort, and in the way he uses it in establishing his own dimensions of space–time. It is interesting to reflect upon Dewey's consideration of space–time in human experience. "Space," he wrote, "becomes something more than a void in which to roam about. . . . It becomes a comprehensive and enclosed scene within which are ordered the multiplicity of doings and undergoings in which man engages. Time . . . too, is the organized and organizing medium of the rhythmic ebb and flow of expectant impulses, forward and retracted movement, resistance and suspense, with fulfillment and consummation." [2]

Against this broad background we can consider how space–time–force function in the arts, apart from other types of experience. Teachers can weave these concepts into a workable vocabulary for they offer a "built-in" language for defining qualities usually considered indescribable. Such definitions are also useful in clarifying children's thinking of space–time–force as conceptual elements that exist in the "real" world and as perceptual elements in the "feeling" world as created forms of artistic experience. They can then understand more readily how these differences are reflected in the expressive qualities of their own work.

Space. On a conceptual level *space* becomes known to a child as it exists in the physical world, through shapes, sizes, relationships. It involves ideas of his body in space and about objects and spatial relationships within the environment in which he must function. On a perceptual level his awareness of space begins with his own body: first, in perceiving his body as the center of reference in relationship to ideas such as bigger, smaller, higher, lower, nearer, farther;

[2] Ibid., p. 23.

second, in perceiving his own movement, which is an essential ingredient of space perception. As he becomes increasingly aware of the dimensions of his own body, he also becomes aware of the dimensions of other people and objects. We see this reflected in the way he creates shapes in painting and sculpture, in his use of space in dance, and in his ideas about space in poetry. Thus, the space he designs is not based on logical or metrical standards, as it must be in "real" life, but on his subjective, expressionist feelings. His own perception of space becomes a source determining how he limits or expands space in any creative effort.

Time. In the physical world *time* is marked by clock and calendar intervals. Whether a child can "tell" time or not, he senses it as units that follow in a continuous before-and-after order. Both clock and calendar time fit into a fixed pattern which is conventionally understood and accepted. On a perceptual level time is directly related to the rhythms of the body—through heart beat, pulse, breath. Just as the space of experience is not defined by geometry, so perceived time is not established by clocks. A unit of time in poetry, for example, may be long or short, great or small, past or present, depending upon a particular mood. We see this expressed in a haiku written by a ten-year-old child:

> Moon shines hills again
> was it only yesterday
> that I was seven?

In the same way, the time it takes for a child to go from "here to there" in dance may be important only in relation to the rhythmic pattern he establishes. As with space it is emotionally felt, in that the time a child uses to convey a mood or idea serves his own perceptions. It is neither pragmatic nor conventionally defined. Rather, it is a created sense of duration which may be compressed or extended. Thus, in any art form, it represents a temporal order imposed by the child, and it exists completely within each created, presented experience.

Force. In the physical world *force* involves weight, gravity, energies in motion, and relationships in space. We conceive of it as the power that makes something happen in physical relationships or conditions. On a perceptual level force is expressed as tension or stress and is experienced as energy. When we speak of an energetic line or a strong color relationship in painting, of tension between the volumes or contours in a sculpture, of the power of a movement in dance or the intensity of an image in poetry, we are expressing a sense of vitality. Perhaps this concept clarifies a comment made in an earlier chapter that art happens when the "right" amount of vitality is brought to bear on the "right" amount of formality.

In the arts force is expressed as the process of living energy necessary for creative production, and as the product of that energy combined with media that make forms come alive. In dance, for example, force is perceived as tension which children feel kinesthetically in their bodies. Because energy is the source of movement, it is also essential in giving it an aesthetic quality. That is, by varying the amount of energy expended and by releasing it in various ways, different feeling tones and textures are produced.

Responding to an actual physical force and creating an internally felt force may be observed in a simple movement exploration involved in pulling. It is the difference between pulling a real object or another child and meeting actual physical resistance, and sensing the tension and release within the body in pulling a nonexistent object. In dance the energy factor is one of the strongest means of communication, for it is responsible for the variations and dynamics of a movement. To see the relationship between space–time–force as factors we experience in daily living and as aesthetic elements inherent in the arts is to adapt Dewey's concept that we use the very materials and energies of nature and transform them, giving impetus by ideas and feelings, into what we may call organized aesthetic efforts.

Thus, the conceptual framework proposed here derives from the aesthetic nature of space–time–force as a structure within which to perceive the similarities and differences between painting, sculpture, dance, and poetry, based on four discriminating factors: (1) definition and description of each art form, (2) distinguishing characteristics, (3) nature of the experiential approach, (4) art elements of each form. Working within this framework allows teachers and therefore children to become aware that although space–time–force exist in the external environment, these same elements are transformed in the arts according to how and what a child wishes to express.

CONCEPTS
AND
EXPLORATIONS

4
PAINTING

Definition and Description

How do we respond upon first seeing a child's painting? How does it strike us as a total visual presence? We respond not to its formal aspects, but to its most obvious qualities, such as the vibrancy of color, the energy of line, the movement of shapes forward and backward, and the suggestive but indeterminate nature of the forms. The impact, then, is sensorial, not intellectual. The painting must invade our senses before we even begin to analyze its component parts or make formal judgments.

We see it as a presentation, not as a representation of objects that can be named or identified. For once we have enumerated the "things" we are looking at—for example, a tiger with orange, black, and white stripes standing on green grass looking at a red, rounded shape (see color plates, Figure 1)—what do we know about the painting? And equally important, how do we feel about it? We have responded by telling a story, rather than by allowing ourselves to perceive that this unrealistic but powerful image of a tiger has come to life not through the use of lines, but by the creation of volumes of intense color and by the way he stands solidly in his own magical spatial world. In this particular painting we are experiencing the shaping of space through colors and volumes which read symbolically as a tiger. But it is not simply a symbol of a tiger; it is a symbol of a feeling about a tiger.

Although we can discuss children's art conceptually, and as teachers it is essential that we do so, we must recognize that it differs qualitatively from our immediate sensory responses. Although painting is viewed here as only one facet of children's aesthetic experience, its uniqueness as an art form engenders its own type of aesthetic sensibility. It is in pursuing its special qualities that we learn how to *see* it, for visual art is made primarily for sight, as differing from our tactile and kinesthetic senses. Therefore in turning to the nature of the pictorial image we can describe those characteristics that make it a living, expressive form.

Painting partly achieves its unique quality by the fact that it has, through historical convention, become bounded by a rectangular form. This derives primarily from architecture, for in the past as now most walls were square and artists painted for the walls of private homes. Frames were used to isolate the picture plane from the surrounding spatial environment so that it existed in its own spatial world. The wall that supports the painting is not in the painting, it is in no way part of the picture space. Thus, the convention of the picture plane forced an edge on the object so that it became a "false" world, taken away from the real world.

In contrast, the cave paintings done in France and Spain thousands of years ago had no edges; they were simply placed in space. They existed within two dimensions in the same way that sculpture exists in three dimensions—the whole wall was their terrain in a seemingly endless space. But once confronted with an edge, we create the convention of a form that is cut away from both the subject and the world. Because we cannot make a picture without a surface, that surface, too, is geometric, whether it be a square, a rectangle, or a circle. Whether separated from actual space by the edges of a paper or enclosed in a frame, the painting is limited to the boundaries of the surface upon which it exists.

It is this characteristic which distinguishes painting from sculpture. Anything that is visible can become the subject of a painting, but this does not hold for sculpture. We may imagine, for example, that a child paints a landscape and cuts out the internal shapes of a house, chimney, smoke, tree, flowers. What he is left with, then, is an arbitrary shape. It is arbitrary in the sense that although it is not square, it reflects the form that the child has selected to paint. This form is called the subject or positive space. But although it may be interesting as a "cut-out," it is no longer a painting, for the conditions of its spatiality have been violated. If a painting only existed in shapes that could be cut out, there would be no way of creating the endless illusions imposed by the limitations of the edges of the picture plane.

Sculpture, because it is three-dimensional, exists in limitless space. Whether we place it in an enclosed space such as a niche or an arch or remove it so that it stands alone, it exists as a piece of sculpture. Therefore, in sculpture we are not dealing with a surface but with mass, as opposed to the superimposition of an illusion on a surface, which implies that there is something on that surface that is not the subject. In sculpture the mass is the subject, and everything else around it is space that moves into it or out of it.

Every art form creates a special type of appearance. Painting is "shaped space," but as we have seen, unlike space in sculpture, this is not space that exists in the actual, physical world. It is a two-dimensional image that appears three-dimensional because of the space that is shaped on the picture plane. It is made visible to us through color, line, texture expressed as volumes or flat shapes. When we speak of space as volume, we usually think of something having a rounded or swelling form; therefore, we associate it more readily with sculpture. Volume in sculpture actually has dimensions of height, breadth, and width, which we can see as well as touch. Although volume in painting may not conform to our conventional ideas, we respond to a sense of volume through the aesthetic qualities of space and force—that is, through the contrast of one color against another, the relationship of light and dark, and the tension of shape against shape.

The seemingly solid volumes in painting do not exist as palpable objects but as a purely visual experience. We know that if we pass our hand over the surface of a picture it remains perfectly flat. Our perception is not enhanced by touching it, for painting is made for sight alone. A painting cannot deal physically with three dimensions. We may think of a collage as being closest to a "three-dimensional painting," but although it has an element of three-dimensionality, it exists essentially as a texture, not as pictorial volume. Even when we are involved with painting sculpture (which many often misconstrue as the ultimate and necessary step) the intent is an added or accompanying aspect to emphasize certain planes or volumes. In any case, each art form is defined by its unitary nature, and other forms used in relation to it are secondary to the primary image.

What children are creating and what we are observing is an appearance of objects that exist in an illusory space. Children see things all around them in the environment which they observe in greater or lesser detail, depending upon the importance they attach to them. What is created in a painting, however, is not a visual record of the "realness" of things, but an appearance of the "feeling-ness" of things. It is a way of abstracting—of exaggerating, omitting, distorting—sensory elements of actual life to form a vision that is no more than an appearance.

Therefore, to make direct comparisons with things in the real world is inappropriate for there are no such things as we know them. Illusion is not "make-believe." We can neither believe nor make believe that there is a little girl, a house, or an animal in front of us. We can only see it for what it is—as shapes and volumes that give organization and structure to the visual space. Although a painting may evoke in us certain associations with objects or events in our own experience, what we are perceiving is a child's effort to organize a visual conception of his subjective experience.

Whether we perceive a shape as flat or as having volume depends very much on how we see it, for our senses do not always agree. Two individuals looking at a child's work may have very different experiences of roundness or flatness. For the most part, the perception remains within the subjective experience of both the child and the observer. The appearance of volume in its simplest terms derives from an attempt to make a roundness. Yet the spatial movement forward and backward that emerges from a color may or may not read as volume. As we have said, although a painting gives the illusion of a volume in space, the volume is not physically there. It is an illusion that follows the dictates of color or the tension of shapes. Nevertheless, we can talk about volume in painting because we have a visual experience that transforms the nature of what we see in the real world into a two-dimensional image—that is the magic of painting.

For example, we look at a child's painting (see color plates, Figure 3) of a vivid blue background (sky?) with variously colored overlapping shapes (clouds?), a green foreground with similarly painted overlapping shapes (flowers?), against which is a little girl in a bright orange dress with long hair flying in either direction. Although she occupies the center of the picture and is facing frontally, she appears to be walking. Both shoes are painted similarly as black amorphous shapes, yet one leg moves in such a way as to give the illusion that she is stepping diagonally into space. The feeling is of a leg thrusting forward, because of the tension of this black shape against the blue sky against the green ground. We may say that one foot reads as a volume and the other reads flat.

On the other hand, some shapes really do look flat and have no sense of volume at all. For example, in Figure 2 (in the color plates), in the upper-right-hand section of the picture plane, a lavender bird, whose wings and head are shaped like an inverse mushroom, perches on the top of three black branches which extend parallel in a downward direction from a solid, black vertical tree occupying the left edge of the picture from bottom to top. The five green leaves on the branches have dark-green veins and each wing has vertical blue lines (feathers?); yet there is no sense of rounded forms or of shapes moving backward or forward. The painting has an aspect of a Japanese print not only because of its delicate colors—the lavender bird on the black branches with spots of green against an orange ground—but because the surface reads as a totally flat form. In this particular painting we may say that there is a feeling of "non-volume," wherein one form sits next to or in front of another without creating any dimension itself.

Neither of these paintings has internal volume, in the sense of a whole movement of the surface. In the painting of the little girl, however, there is the implied movement of the hair flying, and the foot forward that gives us a feeling of volume. Interestingly enough, the birds are not flying. There is no sense of motion for they exist as static, flat shapes. Even though we have attempted to "explain" these paintings, the accompanying color illustrations help us to understand the ever-present ambiguity of the pictorial image. Thus, there are different ways of creating volumes and space which read differently in different pictures. The variety of solutions that children produce in coping with the pictorial image informs us that we must look at each work in terms of what it is trying to say, rather than approaching it with preconceived notions as to what constitutes dimensionality.

Distinguishing Characteristics

SPACE

The visual arts have been characterized as "arts of space" based on the fact that their primary appeal is to our visual sense. But such a generalization also applies to sculpture and dance and is insufficient to help us to understand the unique way that space functions in both the making and perceiving of these forms.

Space exists all around us in the real world, yet unless it is occupied or defined it is amorphous and of itself has no shape. Children, however, learn to orient themselves in space through their senses—that is, they begin to identify spatial relationships by seeing, hearing, moving, and touching. These become empirical factors in their daily behavior as they deal with actual spatial phenomena.

But the space of everyday living is not the space used in forming a pictorial image. Space in painting is not experiential. Although the child may draw from memory images of sight and touch, sound and motion, it is entirely visual space a child must deal with. In essence, the paper facing him when he stands at an easel or works at a table is an "empty space" which he has yet to organize and shape. It is for this reason that Langer asserts that "the space in which we live and act is not what is treated in art at all. . . . Pictorial space is not only organized by means of color (including black and white and the gamut of greys between them), it is created; without the organizing shapes it is simply not there." [1] As an analogy, she likens pictorial space to the space "behind" the surface of a mirror, which she calls an "intangible image." [2]

It is this intangible image to which we referred earlier as illusory space. If, for example, we look into a mirror and then run behind it, the image is not there. If we look at it from one side we do not see the image, neither do we see it if we run around to the other side. Thus, the image and the space it occupies are illusory; the image is not real, for when we are not looking at the mirror frontally, our head disappears.

A painting, like a mirror, is not three-dimensional; it is only there in the front to be perceived only in its frontal aspect. In the same way, if we turn the painting to the wall there is nothing there, for there is no three-dimensional form that thrusts out into space. The surface of a picture is as flat as a razor-edge, yet we can create inside of it a tension of shapes that can only make us feel it is 100 miles deep. It is that feeling of "deepness" that creates the illusion of space.

In a limited sense, a painting is a measure of space but it becomes visible through the expression of a spatially conceived form. Although painting involves the apprehension of flat forms, the process is one of creating shapes that move from two-dimensional forms to the illusion of three-dimensional space. The pictorial image, therefore, exists not only as a flat shape in space (such as we see in simple decorative designs or geometric patterns), but as an *expressively shaped space*. By this we mean that an individual selects certain visual elements of experience by canceling out all others, leaving nothing to see except those forms that reflect his feelings. The nature of the illusion lies in abstracting these elements of sensory appearance from things that have meaning in his own life to form a sheerly pictorial vision. It is a vision of created space, not a re-creation of what a child actually knows about the external physical world. Nor does a child merely reproduce what he sees in nature to make it "fit" realistically within the picture plane. Whether the image is realistic or nonobjective (that is, whether

[1] Suzanne K. Langer, *Feeling and Form* (New York: Scribner, 1953), p. 72.
[2] Ibid.

it resembles something in the real world or looks only like itself), the process of transforming natural objects into pictorial elements is screened through a child's perception—through his mind's eye, not the eye of a camera lens—and is always tempered by his expressive needs. Thus, it is this created illusory space that is most characteristic of painting as a "space-art."

We can distinguish the nature of the pictorial image by examining further the concept of positive and negative space. Within the world of the picture plane, there are shapes that create the subject and those that exist as "nonsubject." Whether the form is abstract or realistic, whatever reads as the subject may be considered as the positive space. If we conceive of picture making in terms of a subject with parts "left over" on the picture plane, we begin to understand that there is always negative space—that is, space left over from that created as the subject. Although this is a fundamental concept in painting, it does not always obtain for all children at all times. In their early experiences with painting, young children tend to treat each object or figure equally, to place each one in its own space, flat and separated from the others, giving the visual impression of a piece of embroidery. In painting, as in embroidery, a child simply starts at one point, adds the next object to the first, and so on, rather than conceiving of the total surface as some kind of unified form.

Four-year-old Sabrina paints a smiling sun, a house, and a smiling girl of approximately equal size "floating" in the central area of the picture; beneath are flowers (solid splotches of color) disconnected from their sticklike stems, which run off the bottom of the paper. All around are energetic "squiggly" lines and contour shapes of various colors which also float on the surface. If we were to superimpose similarly colored thread, we would as easily read it not as a painting but as an overall decorative pattern. No attempt is made here to create volume, for in working purely decoratively there is no need to deal with negative space. However, the moment a child moves into a painting where he is involved in decision making as to what a subject is in relation to what is left over, he is concerned with shaping positive and negative space.

Children can be made aware of the way space functions through exploring very simple problems. For example, we may set up a still life of a plant (with fairly defined stems, leaves, petals) so that children all around the room can see it, or we may provide several plants to be shared by small groups. If the presented problem is to paint the subject matter—that is, the dominant shapes of the leaves, stems, flowers—children will be attending to the positive space. If, in contrast, they are asked to paint only the shapes made by the "air" or spaces between the members, they are dealing with negative space, or that which is left over.

Children can extend this concept by painting on colored construction paper leaving certain areas where the color "works" unpainted. In creating the total image, children discover that these unpainted spaces become essential to the form and may be read as either positive or negative shapes, depending on how they are used. In so doing, children are freed of the notion that the background always "goes back" or is always a negative space rather than a shape that sets up its own tension. In reflecting upon their own work, children are usually surprised by their observations that "all the space is used up," "there's no empty places," "there's lot's of stuff in it." Thus, they gain an understanding that all the space on the picture plane is important and not just what has been selected as the subject, and, further, that the background acts as a unifying factor in helping to pull the pictorial plane together.

In a less obvious or conscious manner, children create relationships of positive and negative space drawn from their own imagery which produce highly expressive forms. Yet the ambiguity in children's painting requires thoughtful consideration on a teacher's part. For example, a child "frames" the outermost area of the surface with linear streaks or slashes of overlapping colors which push out toward the edges of the paper, leaving the space in the center vacant (in terms of color). A well-intentioned suggestion to "fill in" the empty space may be inappropriate either in considering a child's exploratory efforts or in recognizing how space has been "carved out." In this particular instance, it is the frame or border which reads as the positive space, because it is the space the child apparently considered most significant. The center, which is left empty visually, is the negative space, even though it occupies the largest area of the picture, because we feel the tension along the edge. The tension of a painting, and frequently its greatest source of interest, is created by playing the subject against the nonsubject, enclosed by the edges of the picture. Thus, negative space contributes to the tension between positive shape and positive shape; it is defined by the outer limits of the picture plane and by its relationship to the illusory space within it.

A child looking at an object in nature or at a figure of another child modeling

in the classroom may decide that he is not interested in the figure in front of him, but in everything that goes on around it. In the process of painting only the background or environment, the figure remains a silhouette with its outer contours defined by the shapes immediately surrounding it. Therefore, contrary to our conventional expectation that what is centered is usually the subject, the figure, which is left over, becomes the negative space.

As there are no objective rules or measures, what appears as positive or negative space lies completely within the imagination of the child, as it does with the mature artist. Whatever he creates as the subject, which is the powerful or readable form, there is always a tension between it and that which is left over. The negative space is never equal in terms of its readability. However, it is not negative space in the sense of not being an important or primary part of the picture; it is essential in creating the pictorial image and gives expressive power to the total form.

Although we can distinguish the characteristics of positive and negative space, the actual process of picture making is far more complicated. Because of this complexity we have admonished against asking, "What are you going to paint?" before a child even begins to work. Children rarely begin by saying, even to themselves, "I'm interested in this subject and that's what I'm going to make." More likely, they discover what their interest is and how they can visualize it as they work. Demanding a preconceived idea is almost like committing a child to a promise that he may or may not be able to fulfill. After the picture is completed we can discuss positive and negative space (or whatever qualities present themselves) with somewhat more assurance.

FORCE

In painting, visual elements exist in opposition to each other which create an inner tension. As an aesthetic quality force lies in the opposition of one part working against another as *shape against shape,* which is expressed through *color* (the contrast between warm and cool, light and dark), *line,* and the *tension of the interior shapes against the edge of the picture plane* (discussed earlier as positive and negative space). Although space is the essential element in forming the primary illusion, it is space that is produced by the dictates of color and line that is expressed in the tension of shapes. It is this tension we sense as the opposition of "felt" energy that gives painting its force.

When we refer to a painting as "exciting," we mean that it has so much energy that it seems to vibrate from the page. And energy in painting is expressed as tension. Thus, when we speak of a sense of tension we are not implying an antagonistic relationship. On the contrary, just as we have defined *problem* as a postive, qualitative exploration, so we refer to *tension* as the expressive quality that makes a piece of artwork "come alive." Tension may be expressed through any of the elements of a painting, through color, shapes, lines, so that whatever elements appear in a particular painting exist in tension—that is, as something working positively against something else. It should be noted, however, that children use different elements to express tension in their paintings. Although we can define those elements that generally create a sense of force, there are no "right" solutions. Rather, we are dealing with a whole range of different forms of tension children use to express and articulate feelings.

COLOR

What strikes us most impressively in children's painting is their highly subjective, powerful use of color. But a sense of forcefulness does not always imply intense, "hot" colors, for muted delicate color can be equally effective. In any case, we are not responding to color as color, but to how it functions to create a tension of shape against shape.

No picture is made merely by placing marks and colors on a surface with isolated areas of the background "showing through." The paper no longer remains an inert surface, for colors define volumes and shapes. Whether a surface is painted or left unpainted, it enters actively into the color relationship of the painting. Once a child puts pigments or tempera to paper, he is no longer dealing with a material surface but with a surface that becomes animated. What do we mean when we say that color makes form "come alive"? We mean that color, by its own spatiality and relatedness, exists within a surface in such a way as to infuse a feeling of life to the space around it.

Families of Color.   Just as there are "families" of instruments based on their sounds, so can we think of colors as belonging to families of "warm" and "cool." The "warm" family includes those colors closest to red—red, yellow, orange; the "cool" family comprises those closest to blue—blue, green, violet. We must bear in mind, however, that the members of these families are not consistent or absolute; they change, depending upon what surrounds them. For example, even though we call green a cool color, it is possible to make one green cooler than another if we mix blue with it. If we add a dab of yellow, it will feel warmer.

We can observe further that the members of a family are not only relative but relational. For example, if, using a bright red, we make a square on a piece of red construction paper, a red line on yellow paper, and a red circle on blue paper, each of the reds will look different. On the red paper, the red almost "loses" its bright color and appears cool; the blue paper comes through the red, giving it an even cooler or purple tone; and the one on the yellow paper seems most intense because of the contrast and is therefore warmer. What we are experiencing, then, is a difference in the "warmness" and "coolness" of the red because of the change in its intensity in relation to its contrasting background.

Colors have certain properties which help us to understand not only what they are, but how they act. When we ask children to identify objects using words such as *red, blue,* and *green,* we are naming; and *hue* is simply the name of a color. If we ask children to look around at what everyone is wearing and describe the different "whites," for example, they respond in terms of "glossy," "bright," "dull," "dirty." As they observe how dull or bright colors are, they are referring to *intensity,* which is brightness or dullness. We think of pigments as they come out of the jars as being brilliant or intense, but as soon as we begin to mix them together their intensity lessens. We frequently confuse intensity with *value,* which is the lightness or darkness of a color. It is not uncommon for children to describe something as dark when they mean bright even though we would logically associate dark with dull. For example, a child describes another as wearing a "dark blue" T-shirt. However, if we look at all the "blues" the other children are wearing, we may decide that the T-shirt is really an intense blue and is very bright. This makes us aware that one color alone is never what it seems to be but changes in relation to what is around it.

In helping children to understand color relatedness, we can point out that this particular shirt is more intense because it seems to be "bluer," just as another child's blue jeans seem to be the dullest because they have more black in them. Not all hues have the same value and each can be changed so that it reads lighter or darker. It is also possible to produce a color which is green in hue, very light in value, and intensely bright. Yet this same green, depending on what is mixed with it and what it sits beside, may appear dull and grayed. This difference in brilliance is what we call a difference in intensity.

Thus, we begin to see that the appearance of being warm or cool does not reside within the hue of the color itself but is a visual experience. In technical terms, every color has its opposition on the color wheel—red–green, blue–orange, yellow–violet. The greatest tension exists between a color and its opposite in the sense that they tend to "pull apart," giving the quality of separating visually. It is fairly easy to observe these contrasts when the opposition is strong—that is, between colors of equal hue or intensity, but children do not paint by the numbers, and by using more subtle variations there is more ambiguity.

Adults looking at the same painting do not always see these relationships in the same way, and we cannot turn to theory as the ultimate criterion. For example, we may "know" that yellow is warm and violet is cool, but we may "feel" differently in looking at a four-year-old's expressive use of abstract forms where color mixing on the paper has produced overlapping and interlocking shapes. In this instance, we observe that the purple which sits next to the larger yellow shape has been mixed with white and is grayed down, and that the yellow has even more white painted over and into it. Presented with these mixtures, what reads as warm and cool is completely relative and is frequently determined by our own personal perceptions.

We begin an exploration of color with children by looking at the relationships they have created, for in this case, as with all experience in art, practice precedes theory. The purpose of clarifying these relationships is not to make decorators of children, but to make them sensitive to how colors work together in painting, which is considerably different from the way they exist in real life. Any colors can be made to "work" in a painting—the notion that certain colors "go well" together and others do not is related to decorative notions rather than to artistic considerations. Therefore, it is important that we free children from preconceived ideas of what "goes well" in the sense that certain clothes must "match," for such ideas are based on style and convention. As we have seen, there are no absolutes as to whether one color is duller or more intense than another, for colors do not act alone but in relationship. Thus, we need to re-examine teachers' efforts, especially with very young children, in asking for factual identification of the colors they have used. Having a child identify colors verbally does not help him deal with the problem of perceiving his own expressive use of color, nor does it help him to understand how color acts in a particular painting.

Spatial Properties of Color. The primary characteristics of warm and cool colors are their *space-making* properties—that is, their propensity to make shapes move closer or farther away. If we look intently at a painting, we may observe this in two ways: first, that certain colors "pull forward" while others "pull back," and, second, that soft, "smudgy" boundaries merge spatially while hard edges tend to pull apart—that is, softer boundaries give the illusion of nearness or connection and harder boundaries indicate distance or separation between two shapes. As soon as we perceive that a certain color "stands out," we also begin to observe that it appears to be pushing one way or another. It is this sense of "standing out" that gives painting its three-dimensional quality. Thus, not only does the tension of color against color create a feeling of space, but each created color shape has its own direction or thrust on the picture plane.

Within this general context, we can begin to pose questions to children such as, "Which color is closer to you and which one seems further back?" or "Which colors sit together and which pull away from each other?" Although this may be an appropriate vocabulary in the sense of helping children to become aware of one of the inherent problems of painting, it really only becomes functional when applied to a specific painting. For example, we can examine once again the painting of the little girl "walking" toward us on a ground of flowers, because all the shapes are totally defined by color. (See color plates, Figure 3.)

What we read initially is the opposition of the very intense yellow (hair), orange (face), and red (dress) against the cool blue of the background. (This also holds if we turn the painting upside down, which is frequently an interesting thing to do for it frees us from becoming too preoccupied with subject matter.) Because the yellow, red, and orange all appear to have the same intensity, we feel the figure as a unified warm color. However, when we turn the painting upside down, we notice that the yellow, being much lighter and much warmer, jumps away from the blue, and that the red sits more closely with the blue, because it is darker and cooler. In the same way, the green and violet "clouds" read darker and cooler than the cool, blue sky and push farther back into space than the warm, lighter yellow and orange shapes, which appear closer to us.

In terms of their spatiality, the movement of these three "warms" is very much influenced by the *placement* of colors around them. For example, instead of the yellow just following the shape of the hair and pulling out to the sides, it also moves forward and up because of the two yellow "clouds" directly above it. And even though the little girl is moving diagonally to the left, the red of the dress pulls to the right because of the red "flower," which moves our eye in that direction. To check our perceptions, we can cover up the colored shapes surrounding the figure and discover that without these "directional pulls" the figure just sits in the middle of the picture plane.

Through shared observations of their own work, we can make children aware that certain colors sit "above" or "below" each other, as well as "in front of" or "behind." We can begin to develop a spatial vocabulary of color in relation to the way it appears to "pull back," "thrust forward," "curve around," or "bend over." It is a way of seeing that may lead children "from a visual realization of the interaction between color and color to an awareness of the interdependence of color with form and placement." [3] When we speak of colors that "curve around" or "bend over each other," we are referring to some of the ways in which color expresses itself spatially—as *interlocking and overlapping forms*. Yet these conditions also create a feeling of force.

We never really see a single color unrelated or unconnected to other colors, even in children's beginning "embroidery" approach, where each color is seemingly added to the next. Our perception of color is such that it is continually shifting and is always related to the changing qualities of those around and behind it.

One of the magical aspects of a painting is that as we look at it for a longer time, all the relationships with color begin to happen. For example, what first strikes us in Wayne's portrait of himself (see color plates, Figure 4) in a cowboy hat and bandanna is a sensation of undulating, vibrating colors playing against each other. As we look further, we can identify forms such as the intense orange outline of the face, against the dull purple and blue shape of the hat, surrounded by the overlapping, swirling lines of yellow, green, orange, blue. If we allow our eyes to penetrate the surface and even squint a bit, we find that everything begins to move. The face and hat come forward and then recede; then again, the whirling colors of the background seem to swell and pull forward. Thus, we come to realize that colors vibrate against each other, which not only affects their relatedness but creates an ever-changing sense of space. What makes a painting "alive" is that each time we look at it we may see these constantly changing relationships. We may not all see things in the same way, but this is partly a condition of its spatiality, for in paintings which deal with flat forms, what is happening tends to be more immediately evident.

Presenting the diverse and devious ways of color may be a means of overcoming children's initial conceptions that everything must exist in its own space. But because picture making deals with two-dimensional rather than three-dimensional objects, more than one shape can occupy the same space at the same time. As soon as a child places one shape on top of another, he is creating an illusion of space. It may create tension, but essentially it is an *overlapping* of space wherein one form seems to go in front of or in back of another. Children's spontaneous placement of color upon color leads easily to a recognition not only that it creates a feeling of density, but that it may lend a quality of texture. For example, Arturo's white snow "falling" against the gray background "covers" the brown animal (dog?) already textured with brown and black spots to create a denser and more active texture. Although, in general, warm colors tend to come forward and cool colors tend to go back, they are reversed here by the very placement of the white dabs in front of the warm brown "fur." Thus, over-

[3] Joseph Albers, *The Interaction of Color* (New Haven: Yale University Press, 1963), p. 2.

lapping colors act as a source of tension and as a source of sight—that is, they help us to see what is happening spatially.

In contrast, *interlocking* forms act like pieces of a puzzle in that one "fits" inside or encircles another. In observing Danielle's work, for example (see color plates, Figure 5), we see that she approaches a self-portrait as if she were piecing the puzzle of her own image together. In a later description of how the painting took form, she revealed her own intuitive decision to move away from a more conventional beginning—"I drew the round part of the face, drew the face and didn't like it so I smeared it up." Rather than discarding the painting, however, she leaves the "smudgy" shape in the middle. Beginning with a semicircular brown wedge (hair), she connects a larger semicircular green wedge (beret) which curves around to the right. Working from the inside of this large shape, she rounds out the lower part of the face with a thick yellow line and outlines the upper part with a thin brown line, locking the hat and hair firmly around the face. Turning now to the features, the eyes change from little green dots to large, solid brown circles (one slightly above the other), the nose is indicated by a single yellow line, and the mouth is formed as a solid red heart. In connecting the mouth to the eyes, she covers the entire surface with pink but remains within the original outline of the face. Below the chin (there is no neck) the horizontal thrust of the dull-green T-shirt extends almost to the sides of the paper. The negative space of the background, painted in a cool, even duller green, covers the surface except for a narrow area surrounding the cheeks and chin. The light, warm yellow which she now places in that space plays against the cool green. That is, even though it is "locked in" by the background, it pulls away from the green and pushes the head forward. The total effect suggests a feeling of compression in comparison with shapes that seem to "swim" in a void. What is especially interesting is that she created five solid, interconnecting forms that retained their essential shapes throughout the painting process. It is as if she were making the pieces of a puzzle work together, except that the shapes are of her own invention.

These spatial properties become possible through the use of variations in color which come about because of its characteristic qualities. But characteristic does not mean immutable, for even these spatial relationships change, depending upon all the other elements in a picture. We can speak broadly of the relationships that create these tensions, but we must keep in mind that they may function differently in different paintings. Generally, we may say that colors act as "space-makers" by variations of a single color against a background painted in a single color, by variations in brilliance, and by variations of light and dark.

Light and Dark. *Light and dark* do not enter painting in terms we conventionally think of as light colors and dark colors but as shapes. Even within one color there can be variations of light and dark. We observe these accidental nuances as children explore mixtures with black or white, covering the whole surface as if they were painting a wall. But tension exists only when shape works against shape—that is, as positive shape against negative shape or as positive shapes against other positive shapes.

For example, as a child paints a portrait looking into a mirror, he is frequently beset with making his cheeks look round or his nose "stand out." We may suggest to him that one way to "build up a form" is to observe closely which features "go in," which "go out," and how light falls on his face to illuminate certain shapes. What he begins to discover empirically is that each color is not only warm and cool but also light and dark, depending upon what is around it. As they move colors around and on top of each other, one child may discover that using white creates planes on his brown cheeks, whereas another becomes aware that blue and green can create shadows as well as the conventional brown or black.

The exciting aspects of color in all its deceptions and appearances sharpen children's awareness of what happens in a painting, but also make them "see" what they casually look at in real life. For example, conceiving of a shadow as always being dark, they do not see it as having color, much less as having a shape which works against other shapes. But the shaded areas we see in nature are not always produced by adding black or white. They are more likely created by variations in the color of the object. Nor does shadow have the same meaning in real life as it does in painting, where the problem is in understanding how shadow works in creating the spatial tension of an illusionary three-dimensional image. Becoming conscious of the existence of color from the experience of painting to the observation of nature cannot help but enrich children's visual perception.

It is perhaps necessary, however, to distinguish between the conventional notion of *shading* or "modeling," which is "filling in" the outline of a form to represent more or less darkness, and *shadow,* which is the contrast in darkness or lightness built up within the form itself. For example, in painting a figure of a classmate in a gestured pose, we might focus for a moment on the way we see an arm extended in space. We would notice that the top appears to have a darker shadow, which becomes lighter in the middle and darkens again along the lower edge. No matter what color a child selects to use, it will most likely be lighter in the illumined areas and darker in the shaded areas, but the shapes will be defined by color. (Even in a drawing, gradations of black and white imply color.) It is this opposition of light and dark that helps us to read the arm as a volume rather than as a flat, rectangular shape.

Because we are dealing with painting, shadow also functions as a warm color against a cool color, as different values within a color, and as two almost equal colors expressing themselves as warm and cool. Thus, what we observe in the outstretched arm is a dark, rounded upper shape, against a lighter, flat middle shape, against a dark, rounded lower shape. For this reason we can create a feeling of light and dark even while using relatively intense colors. For example, in an eleven-year-old's imaginary portrait (see color plates, Figure 8), we see a figure of a girl which occupies the central, vertical space of the picture plane. Dense black hair cascades down from the top of the head, alongside the body, and runs off the lower edge. This black shape defines the face as well as the purple dress with the white polka dots. The hair, the yellow background, and the dress are shaped by solid colors, and the features in the brown face are formed by variations of light and dark. The shape of the nose, part of one cheek, and the forehead are articulated by a brown of lighter value than is used in the rest of the face. Without being "modeled," the nose comes slightly forward as against

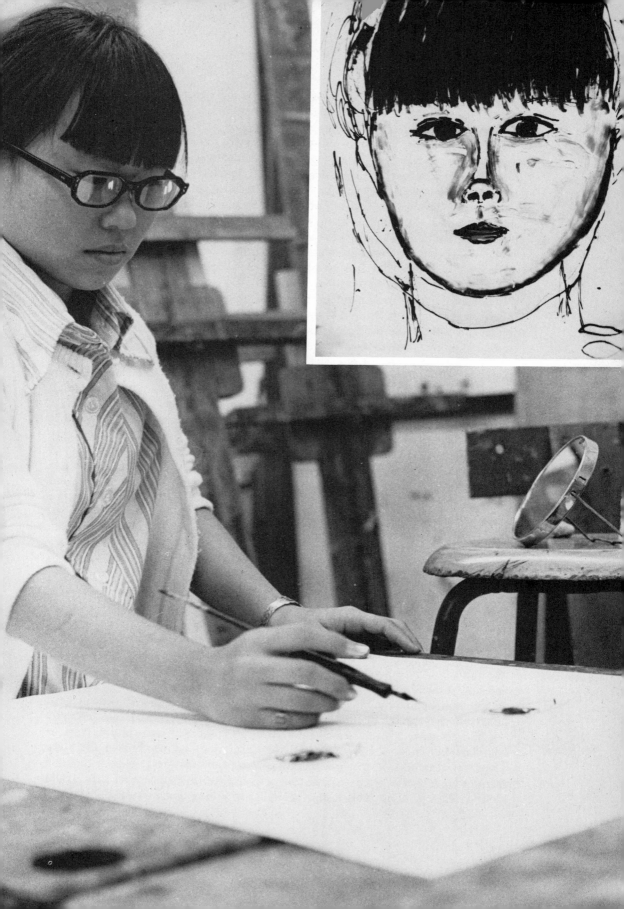

one cheek, which pulls out to the side. Although there is less of the lighter brown than the darker, we read it first because it is what "stands out," in the same way that we read writing or type against a white paper.

We see this more starkly in self-portrait drawings where the problem of light and dark arises inherently from the use of ink, charcoal, or conte crayon. Patti, for example, creates the black shapes of her bangs, eyes, nose, mouth, which carry down as a vertical series of dark shapes against the whiteness of the rest of her face. In this case, we can talk about a movement of "darks" which give form and direction to the shapes. Again, we read the features first, as we would if they were a light or dark color, for we read that which is emphasized.

Unless color is presented as an area of exploration, children are not consciously concerned with light and dark or warm and cool. But when we observe them in the process of picture making, we note that they are continually creating new relationships in conforming to their own needs to organize. Even when they paint over or take out parts without knowing why they are doing so, they are making judgments. And these judgments are based not on what they know in a factual sense but on their associations in a feeling sense.

Associative Aspects of Color.   The associative aspects of color give children's painting its characteristic expressionist quality. If we ask children to free-associate on a color, such as red, they offer such varied responses as "hot," "intense," "flashy," "mellow," "angry"; and to green, they respond "fresh," "grass," "young," "spring," "ocean," "seaweed," "sick." It is interesting to note that what is associated with green bears little resemblance to red. We may consider that these two colors, being opposites, produce different associations. But in a class of ten- and eleven-year-olds, some of the children identified colors with numbers and letters—that is, A with red, B with yellow, C with blue, 12 with orange, and so on, so that although the diversity of responses is not always accountable, we know that it is reflective of very personal kinds of experiences.

Even if we presented all the responses of a group of children, it would become apparent that no two children perceive a color in exactly the same way. The responses would also differ if we asked each one to describe the red of a stop sign, which is a most familiar and frequently observed object.

What does this tell us about the subjective nature of color? In relation to teaching, we must recognize that it is extremely difficult for children (as well as adults) to recall distinct colors, and that the ritualized naming of colors before or while they are working is questionable, for it is the way colors act upon each other that gives them their expressive quality. We are not concerned with looking into the *what,* but into the *how*—that is, how does a child associate with color and how does he make it work? Thus, we do not present him with theories but with conditions that may help him become sensitive to color as the most magical and relative element in painting.

Children arrive at satisfactory color relationships based on exploring various combinations, but not by isolated mixing "exercises" or memorizing the color wheel. For example, in the process of searching they may test colors by mixing them on an adjacent piece of paper but they are still not quite what they would look like in a painting. This testing is similar to jotting down fragments of ideas

Figure 1

Figure 2

Figure 3

Figure 4

Figure 5

Figure 6

Figure 7

Figure 8

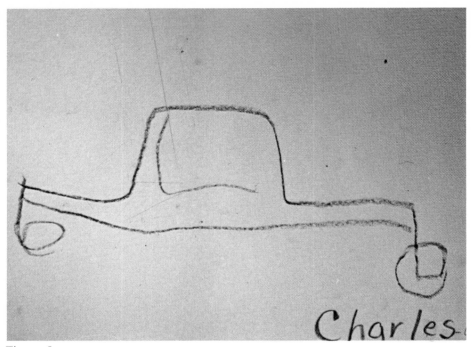

Figure 9

Figure 10

Figure 11

Figure 12

Figure 13

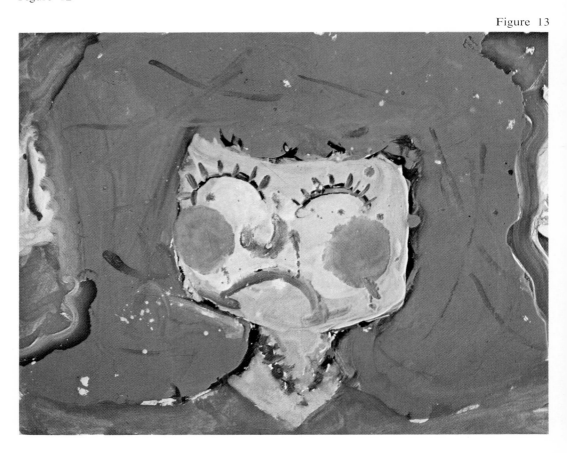

for a poem which, like these color "splotches," may be included or discarded. We can encourage a child's critical judgments by making it possible for him to stand away from his painting occasionally, so that by changing his physical point of view, he sees colors in a different way, and becomes both spectator and critic of his own work. In placing colors together often enough, he discovers how he wants to express himself by experimenting with the properties and potentials of color. He becomes capable of making decisions in an area that can only be learned by "doing." For what is pleasant and satisfactory to each child is based essentially on his educated feelings.

It is perhaps important to note at this point that much of what has been written on children's art relating color associations to certain emotional states has little proven validity for teaching. Neither psychological nor educational research has produced any correlation between choice of colors and emotional feeling beyond the most tenuous implications. Therefore, we must be wary against arbitrary assumptions that yellow means happy, black is scary, blue is sad, and so forth. We can have more confidence in a five-year-old's assertion that "I don't like gray; gray is soggy."

When we say that a child's use of color is expressive, we are not referring to his immediate emotional state. We mean that it is not representational or "true" to the object in nature, but is expressive of the way a child feels about it. It may or may not be descriptive—that is, a sunflower may be yellow or it may be red, white, and blue—but it is not literal. We see evidence of this when a four-year-old paints a house with the curtains of the windows closed, places a thick black line across the top of the paper, and announces, "It's nighttime." Once we release a child from denotative representation—the sky is blue, the sun is yellow, the grass is green—he is free to express relationships that reflect his own feelings.

The way a child handles color is a highly personal matter and each one must settle it for himself. As has been said, systems or rules of complementary or contrasting combinations mean little at the moment of execution, for what "works" is not technical but expressive. Therefore, much depends on the associations and learning experiences of the individual child and on the sensitivity he brings to bear in relation to a particular painting. Although colors tend to act in certain ways, the problem becomes more complex when color is used to create a form, for forms have a great effect upon each other in terms of the kinds of tension they produce. Color cannot be separated from form because form is one of its primary aspects.

Color as line symbolizes objects and feelings and comes into being by virtue of the subjective vision of a child. This does not imply that it is unreal, for once it is created (no matter how fancifully) it exists as part of his reality. Thus, judgments of colors can only be made in terms of their own intrinsic relationship; color is neither imitation nor distortion—it is an invention.

LINE

Line is an abstraction, for it does not exist in nature as it does in painting. In nature we impose linear qualities on edges of objects or boundaries to derive meaning from what we observe. However, children can experience the "irreality" of line kinesthetically by running their hands around the edges of a table, tree, or leaf to discover that they are really dealing with volume. For example, if we place one leaf upon another to draw them, we observe that the two leaves do not have a line between them, but rather, two edges that meet to form a line. What we are dealing with, then, is the edge of a surface which, in turn, sits on top of another surface and is so defined.

But nature does not present us with lines in isolation. We experience them as lines or boundaries of things, defining the shapes by which we ordinarily recognize objects around us. Even if we try to focus upon a line and ignore everything else, it carries over the meaning of the object of which it is an integral part. In this sense, lines contain the properties of objects. Although they demarcate and define objects, they also express ways in which things act upon each other and upon us.

It is the way lines reinforce or counterbalance objects or forms that sets up tension, for in painting they are never independent of external shapes. By their very creation they create shapes. For example, the moment a child makes a simple line moving diagonally across the page without even touching the sides, he has divided the paper and has created two shapes. In so doing, tension is created between the shape above and the shape below, as well as between the line and the four edges of the paper. What we see immediately is the line dividing the space into two parts, thrusting across it.

When children begin to explore the functions of line in gesture drawing, contour drawing, self-portraits, and the like, they begin to observe that lines have different characteristics. In discussing "What is a line?" children from nine to twelve responded in this way:

- Some are wiggley, some are slow.
- It can show gestures—movement.
- It can be something that's straight—that's one thing!
- It can be something that's curvy.
- Even writing is a line—sometimes it's straight, curving, or crossing.
- It can be any shape as long as it's not filled in.
- It can be filled in—stretched out.
- It shows where things are brought out and where they're pushed in.
- Some lines are darker, some are thin.
- It goes on forever, so I've heard.

What these elements reflect is an awareness, if not the vocabulary, of the characteristics of *speed, direction,* and *dimension.*

When we speak of the energy of a line, we are usually referring to its speed and direction. *Speed* does not function in a temporal sense as it does in dance, but determines how long we look at a line. For example, an uninterrupted line, whether horizontal, vertical, or diagonal, is a "fast" line, because it goes directly from "here to there" in space. The "upness" or "downness" of a direction also influences the speed, for, in general, a line moving upward has the feeling of less speed than a line "falling down." (It is perhaps our own relation to gravity which makes us respond in this way.)

Direction gives focus to a painting. Without it, a line is inert and a shape is amorphous in the sense that the work tends to lack power and appears amorphous. Actually, we cannot deal with picture making without direction of lines or shapes. Although children are not aware of this consciously, the moment they put a line on a surface they have created a volume or shape. And whether the form is produced by line or color, it has direction.

Dimensional Quality of Line. The contending opinions of the children cited earlier that a line can be "any shape as long as it's not filled in" or that it can be "filled in" are both alluding to its *dimensional quality.* In a limited sense a line is the result of a mark produced by some medium on the surface of the picture plane. However, if a child begins with one brush stroke and continues to square it out so that it becomes thick, it is a shape. In this sense a line becomes a form, for beyond having the dimension of length (being so long or going so far) it now acquires the dimension of width. But there is no hard-and-fast separation between the two. Line and shape cannot be easily separated, any more than shape and space can be separated from color. We may see the thickness of a brush stroke as texture, shape, or color. Whether we are responding to a shape or a line depends upon how it functions in relation to the total image.

The most vivid exposition of the function of line is to be found in this excerpt from Paul Klee's *Pedagogical Sketchbook.* The clarity of the imagery should delight children and, at the same time, be an enlightening source for teachers. His description of how lines "act" reads like a pictorial journey:

> Breaking away from the dead center (i.e., from the single point), that is our first act of motion (the line). After a moment it stops to catch its breath (broken or articulated line). There is a backward glance to see how far we have come (counter-movement). Tentative starts in several directions (cluster of lines). A river lies in our way, so we take to a boat (wave movement), though there may be a bridge across a ploughed field (plane traced with lines), then through the dense woods . . . meeting basket makers on their way home with their cart (the wheel, a circle). They have a child with the funniest curls (spiral movement). Later on the atmosphere grows sultry and night falls (spatial elements). A flash of lightning brings to mind a fever chart. . . . [4]

Thus, lines are divisions of space, creating the tension of shape against shape, and they are contours that define volumes. But aside from formal definitions, it is the way a child uses line expressively that determines whether it becomes a forceful or static element. Lowenfeld suggests that in children's art especially, lines represent an expression of emotional values. He considers the mere drawing of a line a "creation" because it is expressive of a child's feelings and ideas. Although we tread lightly upon drawing such direct correlations, because art is not immediately symptomatic of feelings, we do observe that lines take many forms and describe many different shapes.

In order to render meaning to a line in children's work, we must look for the different relationships of lines to one another. For example, a line can be a simple direction in space, or it can be formed when two colors meet, and may be thick, thin, delicate, soft, hard, straight, or curved. Beyond this, a line takes on a kind

[4] Will Grohmann, *Paul Klee* (New York: Abrams, n.d.), p. 371.

of emotional expressiveness which we sense as "nervous" or "energetic," vague or wavering, thrusting or collapsing. As an aesthetic quality, we cannot separate the creation of lines from a child's visual and emotional experiences. The different properties and relations of lines that define objects are charged with certain values that reflect children's objective and subjective relations to the world around them. Yet in the painting process, a child has to be stimulated in the discovery that a line is to "feel" as well as to "know"; that is, that lines are not merely representative, but are suggestive of some type of "felt" experience. Through developing his own sensibilities, the child gradually becomes aware that just as a line encloses a shape, so does it also describe an experience.

TIME

Unlike dance or poetry the plastic arts (typically, painting and drawing) lack the element of time. The pictorial image exists through the aesthetic qualities of space and force, yet it is a physically static presence. The basic difference is that time in the visual arts determines neither the content nor the rate of our sequential impressions. That is, pictures do not begin at one moment and end at another, and therefore there is no beginning, middle, or end to the way we perceive them. On the contrary, the very nature of the process is such that we encourage children to be aware of what is happening on all parts of the surface at once, for each element affects every other. Thus, even in the making there is no sequence.

We can, however, distinguish between time as having to do with the essential pictorial image and time as memory or experience. In producing images, children draw from their own memory and experience, which significantly accounts for developmental differences in their work. For spectators time exists as an experience which takes a period of contemplation and has an impact through the extension of its images on our memory. But again, it is not sequential—it is immediate in its presentation.

Experiential Approach

We can consider the nature of children's experience in painting only through the broadest observation of *how* and *what* they produce. Yet most of the literature in this area, beginning with Lowenfeld, ascribes the drawings and paintings that children make at different ages to various developmental schema which find their source in psychology. Although there is some difference among theorists as to the exact chronological age, the implications are that the visual forms that children produce are the "natural" result of growth factors occurring at predictable stages. In all these theories, a "stage" is used to characterize the successive steps in the organic growth of a child's visual perception as the basis of his artistic activity. Thus, for teachers outside of psychology or psychiatry, the implications have been that children's ability to deal with visual symbols proceeds in an ordered and logically observable manner. Theories describing what happens when children create "typical" images offer us another source of insight into a child. But how do we regard such notions of typicality when confronted with our own experience that not all children pass through all stages, or that we cannot confidently identify a child's age from his work?

Such an approach has fostered two fundamental misconceptions in teaching the visual arts (and has also pervaded other forms). First, it has tended to inhibit the fresh perceptions of teachers in terms of the specific qualities of a painting and has led instead to judgments tied to general theories such as "two's and three's are in the smearing and scribbling stage," "fours make head-figures," "fives are more realistic." How then do we respond to three-year-old Ori's self-portrait of a rounded, solidly painted gray-blue head (which occupies three-fourths of the picture plane), two large, dark-gray circular eyes with black centers, a long, vertical nose made by a thick gray shape that partly encircles one eye and thrusts forward into space, a black square mouth, with one orange and one gray ear on either side of the head? The entire form is shaped by inter-locking and overlapping colors. Presumably, three-year-olds have neither the perceptual acuity to draw from an image nor the ability to make shapes move in space. Shall we regard this as an "exceptional" effort or as something a child is capable of doing, given a certain kind of educational environment?

The second misconception perpetuates the myth that children must be left alone to "go through" developmental stages and that the teacher's role is merely to offer materials and stand aside lest she interfere with a child's "inherent creativity." As a result, teachers have tended to rely heavily on psychological guidelines rather than to look at the child and his art as both separable and interrelated entities. In terms of artistic considerations for teaching, there has been a separation of process from product, with the latter regarded as relatively insignificant.

The belief here is that both components of the art experience are equally valuable and must be considered in helping children develop their aesthetic sensibility. To deny the importance of the way children subjectively organize and express art elements through objectively stated forms negates the value of painting as another language. It is insufficient to regard children's work as merely another kind of experience or one that necessarily follows certain stages. An approach that would free teachers from making judgments in terms of predetermined categories would be to view development not as moving in a logical progression, but as interrupted, with lapses and overlapping phases. Children's artistic production moves more in a zigzag pattern than in a steady increment. And we know empirically that as children grow older, they do not necessarily produce work of greater quality, for societal factors which are even more pressing come into play.

The importance of viewing children's art as a developmental process is that they find ways of coping with their own states of feeling, of becoming aware of subject matter about which they feel deeply, and of discovering forms through which to express those feelings. Certain sequential images appear, such as repeating circles or squares or dividing space in certain ways, but these also appear in the work of adult artists. (Perhaps because we are a standing species, it is a way of ordering our perception in relation to the vertical and horizontal axes of our bodies.) In any case, the experience of making a painting is one of looking

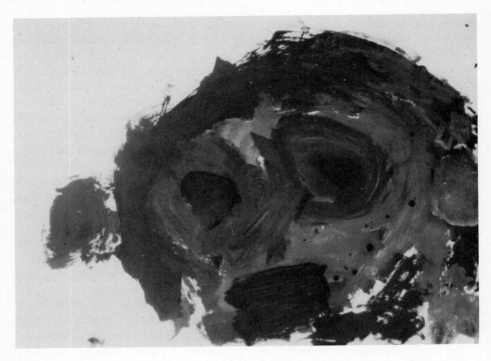

inward to oneself to see the outward world and of abstracting what is visually and emotionally relevant.

CHILD-CENTERED AND CONTENT-CENTERED

Developmental information is useful in appraising a child's growing self-concept in the way he identifies with his own creative efforts. If we are to observe this growth, however, we need to accumulate his paintings and drawings over a considerable period of time. This is reason enough neither to discard work nor to send it home after each session. Sharing it with teachers and peers not only offers children an understanding of another facet of themselves, but helps them to become aware of how they did what they did. Through such exposure, they begin to learn about the generative forces of the art process itself. If we recognize art as both a product of and a vehicle for the expression of human insight, we find an alternate approach to that of psychology. It is, as we have suggested, one which views children's art as *both child-centered* and *content-centered*. Although we are dealing specifically with painting in this chapter, the concepts in relation to content in art can be generalized to include sculpture, dance, and poetry as well.

What do we mean when we refer to "content" in children's art? We know that it is frequently confused with subject matter and that both are usually associated with storytelling. Painting as a language involves *what* is being said (subject matter) and *how* it is said (content and form). In the language of painting, what we are dealing with, then, is *subject matter, content,* and *form* as interrelated entities. In the painting experience it is impossible to separate them—to speak, for example, of emotional content without form, for that is what art is all about. Although each is an ingredient of the other they are not identical, so for purposes of discussion we may identify them separately.

When we turn to the *what* of painting we must recognize that there is no subject that does not include who a child is and how he perceives it. We can, however, distinguish between subject and subject matter. In the opening chapter we drew a general distinction between subject matter in the arts and in other areas of the curriculum by suggesting that "subject" is the individual and "matter" is the education of feelings and the development of sensibility. Now, in relation to painting, we distinguish further between subject as a child's psychological motivations and expectations and subject matter as those objects or events that he makes visible in a picture. As a reflection of a child's sensibility, then, the matter becomes the content, which is the emotional attitude through which subject matter is expressed. We borrow the concept from Shahn that, "Form is the very shape of content," [5] and view it as the total embodiment of the aesthetic qualities within the art object itself.

The relationship among these entities becomes rather dramatic when we consider what children are involved with in making self-portraits. We observe that children frequently put themselves in their pictures, whether or not they identify themselves as such, for they are their own most intimate and interesting subject. When we, in turn, offer an artistic problem of drawing or painting a self-portrait, we make it possible for them literally to "look into themselves" (via a mirror) and to see themselves as both subject and subject matter. Although the subject matter is the same for all children, the content will vary according to the way each child feels about himself, and the form will be shaped by his search for artistic perception.

Subject Matter.   *Subject matter* is whatever object or situation is being drawn or painted. In a self-portrait it is the head and perhaps the shoulders of a child, but it could also be a house, street, still life, or something fanciful. Again, art departs from the conventional sequence of studies in that there is no increasingly complicated or changing subject matter that must be taught, because all things may be equally appropriate to all age levels. By the age of three or four, all the complex elements such as multiple forms, space, focus, exaggeration, color variations that exist in more developed art are reflected in children's work. We see, for example, that a self-portrait is made by a three-year-old as well as an eleven-year-old. Therefore, it is not a question of moving from the simple to the complex. If anything, it is quite the reverse, for even with children's art the attempt is to make the complex simple. That is, for those things that cannot be stated visually in reportorial terms, children must find forms through which to express their evanescent states of feeling. The problem of art, therefore, is to make complicated things simple, not simple-minded.

What we need to understand is that subject matter is not the dominant criterion

[5] Ben Shahn, *The Shape of Content* (Cambridge, Mass.: Harvard University Press, 1957), p. 53.

by which we judge a painting. Identifying objects or giving them a narrative meaning may have no significance other than the practical one of identification, and may have even less to do with illuminating the qualitative aspects of the work. It is perhaps because we are overly preoccupied with labels and titles that we persist in asking, "What is it?" To a very young child, such a demand often imposes a need to respond even though he may have no articulated idea. Even with an older child, it often produces a quickly contrived title or story which tells us little about his attitudes or feelings. Perhaps this is why some adult painters prefer vague titles or none at all, referring to pictures as #1, #2, #3, or Studies in Black and White. We may interpret this as a means of avoiding the general tendency to associate the objects or events in a painting directly with those from our prior experience.

In both adult's and children's work it is the expressive content that animates the form. If this is present, the meanings, which exist on many levels, take care of themselves. A painting is not an inventory of objects, for if that were our criterion a photograph would be more suitable. Nor are paintings anecdotes for the sake of storytelling. An anecdote or incident may excite a child enough to lead him to build a picture around it, and it thus becomes a source of imagery. The distinction is simply between a painting that speaks to us merely by its story and one whose emotional content is such that it appeals to us whether or not we clearly understand its story content. Even when we can readily identify the subject matter in a picture, it is not "like" something else; it is itself.

Yet subject matter is not unimportant, for it triggers a child's responses, initiates his attitudes, and stimulates his efforts. On all levels of the art experience subject matter may be similar, but it may also be of the greatest variety. A painting can express any object or situation capable of being presented in a pictorial image. The only criterion is that a child must identify with it; it must involve him in his own emotional being and have some pertinence to his life. Although subject matter cannot be "taught" or imposed, it can be presented in such a way as to open children's emotions and perceptions of something close but unrecognized. As an example, this author's work with children's painting in predominantly black schools bears out the findings of experimental studies that many black children paint themselves white. Because of their experience that the "important" or powerful people in their lives are white—the policeman, father's boss, mother's boss, the teacher—they consciously or unconsciously associate white as the "right" color to be. It requires sensitivity and guided observation from a teacher to encourage black children to identify with themselves in visual terms.

It seems reasonable to assume that children's artistic needs for expression usually depend on the intensity of their experiences. But a variety of experiences does not necessarily commit a child to painting a variety of subject matter. Nor does the presentation of many different topics guarantee that they will find tangible expression in painting. It may be an imposition on a teacher's part to attempt to establish a one-to-one relationship by assigning topics such as, "What I Did on My Summer Vacation," "A Trip to the Zoo," and so forth. Just as a teacher may select subject matter with which children can identify, so can she gain insight from children's own choices as to their emotional needs and interests. What becomes apparent over a period of time is that a child will transform into a painting experiences that are vital and meaningful to him.

The essence of the painting process lies in a child's faculty to convey through the eye those qualities by which objects are distinguished, and the visual aspects by which he perceives them in nature. This does not imply that a child tries to imitate nature or "copy" reality. Ultimately, his search is for a subjective reality embodying his sensuous response to the qualities of a given moment of vision in a tangible form. Thus the function of painting is not to portray the facts of external reality, but to express emotions or attitudes toward selected aspects of that reality. We may ask, therefore, "How does a child transform subject matter into images?"

For most children the process of picture making does not follow a pattern thought out and determined in advance. Rather, the act of "doing" follows the shifting thoughts and feelings. A child does not necessarily approach media with an image fixed in his mind, for often it is simply the elements of painting that interest him—one color against another, spatial relationships, the action of lines. In the process he uses his hands and frequently his body to do something to whatever elements engage him. For young children, especially, forms emerge in the very process of manipulating media, and whether they are accidental or deliberate, they may lead to new images and ideas a child has not previously considered. To this extent we present problems that stimulate explorations of formal qualities to encourage children to experience art beyond its literal or storytelling aspects. As a result of this encounter an image—either figurative or abstract—may come into being.

What constitutes an image is not merely an arrangement of given materials; it is the emotional content expressed in that arrangement, and it is something that a child forms, not something he finds. Several images may be developing, one of which comes forth from a series of things that he has done. Whatever is created, regardless of the method used, takes on a life of its own. That is, the image begins to come through, and whether or not a child is conscious of its development at every moment, eventually a total image takes place. But we do not divorce the art object which has a life of its own from the child who made it, even though he did not know in the process how it was going to take shape.

Content. Children's arrangements of elements reflect a need to find order for their own ideas and feelings. Otherwise, why do they make changes and shift shapes around? What we assume to be change for aesthetic reasons may actually be due to a need for emotional ordering. Content is not the subject matter of art; it is the expressive relationships each child puts together that shape the content. Thus, there is a difference between subject matter and what is being expressed. When we describe children's art as content-centered, we are suggesting that art cannot be expressed without being formed. This means that expression is abstracted from a whole range of feelings conceived and created through forms. Because much of children's subject matter is abstract, we can consider content as that which sets up a kind of equilibrium having an emotional source, not just a physical sense of balance. When we say that subject matter initiates attitudes, we mean that it elicits emotional attitudes of children toward what they are seeing, thinking, feeling. And it is these emotional attitudes to which we refer as content.

For example, a teacher takes a group of seven-year-olds on a walk around their school, which is located in a church. When they return, they are instructed to paint what they have seen. Any two paintings will show that although both children were exposed to the same visual experience, each child painted what he thought and felt was real to him. One child presents a solid, square white building with a pointed roof and a black cross on top, centered against a blue stripe of sky and a green strip of grass. The general feeling is stolid and restrained. The other paints an orange building with a purple roof and a blue cross, in swirling, tempestuous strokes, all of which pull toward the right side of the picture plane, giving a feeling of tension and energy.

Thus, subject matter (whether drawn from memory or imagination) belongs to the external world. Yet each child, as subject, responds to that material in a distinctive way and transforms it into an object that becomes part of his private, subjective world. We may still recognize it as having aspects that we commonly perceive, but as we have said, it is no longer "like" something else, it is its own image. To be the content of art, therefore, it must be re-created through new forms and not be merely suggestive or reminiscent. The subject matter a child selects may reflect his own interests and needs, yet in a sense it is impersonal, for it belongs to everyone who perceives it. What is personal is the form and content through which he expresses it, for this is completely individual and un-replicable. It is not our ability to recognize what is in a painting or drawing that alone determines our judgments, it is the expressive qualities through which subject matter is transformed that gives it its fresh vision. Nor is subject matter merely the arranging or placing of forms in new ways, but rather it is creating a new experience for both child and observer.

What we are concerned with, then, is *expressive content,* which not only embodies subject matter but is shaped by a child's emotional attitudes, ideas, and feelings toward it. With this in mind, we might become more thoughtful about children's subjective use of size, shape, and distance. If a father, a mother, a house, and an animal are all placed equally on the paper, "correcting" for perspective or proper scale, for example, may be irrelevant, because that is viewing subject matter in a very limited way. It is not dealing with content, which is the way a child (as well as an adult) feels about objects in relation to each other. If we accept content as emotional expression which has been given shape, we need not impose a predetermined realistic vision upon a child, for whose reality are we considering? When we say that something has been "given shape," we mean that a child transforms what would otherwise be an unrelated series of sensations and emotions into new and sudden combinations that may be recognized and given significance.

Form.   Up to this point we have used form interchangeably with shape as created by colors, lines, and spatial tensions. To this extent we have associated shape with form as one of the inherent parts of a piece of artwork. But shape is only one element in an aesthetic form, it does not constitute the whole thing. When we quote Shahn's definition that "form is the shape of content," we are referring to form as the total aesthetic organization, and the overall sensory perception that a child has invested in it. We are using form in the sense that subject matter has undergone a change and the child's shaping and arranging of qualities in relation to each other have organized a total vision.

In the painting process form is a way of perceiving, feeling, and presenting the experience of subject matter so that it becomes translated into a pictorial image. As we noted earlier, we cannot really separate what is done from how it is done, for subject matter is what it is because of the way it is expressed through form and content. How, then, does form come about? We may say that form is the ultimate expression of the transforming role of the painting experience. By this we mean that a transformation occurs as a child works in that the shapes which finally emerge embody the emotional content of a particular painting. It is in this sense that we speak of "expressive form" as something formed and as being imbued with feeling.

Thus, to find a form that embraces the emotional content of subject matter is both the process and product of every artistic effort. This does not imply that every form is resolved, for we are not concerned here with judging quality. Nor does this only apply to figurative objects. If the subject matter of a child's work is only paint itself, its content consists of the exploratory energy which he invests and perhaps even in the accidental qualities revealed by the paint. Nonrepresensational works may be as powerful or weak as representational ones. It is not the subject matter that is the determining quality. If they are exciting and vital, they are so for the same expressive reasons—the same qualitative elements apply to both. Langer states it very well when she writes, "A work of art is an expressive form created for our perception through sense or imagination, and what it expresses is human feeling." [6]

Elements of Painting

Although the elements of painting usually refer to color, line, and texture, certain secondary properties arise from the way one form relates to another, or to several others, in making space visible. In this context we shall discuss *balance, proportion,* and *rhythm,* as factors that serve the conceptualization of an idea or emotion. Teachers tend to approach these elements mechanically, based on misconceptions of adult art. For example, a confusion of balance with symmetry may obscure the sometimes vital imbalance and asymmetry which characterize adult art as well as much of children's painting. Asymmetry is a kind of balance which sets up a dynamic force between forms rather than a static, formal relationship. In each case, it is important that we do not reduce them to technical devices, for all discernible elements contribute to the expressive power of the pictorial image.

BALANCE

In an earlier section we defined force as an opposition of tensions or energies expressed as countermovement. But such opposition is not to be sought through

[6] Suzanne K. Langer, *Problems of Art* (New York: Scribner, 1957), p. 15.

formal balance. Rather, we are suggesting that tension, which is essential in a picture, implies a breaking away from balance. If a painting were totally balanced, there would be no tension. What we are looking for in children's painting is not the equal placement of objects or shapes on a surface, but a sense of *equilibrium* which brings together the force of forms, colors, and movement within the work itself.

We may also associate balance with a kind of *weight* given to a painting, which produces a sense of equilibrium. It is not that colors, textures, or shapes are physically heavy in the way that a collage actually protrudes from a surface. It is because darker colors, rougher textures, and larger shapes give the illusion of being visually heavier than lighter colors, smoother textures, and smaller shapes. Balance, then, is created by the tension of large shapes in countermovement against small, warm colors against cool, light against dark, texture against texture.

Children's greatest power is in creating a psychological equilibrium through their very subjective use of space. For them, the problem is nothing other than being expressive. They are not concerned with composition as adults may consider it, nor are they concerned with consciously creating an equilibrium. Rather, they are involved in trying to transform what they remember and see and what they think and feel into a kind of expressive whole. We may think, then, in terms of *expressive balance,* which is based on a child's interest and is reflected through his focus on and placement of things on the picture plane. In this way he indicates pictorially that certain shapes or figures are more important to him than others. Thus, a feeling of balance has to do with the nature of a child's perception in relation to particular subject matter, and does not follow arbitrary rules of composition.

Balance, along with other traditional notions such as symmetry and perspective, needs to be reconsidered in relation to the emotional content of a child's vision. We recognize that they sometimes work in a painting or drawing, depending on what a child is trying to do. But children's worlds are not balanced; they are always in a state of ambiguity. In today's world especially, children are learning so fast, trying to organize their ideas and emotions, that to impose these elements abstractly is inhibiting. To expect that children conform to such adult preconceptions is inappropriate.

PROPORTION

The most common misconception about proportion is that the relationship of forms must be expressed in terms of their naturalistic sizes. But as we have stated throughout, the child is the point of reference for his perceptual world, and therefore size and shape are screened through his emotional attitudes. Children express ideas of size and shape by transforming what they see into what they feel, for they are motivated more by subjective, expressive needs than by duplicative efforts. They are more concerned with the imaginative and emotional qualities of experiencing what is important to them than with transcribing it literally.

A major characteristic of children's art is that it is rarely depictive of the way objects or events appear to the eye, but of the way they appeal to the sensibilities.

Thus, children's approach to proportion is based on its emotional or functional importance. We are using *functional* in two ways: first, as conveying the function of what is being done, such as parts of the body which are performing certain crucial actions or making certain gestures, and, second, as expressing a child's emotional intent. For example, to a very young child, head and hands are more important than neck and shoulders, for he perceives their functions more directly. Similarly, in portraying his family, he may place his sister next to him but upside down, because that is the way he feels about her.

We frequently notice that the exaggeration of significant parts, such as making the hands and feet or mouth large, is accompanied by the omission of less important parts, such as a nose or ears. Of course, judgments of exaggeration, omission, or distortion refer to the way adults see things. When a child makes a person as large as a house or a figure as tall as a tree, he presents us with relative proportions very different from our own. Yet what he is creating is a pictorial image of the experiential size and significance that objects and living beings have for him. In so doing, he transforms the truth of what he knows to the truth of what he feels, convinced that both are real.

Children do not sense the discrepancy unless it is pointed out to them. Therefore, what we may judge as a lack of proportion may as well be viewed as a child's vision of the size and placement of objects. Naturalistic conceptions find little place in children's drawings and paintings, for they see the world differently from the way they portray it. In becoming aware of the difference between the representation and the thing represented we may gain insight into a child's "real" experience.

Although size is a subjective element, it is also affected by an objective condition that may influence the way a child expresses proportion. It is simply that different sizes of paper have different effects, just as using large brushes produces qualities different from those produced by small brushes. A 20- by 20-inch piece of paper is not necessarily preferable to one 8 by 11 inches, but each surface provokes different responses. Since children perceive elements in terms of their expressive function, we must provide avenues for the most diverse artistic expression within a medium. Even very young children must be given the opportunity to select paper of different dimensions (as well as brushes of varying size) so that they can experience different possibilities in working large and small. More particularly, we may observe that some children function only with one or the other. To children who have already found expression on large surfaces, for example, a teacher may offer even larger sizes to open exploration further. What we are suggesting is that teachers need to consider size in both of its aspects— as the size of various parts as they relate to each other within a picture, and as the size of the picture plane itself.

Thus, children's relation to size reflects a visual impression, not a camera image, and so does their approach to space. Just as a child makes those figures or shapes larger to which he attaches more emotional significance, so do objects which recede tend to be considered less important. Children do not conceptualize space in terms of *perspective,* which is a technique for making objects appear to move back in space by giving the illusion of distance. Perspective is a convention developed during the Renaissance as a means of representing objects not as we know them but as we see them. Simply stated, artists at that time decided to project an image of reality in which objects close to us were made bigger than those that are farther away.

A convention in this case is merely a system devised for a way of seeing; it is not an absolute condition. In Oriental art, for example, perspective is reversed, in that objects and figures that move farther into the distance may be larger. Yet we in the Western world have no difficulty in recognizing in a Japanese or Chinese landscape that the tree closest to us may be smaller than the mountain which is looming behind, which not only is farther away but becomes larger as it moves spirally into space. It would enhance our own perceptions to recognize that our ways of seeing are based on conventions that depend on the time and circumstances in which we live. Therefore, rather than impose a "method" of seeing upon children, we need to encourage them to see freshly.

RHYTHM

Finally, we turn to rhythm as an inherent organizing factor in all art forms. Although it is easier to observe in dance and poetry, it functions in painting and sculpture as well. In the visual arts we become aware of rhythm by perceiving how the qualities of color, line, texture, and shape are repeated in a certain order or pattern. Thus, we see rhythm as *repetition* of qualities stated over and over again with varieties, much like a musical theme is composed. But it is not something a child deliberately sets out to do; it is a product of his attempt to cope with the picture plane in terms of organizing his perceptions and states of feeling.

Without a rhythmic structure, however, lines, textures, colors, and shapes within a picture would be chaotic and have no relationship to each other. Yet, as with proportion and perspective, we must recognize that rhythm has no relation to schematic renderings isolated from the expressive intent of the total image. That is, attempts to "teach" rhythmic structure by putting colors, shapes, or lines in prescribed combinations tend to disassociate it from other problems of art such as subject matter and emotional content. For children, such an approach is mechanical because it substitutes modes of abstract design for children's own rhythmic, organizing expression. Rhythm cannot be ritualized, for it is a "felt" experience.

The elements we have discussed here are merely a means to an end, they are not technical ends in themselves. Children may or may not be aware of their existence in the process of picture making, but to isolate them from the composed "wholeness" of the form is to focus on what is in the work rather than on how it functions in terms of expressive qualities. The fact that they occur gives a teacher an opportunity to help a child know and appreciate what he has done toward making a picture interesting. Just as a child creates relationships of color, line, and texture, so does he use these elements not as skills or techniques, but as aesthetic, expressive qualities. Thus, the whole arrangement of a picture is expressive—the placement of figures or objects, their size and shape, the empty space around them—everything plays a part.

PROBLEM: To observe the physical properties of color

TEACHER: Let's talk about what you know about color. Anything you think, even if you don't know, just your feeling about color.

CHILD: Like if you have a color green and you put orange or white in it you get gray; you can make different colors with it.

TEACHER: Okay. You can mix colors and make different colors out of them. What else?

CHILD: Also letters. When you think of a letter A you might think of blue or red.

TEACHER: That's an idea. What do you think of when you think of A?

CHILD: I think of red.

TEACHER: What do you think of when you think of B?

CHILD: Yellow.

TEACHER: C?

CHILD: Blue.

TEACHER: Three?

CHILD: Green.

TEACHER: Twelve?

CHILD: Orange.

TEACHER: Why do those colors or numbers have these feelings for you?

CHILD: Maybe in your life certain numbers are associated with certain colors, so it sticks in your mind, and you don't know that when you say it.

TEACHER: Right. Maybe every May you went out in the country, so you think green because it's grassy and it's springtime. Who knows why? But it is interesting that you raised that because a lot of people in the past, very famous artists and writers, have had those feelings about numbers and colors too. What else about color? What other kinds of associations do colors have for you? Let's just throw out words. If I say "red," what do you think?

CHILD: Mellow.

TEACHER: Anybody think of anything else red?

CHILD: Hot.

CHILD: Intense.

CHILD: Flashy.

CHILD: Angry.

TEACHER: Anything else? What if I throw out "green"?

CHILD: Fresh.

CHILD: Grass.

CHILD: Young.

CHILD: Spring.

CHILD: Ocean.

CHILD: Seaweed.

CHILD: Beautiful.

CHILD: Sick.

CHILD: Leaves.

CHILD: You can associate different colors with different moods or feelings.

TEACHER: Yes. Notice that no one said anything associated with green that was in any way close to red. The words that came out were very different in associating green with red. Suppose I say "white."

CHILD: Nurse.

CHILD: Cold.

CHILD: Dull.

CHILD: Bright.

TEACHER: You are thinking of two very different kinds of white. You're right; colors do have all kinds of feelings attached to them. Let's take the idea that somebody said "dull" and somebody said "bright" for white, and I said, "You must be thinking about different whites." Look around at what everyone is wearing; look at everything white. How can you describe these different whites?

CHILD: Glossy.

TEACHER: What else?

CHILD: Dirty.

TEACHER: What else?

CHILD: Bright.

CHILD: Cream.

TEACHER: Let's think about something else for a minute. We've been talking about things like red, blue, green, etc.; we've been *naming* colors. Colors have certain properties—certain things about them that we're going to explore today. One of them is *h-u-e*. Have you ever heard of it?

CHILD: Yes.

TEACHER: What does it mean?

CHILD: It's like the tone of a color.

TEACHER: What's the tone? (*No response.*) *Hue* is simply the *name* of a color. So when we talk about red, yellow, blue, that's the hue. Now somebody raised another issue. Someone said "dull"; somebody said "glossy." I'm going to change glossy to bright. The minute you start talking about *dull* and *bright* you're talking about another property of color we call *intensity*. What has intensity got to do with it?

CHILD: How dull or bright it is.

TEACHER: Exactly. Think about red screaming as brilliant as can be coming out of a jar; that is really an intense red. The minute you start mixing other colors with it, it still may be very intense, but the intensity of it as red gets less. There is another property in color that is related to intensity, because people mix it up with intensity, and that's called *value*. Value has to do with what we were talking about before—tone, which is how *light or dark* something is. Think about it for a minute.

TEACHER: Think light and dark; think dull and bright. People very often say "dark" when they mean "bright."

CHILD: "Dark" when they mean "bright"?

TEACHER: Yes, somebody will say, "She is wearing a dark blue dress," and when you look at it, it's a very intense blue dress, it's very bright. For example (*pointing to children around room*), if you look at her pants, his shirt, his shirt, and her shirt, those are all dark blue, if you think of blue going from this blue (*points to one shirt*) to this blue (*points to another shirt*). Are these dark or light?

CHILD: Dark.

TEACHER: They are all dark. Which would you say is the most intense blue?

CHILD: Hers.

CHILD: No, his.

TEACHER: How many people think his shirt? Her shirt? Don't be afraid to say it. One thing about art is that there are absolutely no absolutes—what does that mean?

CHILD: Nothing is . . .

CHILD: . . . completely right or completely wrong.

TEACHER: Nothing is only one way. I sort of feel that her shirt is more intense because it seems to be "bluer." The other one seems to have more white in it. Do you see the difference? You might say that his shirt is about as dark as that but it's duller, it's got less blue in it, it's got more other colors.

CHILD: It also doesn't look as dark as this because it has the white around the neck and sleeves.

TEACHER: Ah! That is a very important part and that's something you're going to discover today when we talk about colors not being absolutes. It means that colors change, depending on what's around them.

For example, let's take a little blob of this brilliant red and put it anywhere in a room like this. If this room were painted black it would look one way, but if you paint the room an absolutely brilliant magenta and then drop a spot of red in it, it will look very different. If you mixed orange in that red it would still look different. Have you ever had the experience of buying a piece of clothing, let's say a shirt, and you're wearing a certain color pants when you buy it? And when you come home and try it on with pants of a different color it looks completely different?

CHILD: Things look different in different light.

TEACHER: Or the light changes the way it looks, right? So there is no absolute about color. One of the things that changes it is what surrounds it. The other thing that happens is that color has what we call *space-making* properties. What do you think that has to do with?

CHILD: It can make something seem smaller or bigger, depending on the color.

TEACHER: I wouldn't say so much smaller and bigger as *back and forth*. In other words, color can make things appear to move closer to you or far away.

Now come over here and sit facing these three papers on the board (*red, yellow, and blue construction paper*). What's really important about the first thing you'll be doing is *how you observe*. We're not too concerned with what they end up like as a group of paintings, even though they'll be interesting as shapes, colors, and lines. We're interested in having you really think about what you're doing and observe very particular things; for example, we were talking about the observation that color changes, depending upon what's around it. (*Teacher paints red square on lower part of red paper, long red horizontal line on bottom of yellow paper, red circle on upper right side of blue paper.*) Do those reds all look like the same color?

CHILDREN: Nooooooo.

TEACHER: How do they look different? First of all, the people sitting at the edges should move in close toward the middle because where you sit really affects how you see things.

CHILD: The red one on the yellow paper is more intense—it's clearer, it's more pure; in the red line on the blue paper, the blue's showing through and . . .

CHILD: . . . the one on the blue paper is standing out.

TEACHER: Now you're talking about two different things. When you say *"standing out,"* you're talking about the way it *makes space.* What I asked is, does the color look any different? You are talking about the intensity of the color when you say it looks more or less intense. Does the hue look different?

CHILD: Yes.

TEACHER: How does it look different?

CHILD: It gives you a different feeling for the red.

TEACHER: How does the red look different? Can you describe how it looks on the red paper, for example, in terms of the color itself?

CHILD: Like on the yellow, it's bolder; like on the blue it looks really dull; the blue paper is a dark color and the red paper—well, the red is really a dark color too but it doesn't look as red. . . .

TEACHER: If it does look red, what does it look more like?

CHILD: Purple.

TEACHER: Okay. Now you're talking about several different things. One is the idea that on the red paper you have a red that is quite dark, and you have this blue paper which is much darker than the yellow as a field (*background*). So you have a contrast of light and dark between the red paint on the different backgrounds. On the red paper you have very little contrast between red and red, and on the yellow the contrast is tremendous; it's almost like white and black. So you get this type of intense color (*yellow*), which changes the intensity of the feeling of the red. And it also starts to be what Steve was talking about—it moves in space and begins to do what? What happens to the red color on the yellow paper that doesn't happen on the red or blue paper?

CHILD: It stands out.

TEACHER: It really stands out; the red begins to *pull away* from the yellow.

CHILD: Your eye goes to the red.

CHILD: In the yellow the red stands out more, but with the red on the blue paper, the red just sort of sits there.

TEACHER: What about the red on the red paper? What I'm asking you is about the relation between light and dark.

CHILD: They are both pretty dark.

TEACHER: Yes. There is a fairly close relationship between the red of the color and the red of the field. Does this red on the blue paper look like this red on the red paper? How is it different?

CHILD: Because you can still see a little touch of the blue behind it and it makes the red shape look more purple.

TEACHER: And what does this red shape look like?

CHILD: The red on the red paper looks just like—plain; it looks just like it even though it's not the same red.

CHILD: It just looks dark. On the blue paper it looks more purple.

TEACHER: Would you imagine that we could carry on such a long conversation about three little marks on three pieces of colored paper? I think that's really exciting, don't you?

CHILDREN: Yeah, yep, yes.

PROBLEM: To explore colors acting physically and spatially in relation to each other

TEACHER: We've talked about the differences in colors, depending upon *what other colors surround* them and we've talked about the differences in *spatial feeling*. The minute you say something *stands out more you're* beginning to see that it is *pushing* one way or the other; you're saying it is closer to you than something else that is further back.

CHILD: If you're talking about forward or backward that's one kind of standing out, but if you're talking about seeing it better because it's. . . . Let's say you have a whole bunch of people wearing black shirts standing around in a big group and one person is wearing a white shirt, that person is gonna stand out an awful lot and you can see it better, just like that red jumps out on the yellow. . . .

TEACHER: Right.

CHILD: But there is another kind of "standing out." Like if you draw a box. . . .

TEACHER: You mean make it three-dimensional?

CHILD: Three-dimensional, that kind of standing out.

TEACHER: Yes, there is a difference, you're right. When I say "standing out" in terms of a color making space, I'm talking about your idea about the box except that the box is one way of making space, and using color is another way of making space. People who don't know a lot about art think that a box or a three-dimensional object is the only way of showing something making space. For example, the box you're talking about goes back to fifteenth-century Italy where a number of artists sat down and devised a system, and said, "This is the way we're going to show space"— and that's the whole idea of perspective. But there are ways artists used before that to create space and there are other ways that artists have used since then. Where you live in terms of what culture you are in determines how you make space. Our ideas come so much from the Renaissance in

Italy that when we're drawing and something is close to us, we make it bigger than something that is far away, isn't that so? If you're drawing two trees and one is close and one is far away, you make the other smaller. But do you know anything about Chinese art? If you look at a Chinese landscape, what happens?

CHILD: Most Chinese art is about nature and it has a lot of people in it.

CHILD: When it is a landscape it curves up and, when it has people they are very small, and the people that are far away are bigger; the people who are closer are smaller.

TEACHER: It's really the exact opposite of our convention of seeing. By convention, I mean a rule that somebody sets up. Even Western people have no trouble looking at a Chinese scroll and saying, "Oh yes, that mountain which is bigger is further away than this tree which is closer and smaller." It's just the opposite of our Western idea. The way we're going to use color today is another convention of making space. It is a way of seeing it that artists in this century have become involved in. An artist changes the way he works, depending upon the time in which he lives. People today don't paint the way they did in the fourteenth century. Everything is different—the light is different, the surroundings are different, so how can we paint like someone who lived in the 1400's? In this century, artists use color in terms of "standing out" in a very specific way to make this distance of space.

CHILD: Not necessarily in a line.

TEACHER: Exactly, let me show you because I think you'll see it much more clearly this way. *(Teacher, using pink paint, puts small square in the upper left corner of red paper; large curved shape in center of blue paper; S-shaped squiggle on upper right side of yellow paper.)* Do they look the same on all the papers?

CHILDREN: No.

TEACHER: If they don't, can you describe the differences in the color?

CHILD: The pink on the red paper looks pink except that the paper is pinkish-red too; the pink is light and it looks different on the yellow paper.

TEACHER: How different? Squint your eyes and look at them. How do you describe this pink as different from that pink?

CHILD: The pink on the yellow looks more pink than the one on the red, which looks more dull 'cause all around it is pink and red and stuff.

TEACHER: You're saying it looks duller on the red and brighter on the yellow?

CHILD: Yes.

TEACHER: *(To other children)* What do you think?

CHILD: I think it looks brighter on the blue paper because it offsets it.

TEACHER: What about the color itself? Does it look more yellow or more orange, or more blue or more anything on one paper than on any other?

CHILD: Yes, it looks more "bluisher" and . . . .

CHILD: . . . darker.

CHILD: "Bluisher" on the blue paper . . . .

CHILD: Lavender.

CHILD: It looks more orangy.

TEACHER: It looks more orangy on the blue paper and what on the yellow?

CHILD: It looks more pure color on the yellow; on the red it kind of gets bleached out.

TEACHER: You can begin to see that the differences you're observing in the colors are because of what's surrounding them. Let's get back to someone's idea that a color stands out more. I want you to see what happens to color spatially. When I put a mark down on these papers, the first thing is to look at the hue, and how it is different on each piece of paper. The second thing is to imagine that these three pieces of paper are three-dimensional boxes that come out into space like boxes of Jello that are colored red, yellow, and blue.

I'm going to paint these color shapes on them and they are going to swim around in their own space because of their color, but they're going to arrive at some position back and forth, front and back. *(Teacher, using green paint, puts curved line on red paper, beginning from bottom left, horizontally halfway across; outline of green rectangle on lower left of blue paper; small solid square at left edge of yellow paper; paints orange vertically over original red line.)* In this red field, which of these two colors is forward and which is back?

CHILD: I think the red is forward and the pink is back.

CHILD: I think the pink is forward and the red is back.

TEACHER: How many people think that pink is forward and red is back? *(She asks reverse question.)*

CHILD: When I look at the pink curvy line it looks like the red is back.

TEACHER: If I had used a huge amount of the pink paint, I think everyone would see that pink is forward and red is back; but because it is just a little bit (remember it's never just one thing; there are all these other colors that come into play), it keeps shifting. The size of something will change the way you see it. Because the pink is little and dull against the bigger and brighter red, you get this kind of switching back and forth. The other thing that is important is *placement*. Which is in front on the blue paper?

CHILD: The red.

CHILD: Yeah, the red.

TEACHER: Does anyone say that the pink is forward?

CHILDREN: No.

TEACHER: Usually things that are lower down on the paper . . .

CHILD: . . . are further forward.

TEACHER: Also, because it's bigger and brighter.

CHILD: Another reason we couldn't agree on the red paper is because of the shape of the curved line.

TEACHER: Yes, *shape* will have something to do with it too. Now, which is doing what on the yellow paper?

CHILD: The red is closer.

TEACHER: Anyone think anything different?

CHILD: I think the red is inside and the pink is just indented into the wall.

TEACHER: So which is closer to you?

CHILD: The pink one.

CHILD: I think the red one is.

TEACHER: Here's a situation where they're both about the same amount, yet one is much darker than the other. But where they're placed is important. You can think of it in several different ways; you can think of the red as being a dark hole in the yellow paper, which will push it way back and the pink would be forward; or, I can think of it almost like a comet that starts out in the front and is shooting back, and this pink shape is just kind of wiggling along back there, kind of quietly.

One of the exciting things about painting is that if you sit in front of one painting for a very long time, all of these things begin to happen, in the sense that you see them immediately; you see "here's blue, here's yellow, here's red," and all of the places are kind of defined and it's there. If you look at it long enough and really think about what's happening, the thing begins to move. If a painting is really "alive," it's constantly changing and every time you look at it you'll see different things. If the red seems forward, it will suddenly seem back. If the pink pulls back, it will suddenly come forward—the whole thing will kind of be shifting around because colors vibrate against each other. Not all the time but sometimes. With some paintings everybody will see what's happening right away, but in others it is not clear to everyone the same way; you can see it lots of different ways. Now look at the way these colors move in relation to one another.

CHILD: On the blue paper the blue that's inside the green rectangle looks clear and brighter, more intense, than the other part of the blue paper.

TEACHER: Both blues are the same color; yet surrounding it by another color (*green*) not only makes it more intense, but it does something else to it spatially. What does it do?

CHILD: It closes it off.

TEACHER: Besides closing it off?

CHILD: It lifts it up.

TEACHER: Yes, it pulls it up. I really feel that the blue outside of the rectangle is swimming around compared to the blue inside the rectangle.

CHILD: The blue inside the rectangle looks like a pure color. If you look at the rest of the paper, it looks like it has white in it.

CHILD: The green on the yellow paper seems so fresh and seems like spring; on the red one it looks horrible. . . .

CHILD: It looks like a different color on the red.

TEACHER: How can you describe the difference in the color?

CHILD: It's more fluorescent on the yellow. On the red it kind of looks more dull.

TEACHER: Which one looks greener?

CHILD: On the yellow paper it looks greener.

CHILD: And on the red it looks yellower.

TEACHER: Now, think of the idea of space that we talked about, and let's look at the green shape. Which color is the furthest forward, which is the furthest back, and which is between the two?

CHILD: The pink one looks forward the most.

CHILD: I think the green and the red are almost sort of the same and maybe the pink is a little bit forward.

CHILD: The green is the closet one to you.

CHILD: I think the green is closer than the red and the pink looks the farthest away.

CHILD: I feel that the green is the closest and the red is the last and the pink is in the middle.

CHILD: I feel that definitely the pink is closer.

TEACHER: Definitely?

CHILD: Yeah.

TEACHER: There is no such thing as definitely.

CHILD: Definitely pink is closest and then green is farthest and red is in the middle or vice versa.

TEACHER: Let me ask you this, do you feel that some of these shapes sort of move around? They don't necessarily have to stay flat shapes parallel to the picture plane. For example, in this pink shape on the blue paper this edge could be back in space; the edge is curving out so that the whole form is pulling back to the left. This red circular shape could be spinning around and shooting forward or shooting back. All kinds of things can be happening with them, they are not only flat shapes. So there are infinite possibilities in the way you look at color.

PROCEDURE

TEACHER: Let me talk to you about mixing colors, then we'll talk about what we're going to do. Two of you will be sharing these pallets (*muffin pans*). You'll all have your own cans of water, your own brushes, and some paper towels. You will need empty places in the pallets for mixing colors; some of the pallets have them and some don't. If you need more places to mix, there are extra muffin tins on the shelf that you can use. When you are mixing paint, you start with the lighter color and add the darker one to it. Let me show you what I mean. Supposing I want to mix this white with this red. Now, if I had started with the same amount of red as with white and tried to get this same color, I would have had to use five times more white.

CHILD: If you were making that same color pink and you started with the red, and then wipe the brush and put the red in there first, the entire white would get red.

TEACHER: You mean if I had not cleaned the brush first?

CHILD: Yeah.

TEACHER: Actually these paints are thick enough that you don't have to worry about that. If you use too much water on your brush, your painting will become too watery. You just have to "feel" how the materials work.

Choose three pieces of construction paper to work on so that you can put one color shape on all the papers at the same time. Each color doesn't have to be the same shape, but it can be if you want. Mix as many colors as you wish and each time you put a color shape down, observe the *hue*.

And observe what happens spatially. You can mix and get fifty shapes on each paper and get them really close; however, one thing you should not do. . . .

CHILD: Run them into each other.

TEACHER: Right. You should not do this—what did I just do? *(She dabs orange over red.)*

CHILD: Overlap.

TEACHER: Why?

CHILD: 'Cause it makes you say that one shape is behind another.

TEACHER: It doesn't make any difference what colors you use. For example, this orange could be any color and it would be in front of that red because of the way it is placed; it's *placed physically overlapping* in front of it. What you're going to do in this particular problem is see what happens to the space only because of what's happening in your head and in your eye.

CHILD: I don't understand what we're suppose to do.

TEACHER: Let's say you put two shapes on the paper—two circles—the same color, the same size, and space them equally in relation to the top and the bottom, the sides, and together, right?

CHILD: Yes.

TEACHER: So that all the spaces are equal. The two shapes are the same size, same color, and same shape. Then you say to the shapes, "I want this one to go back and that one to come forward." Then you're going to completely cover the paper around the shapes with other color of shapes so that when you are finished, the paper is all covered with colors and shapes. And by the colors and shapes you choose to go around those original shapes, you're going to try to make the one you want to "go back," go back, and the other one you want to "come forward," come forward.

PROBLEM: To paint an imaginary portrait exploring the spatial properties of color

TEACHER: How would you describe this painting? [*Matisse,* New York: Skira, 1959, "Woman with the Hat," p. 38.]

CHILD: The artist didn't use any particular lines; he used different colors to make the face.

TEACHER: What does the yellow at the tip of the nose do to that nose?

CHILD: Makes it stick out.

TEACHER: Yes, if he had used green for the whole nose, it wouldn't push out like that. *So colors make forms push in and out.*

CHILD: He uses colors in a smudgy way.

TEACHER: What does that mean? Are the colors around the hat very different from what is happening in the head?

CHILD: The colors have no sharp edges—they sort of run into each other.

TEACHER: These are among his early paintings. What is he doing with color here? [*Miro,* New York: Skira, 1965, "Portrait," pp. 22, 23.]

CHILD: It's like the other artist except the space is broken up into definite shapes but within each shape the colors are smudgy.

CHILD: He's breaking it up.

TEACHER: What do you mean?

CHILD: He's breaking it up in different shapes.

TEACHER: Right, he's breaking up the face in different shapes but the shapes are very clear and definite.
Look at this picture [*Matisse,* "Gustave Moreau's Studio, 1895," p. 22.] What about the color between the shapes in the face and the body?

CHILD: It's smudgy.

TEACHER: Yes, it's a lot of different colors that are smudgy. What do you see in this painting? [*Miro,* "Portrait."]

CHILD: Shapes are sharp.

TEACHER: Yes, this is the other extreme from the first painting I showed you by Matisse where he uses all smudgy colors in the face. This painting has very different shapes and the color is different within the shapes. What else do you see here?

CHILD: There's shapes behind him.

TEACHER: Yes, the shapes and colors around it are very much like the shapes and colors in the face and figure.
What do these look like to you? These are his later paintings. [*Miro,* p. 83.]

CHILD. Ugly.

CHILD: Childish.

CHILD: Before, he did what he saw, now he's doing what he's feeling.

CHILD: Here the face and outside are really the same.

TEACHER: You're going to paint a painting of an imaginary head; it can be human or part human, part animal, but the head must take up most of the paper. The space around the head must have something to do with the shapes in the head. You can even put something on it like a hat or hair and you can include shoulders.

PROCEDURE

TEACHER: There are eight colors in each tray (*muffin pans filled with pre-mixed opaque colors*). Do you know the name of every color? What's that one?

CHILD: Magenta.

TEACHER: What do you think magenta has a lot of in it?

CHILD: Red.

CHILD: Red and white.

TEACHER: Whenever you mix colors, you usually start with the lighter color first; the reason is, look what happens if I start with red first. *(Children are standing around a table; teacher mixes colors on a piece of paper.)*

CHILD: You have to use lots of white because red is so strong.

TEACHER: So if I use white first and then add red, does this look like magenta?

CHILD: No.

TEACHER: What other color does magenta have in it?

CHILD: Blue.

CHILD: It needs purple.

TEACHER: We don't have purple; so if we add blue, what color does it become?

CHILD: It becomes more purple.

TEACHER: If I start with yellow and want to mix in green, just a dab of green will change it, but if you put green in first, you'd have to use a lot of yellow to change it.

We're going to paint on large paper (*18 by 24 inches*). When you paint, cover the surface with color so completely that the paper is kind of a support for the paint. If you want the paper to show through, make that a part of your picture.

You will share the trays. If you want to mix colors, come and get an empty muffin tin. Get some brown paper (*on roll*) to put under your paper.

Someone asked if they could outline with a pencil and I said no, because if you outline something, you'll stay within the lines. This problem is very flexible and I want you to work freely.

OBSERVATIONS WHILE CHILDREN ARE WORKING

TEACHER: Instead of finishing with the head first and then discovering the space behind it, I would suggest that you work back and forth from the head to the background.

I think it's fine that you're leaving the head and working on the background.

We really shouldn't think of background as always moving in the back because it's really an important space, because maybe the head will move backward. It's good that you're working on both spaces at the same time because you can see how one affects the other.

Donna is mixing colors on the brown paper before using them. Are you doing this so you can see what they look like before you use them?

CHILD: *(Nods head.)*

TEACHER: *(To class)* Look up for a moment. Elizabeth covered the whole surface of her paper with white; now whatever colors she uses over it becomes mixed with the white.

Jason is using colors that are slightly mixed in the pan and is exploring the way they look as he paints them in stripes. You're not making a shape yet, you're exploring the way colors work, right?

Donna, as you make your mask, fill in all the white spaces. There's a difference between painting a white shape and leaving the white of the paper.

There's a difference between putting down a line and leaving it and never having it change (like an outline) and putting down a line and placing a color next to it; when the color that goes over the line has to change, then the shape of the color changes so that the edges grow between the "backness and forthness" of the two areas. So what you see is the possibility of shapes growing and changing rather than just a one-shot placement of color.

If you draw it with painted lines you need to put color in it.

If you like to work in closed-up shapes and colors, that's fine; or you can work with looser shapes and more smudgy colors.

DISCUSSION

TEACHER: How do you feel about these paintings? Just throw out words that come into your head.

CHILDREN: Weird, crazy, imaginative, feelings.

CHILD: No one painted how they saw it, but how they feel.

TEACHER: Let's take the words you threw out—crazy, weird, feelings—what is it about these paintings that makes you use words like that?

CHILD: They're not very common.

TEACHER: They're not very common in terms of seeing people that look like this, but it has to do with the way they are painted. Some have sharp edges, some have smudgy colors; in some, the shape of the head works with the space around it; in others, the head covers the whole surface of the painting. Some of you had everything painted except one small section of the paper. If you leave it, it's like looking into a hole in the paper. Why were some people afraid to fill everything in?

CHILD: Afraid you'll wreck the face.

TEACHER: But as a result of filling in with color, lines and colors pick up from each other and it becomes a very active painting. So instead of putting down dots for eyes, nose, mouth as separate things, you went back and repainted them as part of the face.

Look at the three portraits of the girls. All of them started out with something, didn't like what they had, so they completely painted over the surface to find what they liked. You have to get used to changing so that a painting grows and develops as you work on it.

CHILD: It's hard to tell in Tina's head where the head stops and the background begins.

CHILD: This could be the whole head.

TEACHER: The space around the head had to have something to do with what was going on in the head, so it was better not to just make the head, but once she got the space around it, she could work back and forth.

CHILD: In Donna's, she used the hair like an important part of the painting.

CHILD: Danielle's has almost no background space at all.

TEACHER: It becomes a series of triangular shapes—all flat shapes.

CHILD: In Elizabeth's, it looks like the negative space was painted first and then the head was painted into it.

TEACHER: The inside space and the outside space are the same. Look at the "mushy" way it was painted. *Mushy* means there are no sharp edges. The cheek has a bit of an edge, but it's not sharp. In Wayne's painting, notice the way the ears, nose, and mouth are very definite shapes.

CHILD: The head becomes the whole painting.

CHILD: It's the brushwork that makes the head—it also makes the nose.

TEACHER: How did you get your "mushy" edges, Elizabeth?

CHILD: I started with painting the head, and didn't like it, so I smeared it up to use as a background and painted over it.

PROBLEM: To paint a self-portrait with a hat using colors as shapes

TEACHER: When you look at yourself in the mirror, think about how the shape of your head changes when you put something on it. Look at how it changes, depending on how it cuts the form—whether it becomes a circle or a triangle, or whatever. (*Children choose hats from a box of materials.*) Work as you did last time so that your head fills up the whole paper. We're using our own heads because they're available; don't get "up tight" because it's your head. Don't worry about making it look like you— making it "right"—think of making shapes and colors. Remember the pictures we looked at last time? Those were real people that the artist painted but we see them as colors and shapes.

OBSERVATIONS WHILE CHILDREN ARE WORKING

TEACHER: Look at it—you've followed the problem in that the way you've painted the head and painted the brush strokes of the background are the same, but how have you painted the head?

CHILD: Solid.

TEACHER: Squint and look at it.

CHILD: It all runs together.

TEACHER: How can you separate the head from the background somewhat so that you can read it more clearly as a head?

CHILD: Make it more solid—not have the spaces show through.

TEACHER: Also in your choice of color. Looks like you need a different color here (*along side of the face*) to really separate it from the background.

(To another child) When you start another painting, take a different hat this time. *(Child takes a black felt hat with a floppy brim and ties a red paisley scarf around the lower half of his face like a bandit.)*

DISCUSSION

TEACHER: Who would like to start the discussion—what do you think about these?

CHILD: Wayne's looks so "proportionally"—it looks realistic.

TEACHER: Why do you think so?

CHILD: Without that line around the face it would look different.

TEACHER: What does that line do?

CHILD: It divides the neck from the head.

TEACHER: So what does that plane do? What's a plane?

CHILD: A surface.

TEACHER: What do you think about the difference between the way the head is painted and the hat is painted?

CHILD: The hat is painted in globs of color; the face is divided into really small pieces.

TEACHER: While he was working on it, all that space around the head was painted the same as the head was painted. You couldn't see it because it was all split by little lines. Now, you see the head swimming in these other colors; you can all see the splotches that make the cheeks pull out. Tina, when you say "realistic," do you mean that he's used color and brushwork to make the face move in and out kind of in a sculptural way?

CHILD: I like it because it looks like it's been raised or something.

TEACHER: Why does it look that way?

CHILD: 'Cause of the different splotches of color.

CHILD: It looks like finger painting.

TEACHER: Did you use your fingers, Wayne?

CHILD: No.

TEACHER: So it was just a question of getting the paint thick enough.

CHILD: The circular lines on the outside stand out more than the head.

TEACHER: That's different from what usually happens. In this painting, the negative space which we call background really comes forward. What happens when you squint at it?

CHILD: The head almost disappears.

TEACHER: That's because it's all painted in the same way.

CHILD: The others are like magic; Elizabeth's looks like a person.

TEACHER: What makes it more like a person than the one that you did, Karen?

CHILD: Nose, eyes, lips.

TEACHER: Okay, the shapes of the features. What else?

CHILD: She made the eyes like they look on other people.

CHILD: It's smudgy.

TEACHER: I think it's more real in the sense of colors and shapes, but if you look carefully at the eyes, for example. . . .

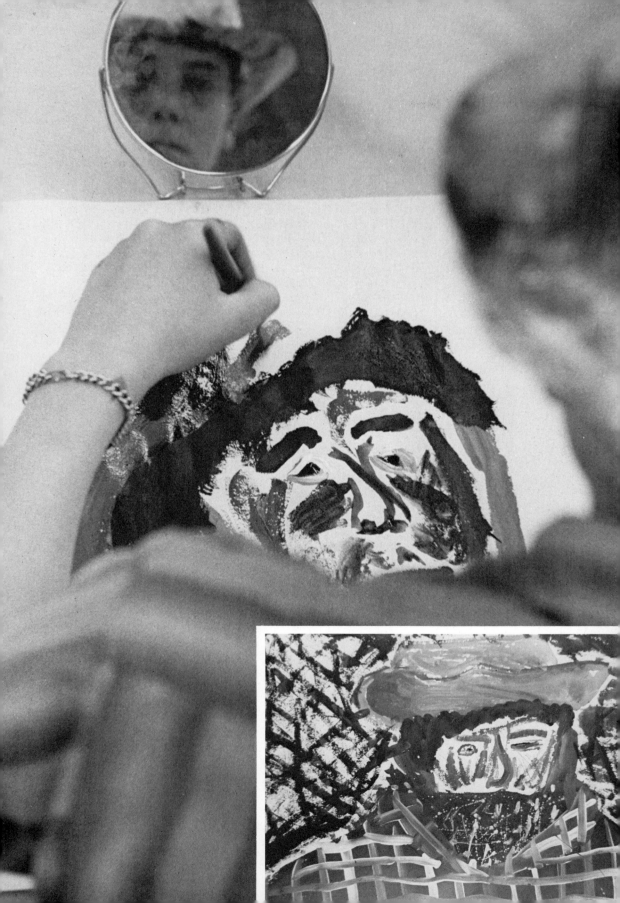

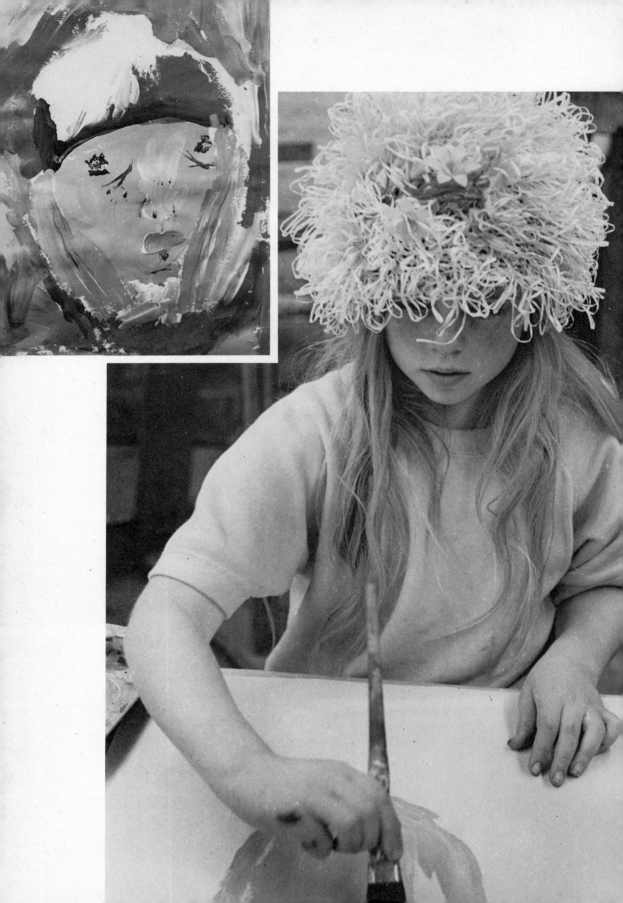

CHILD: They're just dots.

TEACHER: So if you start looking at each part separately, you can see it's not real. She has painted the top of the lids and she has used colors around the irises so it looks like they're really peering out at you. But both eyes are not the same. The features in your face are not really symmetrical. What is symmetrical?

CHILD: When both sides look alike.

TEACHER: That's what makes it look real because people's faces aren't the same on both sides.

Danielle, tell us how you did yours. What did you do first?

CHILD: I drew the round part of the face, then I drew the face and didn't like it, so I smeared it up.

TEACHER: But she didn't throw the painting away when she didn't like something. It's not that I'm interested in saving paper but when you put something down that you don't like, it doesn't mean that it has to stay there. If you don't like what happens, change it, don't throw it away.

How did you paint the hair and hat?

CHILD: I started with the hair—the brown part, then I put in the hat next to it.

TEACHER: Notice how the shape of the hair looks like her—she saw the hair and hat as two separate shapes. First, she painted the hair, then the hat, then put them together. She painted not what she knew was there but what she saw.

PROBLEM: To paint a figure in an environment so that the negative space becomes as important as the positive space

TEACHER: We started with imaginary heads, then painted self-portraits with hats, and now we're going to continue with a figure in an environment. I'm going to show you some paintings and ask questions about them. [*Matisse,* New York: Skira, 1959: "Zulma," cut and pasted paper, 1950, p. 121; "Small Blue Interior," 1947, p. 116; "Plum Blossoms, Green Background," 1948, p. 115; "Woman with Etruscan Vase," 1940, p. 109; "The Painter's Family," 1911, p. 67; "The Dinner Table," 1908, p. 61.] Is there anything that is common to these pictures?

CHILD: It's the same artist.

TEACHER: Yes, his name is Matisse.

CHILD: He was seeing all shapes—circles and squares and triangles, and making them look like bodies but they were really all shapes.

CHILD: The first and second pictures look more like colors and shapes, not like people.

CHILD: The last pictures look more like people.

TEACHER: I reversed the order in which he painted them. I started with his later work and then went back in time.

CHILD: It's neat the way he shows the wallpaper and the table the same.

TEACHER: What else can you see?

CHILD: They're weird.

TEACHER: How?

CHILD: *All the space is used up.*

TEACHER: What do you mean?

CHILD: There's lots of stuff in it.

CHILD: There's no empty places.

CHILD: The table repeats the same thing in the wallpaper. ["The Dinner Table."]

TEACHER: There's lots of objects in them and the objects themselves have a lot going for them in terms of colors and shapes. In all of them, where is the figure?

CHILD: All over.

TEACHER: What is it surrounded by?

CHILD: Background.

TEACHER: Where is the figure?

CHILD: It stands out.

TEACHER: How? What is it surrounded by?

CHILD: His habitat.

TEACHER: Yes, an environment of colors and shapes. Is the figure treated differently from other colors and shapes?

CHILD: No, he's part of it.

TEACHER: The artist is not trying to show that it's flesh color or eye color; he's painting the figure in the same way he's painting the environment. Look at the way the shape of the hair repeats in the trees and the wallpaper.

CHILD: The dots are repeated from the outside of the tree in the window to the flowers in the inside on the table.

TEACHER: Look at how the figures ["The Painter's Family"] become big colors or shapes in this big pattern; suppose he had real people in the painting and he used the real color of her hair.

CHILD: You wouldn't see it against the wallpaper.

CHILD: You almost don't see the figure in this one. ["Woman with Etruscan Vase."]

TEACHER: Everything repeats. His idea was to paint shapes and colors; he stuck the person in at the last minute. He also does something that lots of artists do—uses his own drawings to include in the painting.

Look at his hair ["Plum Blossoms, Green Background"]; it's part of the wall. Look at how his shirt becomes an extension of the table top.

CHILD: He has a window in most of them.

TEACHER: What does that do?

CHILD: It makes you notice the background.

TEACHER: What's happened to the figure in this one? ["Small Blue Interior."]

CHILD: It's just like the flowers.

CHILD: It's all shapes.

PROBLEM: To explore the relationships of shapes in a figure and environment where both are treated equally

TEACHER: We're going to take this idea of a figure in an environment. You will not be concentrating on the figure, but on the shapes and colors. The figure may occupy the largest part of the painting or it may occupy the smallest part, it's up to you. Work on colored construction paper so that when you finish, the whole surface will be covered except what you choose to leave as a shape. We'll have different people in the class modeling against a similar background of colors. Don't try to get the colors exactly as the person is dressed but try to stay in the same family of colors.

PROCEDURE

(On a stand in the front of the room against the board, Karen is wearing a T-shirt over a darker-red paisley long-sleeved shirt, plum-colored pants, white sneakers, and white socks. Against the board, a red-and-white checked drape hangs next to a solid red drape, with a square cloth of teal blue in center. Karen leans against the board, sitting with one leg bent at the knee, the other leg resting on a stool.)

TEACHER: Each two people share a tray of paints. Get your own water and pick the size brushes that you think you may need. Don't just start with Karen and paint her. Look at the whole thing—paint what you see up there and stay within the family of colors. You're going to work fast—15 minutes to a painting.

DISCUSSION

CHILD: This one didn't come out. I can't change it either, can I throw it away?

TEACHER: Why can't you change it? Some of you didn't get far enough into your paintings because you were working too slowly; some are lovely. Come and look at these—neither of them got finished but you're getting the idea.

Now you're all beginning to get the idea. You know what fifteen minutes is—you can't work only on one section in a problem like this, you have to work on the whole thing at once. Now let's change the colors. Who wants to pose?

(Child wearing blue jeans and light-blue shirt volunteers. Teacher places a blue drape across the board and a blue cloth on the "model stand." As the child takes a pose lying down, the teacher places a blue and purple paisley drape over her legs.)

TEACHER: *(To the class)* Before you start, squint your eyes and look at it. What happens when you squint?

CHILD: It blurs all the colors together.

TEACHER: If you look up there and see a color shape and you think your painting would be better without it, don't put it in. Start putting blobs of paint right on your paper and then if you don't like them, change them on your paper instead of mixing them separately on another piece; then you can see what happens as they change colors. *(Children make four fifteen-minute paintings of children posing against a background of materials of vivid textures and colors.)*

OBSERVATIONS WHILE CHILDREN ARE WORKING

TEACHER: If you're going to put down a big shape like that, instead of dabbing it along because the paint is thick, use a larger brush so that you can put it down in two or three sweeps.

The figure works well over in the corner like that so you get all the colors and textures over here and the figure over there, and this very empty space that it kind of balances against; it's beautiful.

In these two paintings, the figure and the space around it really look like one huge garden. The figures are all bits and pieces of flowers—you really have a sense of being in a garden. Have you ever been to the botanical gardens at UCLA? It's very packed with growth and sometimes the sunlight comes through all the trees and plants and if you see people there, they become kind of broken up into pieces like the leaves of the trees because of the way the light bounces back and forth.

DISCUSSION

TEACHER: Look at the way the yellow paper was used. It's so much a part of the painting that you have a feeling that it was painted on there. And look how she's left in places like a line that sort of comes through and disappears.

Look at the way the blue of the paper becomes the whole shape.

CHILD: You get a feeling that the figure is "squeezed" in by the environment.

CHILD: I thought she painted the umbrella in but it's really the black paper.

TEACHER: She's been able to take the space of the paper she started with and make it an important part of the picture; you thought she painted it in because she used the space so well.

PROBLEM: To paint objects from a still life as relationships between shapes, sizes, and colors rather than realistic forms

TEACHER: How would you describe what you see up here?

CHILDREN: Weird, abstract, sickening, strange. . . .

TEACHER: Why do you say weird?

CHILD: They are out of place compared to real life.

CHILD: Out of place or out of proportion?

TEACHER: What do you mean by "out of place"?

CHILD: Well, in real life a lady could not bend her leg so far that way, or have only a black head and neck and be skinny and all. . . .

TEACHER: So the proportions are different from real life. What do you mean when you say it's "out of place"? I think that's true but I want to know what you mean.

CHILD: You don't see it anywhere.

TEACHER: You might see a mannequin in a store window.

CHILD: Yeah, but not like that.

TEACHER: Or you might see an ice skate somewhere. So that all these things are taken out of reality and put into a different context. . . . They're out of proportion and what else?

CHILD: Sickening.

TEACHER: Why?

CHILD: Because it is so different and so out of place, it is just sick.

TEACHER: Does it make you feel sick?

CHILD: No, when I look at that I think of somebody that's sick.

TEACHER: Do you mean sick like they should go see a doctor, sick in the head, or what?

CHILD: I mean like maybe a deformed person.

TEACHER: That's not really the same as sick, is it?

CHILD: Deformed is back to proportion.

TEACHER: Right.

TEACHER: You are all really focusing on the figure now. I would be surprised
if you said something about the striped material in the background, because the figure is so prominent.What does *prominent* mean?

CHILD: Stands out.

TEACHER: Yes, really makes you look at it.

CHILD: It's the biggest thing.

TEACHER: Right, it's the biggest thing there. So now we are starting to talk
about *size,* about *scale,* the relationship of the size of this compared to
the other doll (that's scale—big to small), *proportion.* What else could
you say about this?

CHILD: The stripes don't go. They clash.

TEACHER: What do you mean clash? Does your mother say, "Don't you dare
put on striped pants and a checked shirt"? That happened to me when
I was little too. But I think things have changed because I see lots of
people walking down the street wearing two or three patterns together.
You know who does this a lot, the Japanese. They have influenced us
greatly in things like design. If you look at a Japanese kimono there might
be four or five designs going on at one time with checks, stripes, and
solids, and there is no sense of clash; it's just very beautiful. I think the
idea of checks and stripes "not going together" or clashing has to do
with your education . . . the way you are brought up to think. What
else can you say about this still life?

CHILD: The colors are . . .

TEACHER: What about the colors? *(No response.)* Are they light or dark? Dull
or bright?

CHILD: They go together except that they're all faded.

TEACHER: They all kind of work together. That's a good description.

TEACHER: Someone said they are generally dark except for certain light areas.
If you squint at it, you can see the white of that square shape, the leg,
the checks in the dress, the hat—they become lighter shades in a darker
field.

CHILD: The whole thing is not even geometrical shapes—things are on different
sides and on different planes. And there are big shapes and smaller
shapes.

TEACHER: Now you are talking about what is going on in the whole *composition.*
The first thing you respond to when we were talking about things being
weird or peculiar were the individual things themselves—the figure, the
ice skate, the doll, and so forth. But what he is doing now is describing
an arrangement very generally. How many of you have heard the words
still life? How would you describe a still life?

CHILDREN: No people or animals . . . no movement . . . no living thing that
has flesh.

TEACHER: That's really not quite true because if you remember we had an arrangement of forms and shapes like this and a real person (somebody
in the class) pose in that arrangement. When we looked at those paintings
by Matisse last week we talked about the fact that the people in the painting were no different than the apples, pears, flowers, and so on. They

were treated as colors and shapes, just as other things were, so they were part of the whole still life arrangement.

If you look at paintings that are four or five hundred years old, you will see certain things in real life that were taken from those paintings, like apples, fruit, and so on. Those were the things people had around them and those are the things they used. When an artist wanted to paint and he didn't have any money to hire a model and didn't want to paint himself, he'd look around the studio and grab a hunk of cheese, a piece of bread, a rabbit someone just shot and had hanging on a hook; he would put those out and set up an arrangement. Most of us don't have rabbits that have just been shot hanging around, so instead we might find a part of a car, a mannequin, a plastic pillow, an old hat—that's part of our environment.

So a still life is really what he was describing—an arrangement of forms and shapes in space. He was talking about things starting to stick out and go back—so there is a *spatial order* to it, there is a *size* or *scale* order to it, there are big things or small things and things in between, so there is a *shape order*. (He was talking about big shapes and smaller shapes, remember?) There are *color relationships* and *light and dark relationships*. That is really describing what a still life arrangement is, whether it is alive or dead or moving doesn't matter. We could have live flowers in this one. We would set up a fan that would make all that stuff move and it would still be a still life. You are thinking of the words *still* and *life* and taking the meaning from that, but a still life can have *real* things and *moving* things in it, like the bowl of fish in the Matisse painting, but they would be moving, right? So it's really the relationship of the forms, shapes, colors, and sizes that is important.

PROCEDURE

TEACHER: When an artist paints from a still life, just as you're going to paint from a still life, the idea is not necessarily to make everything exactly as it is there. The idea is to look up there and to think about all the colors and shapes and say to yourself, "How am I going to translate what I see there in terms of all these things onto a piece of paper?" As a second part of the problem you might look up there and say, "Gee, there is just too much, I can't deal with all that; I'm just going to take a part of it." You may just decide to take part of one object and part of another object and make them work together, so that you're not making a whole form, just pieces of it. The only thing I'm going to ask you to do is to keep within the idea of color, of scale relationships, of shape relationships, and of space relationships.

In other words I don't want you to take the shoe, the flower, the doll and rearrange them on the paper. If you take a part of it, I want you to keep those things very much like what's going on up there. When I say, "very much like," that doesn't mean exactly to the letter. Supposing you're painting and you're coming along to this part and you say, "I don't

want to put the doll in—it's just going to squeeze the whole painting"—
well, leave the doll out. When I say "within the range," it means somewhat
like what's going on, but feel free to change things if you have to so
you'll have a better painting.

Now, there is just one other thing I want to tell you about before you
paint. Remember when you did self-portraits and I suggested that you not
spend a long time on an eye, a nose, a mouth, but really try to work on
the whole thing at the same time? The same applies here. If you spend a
half hour on that basket with the flowers and then you move on to another
thing, you will suddenly notice that the basket of flowers is too big or too
little, too high or too low, too left or too right, and you're not going to
want to change it if you spend a half hour working on it. So the best way
to work is to put down big color-shapes first; really get them all over the
paper. Let's say, put down a piece of red that's going to be the dress, and
a piece of purple that's going to be the hat, and a piece of green that's
going to be something else, and then keep going back and changing and
moving. So that at the end if you want it very detailed, you can put in the
details, but that is later on, that's after you've gotten the whole thing
organized. At the beginning I would deal with the biggest movement you
see from left to right, from up to down, from backward to forward. Any
questions?

CHILD: How long do we have?

TEACHER: The whole period. It's not like last week when we only had half an hour. You should think about what you did last week because some of your paintings are extremely well organized in terms of shapes, color, scale, and movement. The fact that you work longer on a painting doesn't necessarily mean it's going to be better, but you have the whole period if you want it. You are too crowded here; take space at the tables so that you can move freely.

OBSERVATIONS WHILE CHILDREN ARE WORKING

CHILD: What do you mean by just painting pieces of things?

CHILD: When there is no whole form in it? What do you mean?

TEACHER: No whole body, no whole doll, no whole pillow, no whole anything.

CHILD: You mean like a part of the pillow that's behind the doll's head?

TEACHER: If you take pieces of forms so that you get a piece of one next to a piece of another, you are really expanding the whole picture. You took a relatively large part of the still life and you have whole forms within it. *(To another child)* In this painting everything is going to go out beyond the edges; it's like you were painting on a piece of paper ten times as big as it is and you're going to blow up pieces of the forms. Do you understand?

CHILD: So there is more than one thing in it?

TEACHER: Yes, but pieces of things; for example, in this area of your painting you're taking a part of the dress and a part of the background and a part of the figure, but there is no place where you can look and say "this is a dress, this is a figure." Do you see what I'm saying?

CHILD: Yes.

TEACHER: You won't know what anything is because you're blowing it up in scale on the paper, understand? *(To another child:)* See how this color butts against this one and this color pushes against that one? The edge is between one color and another color, right? In this part it doesn't work the same way. It looks like it is paint on top of paper instead of just the paper showing through; here it's paint next to paint. That's different than paint next to paper, see?

CHILD: Yes.

TEACHER: So if you want this color here, fine, but you should mix up some paint instead of just having the paper show through.

CHILD: You mean the color of the paper?

TEACHER: No. In your particular painting it shouldn't be just the color of the paper.

(To another child) Look what that orange does, it makes everything else hop around and vibrate because that really comes alive now; before it was just a hunk of paper.

CHILD: It's jumping out of the paper with the orange stripes.

TEACHER: If you want this kind of very fast, energetic mark you can do it this way. All I am saying is that you need more paint on the brush.

CHILD: I can't get the idea of only making parts of things.

TEACHER: Make a little hole with your fingers, like a telescope, move it around and you'll see pieces of things.

CHILD: She's got it too big.

TEACHER: Don't make it so big that you see too much. Do you see little pieces of things?

CHILD: Yeah.

TEACHER: Keep moving it around until you find some place you think is interesting and do a painting—big—on the whole paper of just that one little area, you understand? *(To another child)* What's happening here?

CHILD: I know what I'm doing but the shape of the foot is not right.

TEACHER: What's happening is that you're forgetting about the heel. When you're expanding a shape like this, the heel would be out of the picture but a piece of the foot would come back in.

CHILD: How do you make a telescope with your fingers?

TEACHER: You can make a small hole with a piece of paper or use your fingers and look so you don't see any complete form, so that you are actually seeing the space between forms. In essence, you get an abstract composition and when you blow that up in scale it becomes the whole painting. So what you have is shapes and colors that are not really recognizable objects.

96

DISCUSSION

TEACHER: Anyone have anything they want to say about them?

CHILD: I think they are sort of strange.

TEACHER: What's strange about them?

CHILD: Every one is so different. The lines on that one go up, and on this one the lines go down.

CHILD: That one is sort of scrunched down. This one makes you feel like you are sort of in a real world; it sort of makes pictures of things.

TEACHER: Why is that, do you think?

CHILD: Because of the lines and the colors.

TEACHER: Don't you think it's great that they are all so different? Wouldn't it be terrible if they were all the same?

CHILDREN: Yes.

TEACHER: It's interesting that you said that in yours the lines are all moving up, and in the other they are all going down. Why do you think that is? What gives you the feeling of lines going up and other ones coming down?

CHILD: The lines in the body sort of look like it's going up—sort of drifting up.

TEACHER: And in this one?

CHILD: This one is still.

TEACHER: It is really sitting solidly; that's a really good observation. What about the body in that one?

CHILD: That one, I'd say it was. . . .

TEACHER: In terms of up or down what do you think about it?

CHILD: It's sort of flat.

97

TEACHER: What else? If it's neither up nor down, what is it doing?

CHILD: It's floating.

TEACHER: It's sort of floating like in a body of water. Look at the figure in the very last one, what's happening to it?

CHILD: Like it's kind of buried there.

TEACHER: It's much less recognizable as a figure than the other ones, isn't it? It becomes less separated from the things around it than in these. In this painting you have this object that becomes recognizable as somewhat of a figure from among other stripes and forms, whereas that one is much less like a figure than any of the others. Do you see that?

CHILD: Except for that one. *(He points to painting.)*

TEACHER: Oh, you think that one is less too, why?

CHILD: Everything takes on the same. . . .

TEACHER: The reason is different on this one than on that one. Here, you just don't look at anything and say, "That's a figure."

CHILD: All the rest have a bunch of stripes with big thick lines.

CHILD: But on that one it looks like they took their fingers and . . . .

TEACHER: Are you talking about different textures, about different actions of paint?

CHILD: Makes you think of something dark and maybe sad.

TEACHER: Let's see if we can find out why the figure is more like the things around it here than it is there. What do you think it has to do with?

CHILD: Color—between the background and the objects.

TEACHER: I don't really think it's color; it has to do with the way it's painted. That one is painted much more loosely than any one of the others. When I say loosely, I mean the edges between colors and shapes are not very sharp. There is a lot of moving back and forth so that everything becomes an all-over pattern of shapes and movement and thick gloppy paint, and colors running into other colors. So the only thing that is kind of clear in terms of the figure are the legs, because they become a very light, clear color, and the rest of it is much darker and much more active. In that painting the shape sticks out among the other things much more than it does in this one.

I want to say one thing about the way you painted these. There were three or four of you that thought you were finished but had still left some of the paper showing. We talked about going back and covering it with the same color of the paper or another color. What happens to the painting when you do that?

CHILD: If you leave the paper showing it looks like the color of the paper but if you paint it it looks like another color in the painting.

TEACHER: Right. It becomes much more of a painting this way in the sense that it is really woven together with scale, color, and shapes. Last week in the figure in an environment, you left pieces of the colored paper showing and they functioned as colors within other colors and shapes. But today, everybody left over pieces of paper, but the minute you put the color of the paper in paint, or another color and shapes on it, it really began to fill out as a whole painting. I want to say one word about those few who did the second problem, which was to take a very small area in the still life and blow it up in scale so that there was no one whole form. What happens when you do that? What's different about these three paintings?

CHILD: They look sort of like a big piece of something—like a big, huge piece of a puzzle.

TEACHER: What else?

CHILD: It's not a picture of real things anymore.

CHILD: Much bigger shapes.

CHILD: These three don't give me a feeling of a complete picture.

TEACHER: Why?

CHILD: It's like if you're looking at the things in regular size it just looks plain, but when you blow it up it changes.

TEACHER: How is it changed?

CHILD: It becomes more noticeable and more—I forgot the word.

TEACHER: Abstract? Let me ask you a question about the third one at the top, which is stripes—what's incomplete about that? Does it look like an incomplete painting?

CHILD: Who painted it?

TEACHER: Tracy, do you feel that is an incomplete painting?

CHILD: No.

TEACHER: I don't think so either. I am looking at it and I'm trying to think of what she could do to make it more complete and I can't think of anything.

CHILD: What is it?

TEACHER: It was part of the arrangement of the still life; it was part of a foot. That big bottom orange shape is the foot of the mannequin; the stripes were part of the background. The point is that it can be a painting that is made up of colors, shapes, sizes, and scale and be a complete painting without looking like the real thing.

CHILD: When I said it wasn't complete I didn't mean like it wasn't finished.

PROBLEM: To draw a self-portrait using line to enclose shapes to describe features

TEACHER: What is a line?

CHILD: It can be something that's straight, that's one thing.

CHILD: It can be something that's curvy.

CHILD: It can be any shape as long as it's not filled in.

CHILD: It goes on forever, so I've heard.

CHILD: It can show a gesture, a movement.

CHILD: It shows where things are brought out and where they're pushed in.

TEACHER: So lines create space.

CHILD: Sometimes it shows you where things take place, like in a chair.

CHILD: Everything has lines.

CHILD: Not everything.

TEACHER: What is a circle?

CHILD: It's a connected line.

TEACHER: Even writing is a line, sometimes it's straight, curvy, crossing.

CHILD: They swerve—rivers are lines.

CHILD: Lines connected make a shape.

TEACHER: So what can a line do?

CHILD: It can be filled in.

CHILD: It can be stretched out.

CHILD: It can make a gesture.

TEACHER: What do you mean by *gesture*. If I go like this (*waves hand*), do you know what it means?

CHILD: Means goodbye—a wave.

TEACHER: But if we didn't speak the same language you would still understand. So a gesture isn't just a movement, it speaks a language without words. When we made gesture drawings, what were we doing?

CHILD: Drawing an outline.

TEACHER: No, we were not just interested in drawing an outline, but in a sense of feeling the way a shape moves, so that the gesture captures the feeling of the person. If you were drawing a relaxed pose and you used a hard line, it would be difficult to express a relaxed gesture.

Today you're going to observe your head by drawing all the different parts that you see, using the kind of marks you used in gesture drawings.

PROCEDURE

TEACHER: Work with one medium on each drawing. With ink, use pen or brush on white paper; with charcoal, use textured paper; with pencil, use newsprint. Use all the materials to see what kind of gestural marks you can get. Some just accidentally make marks on the paper so instead of erasing them, use them in your drawing. Don't worry about getting it to look like you.

What's different about each of you?

CHILD: Different features.

TEACHER: What else?

CHILD: Different shapes?

TEACHER: Yes, eye shapes, nose shapes, but there's something else, what is it?

CHILD: Size.

TEACHER: Right, the size of something in your head compared with something else in your head. When you say someone has a big nose, what does that mean?

CHILD: Big compared to someone else's.

TEACHER: No, it's only in relation to other features in the face. Look at this drawing that I am making.

CHILD: It's an eye.

TEACHER: No, it's only an idea of an eye. The white doesn't show around the iris in anybody's eye but a baby's. What makes the difference?

CHILD: The lids.

TEACHER: Yes, and another thing that makes a difference is the inside corners.

∠ ∠ ∠ ∠

You can see that they are very different from each other so you have to look very carefully. You can see that your eyes don't look anything like the first drawing I made.

How does your hair grow? What does your hair look like? You really need to look and see how it grows.

CHILD: His grows forward; hers grows to the other side.

TEACHER: You need to look at it like different forms, so you don't think of each individual hair but how it is shaped on the head. Don't start with an outline like a circle; you're going to build up the form of a head with all the different gestural marks you tried last time. Keep it very loose at the beginning so you can change things. Use the whole paper for the head. Think not only of the features, but of how all the lines and different marks

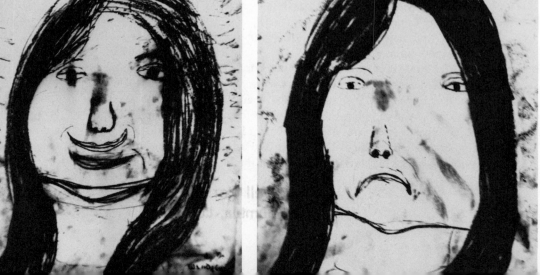

can show that something is going this way and something is going that way. You'll discover that your eyes may not be the same size—maybe one is higher than the other. Start by making a bunch of marks.

OBSERVATIONS WHILE CHILDREN ARE WORKING

CHILD: Some are darker; some are wiggly.

CHILD: Some are thin; some are slow.

TEACHER: Notice that even the way you hold the pencil changes. Sometimes it's on its side; sometimes it's straight.

I want to show you something about erasers. Everyone look here for a minute. Everyone thinks that erasers are for taking things out, but you can use it for changing the texture of the form; it really becomes another tool. For example, if you rub it on the pencil or charcoal, it makes lighter lines in a dark area instead of the reverse. I'm making it lighter with the eraser but it still isn't as light as the paper; all I'm doing is showing a little bit of light in the cheek.

(To child drawing with ink) You can do the same thing with ink but instead of taking away, you have to add more. People are afraid of ink because they think they can't change it. Use the accidents that you have here by adding more so that the marks that were one thing become something else.

Don't start with the outside; work from the inside out and keep it loose.

You did what I was talking about, Patti, the baby with the big white spaces. You've made your eyes look like that, but look at your irises and your lids. If you bring the lids down it's going to make your forehead larger.

Look in the mirror—do your eyes look like that?

CHILD: No.

TEACHER: Then you have to make them closer. Look in the mirror while I'm talking to you so you can see what I mean. If that's the edge of your nose, then make the eye come in.

You have the nose and mouth of one person but the eyes of someone else. Look in the mirror.

Laurel, look at your forehead; now look above it. You've got your hair covering your forehead but it really begins back here. You need to give yourself more forehead. Notice that your mouth is wider than your nose.

Do you think that mouth looks like your mouth? You've drawn a round line but there's no space between the top and the lower lip.

Scott, look in mirror. You top eyelid really comes down low over your eyeball—I don't see that in your drawing. You've made your eyes from top to bottom much larger than they really are.

What you've done, Jane, is take a drawing that you didn't like, destroyed it, and made a good drawing out of it. You took the nose and the space underneath it and made a great shape out of it; the cheek and chin becomes another big shape. You can say, "It doesn't look like me," but if you put it on the wall you'll see that the nose, cheeks, and eyes look very much like you.

It has very much the quality of you but you're making it too small, you're cutting off the top of your head. You might do what Janie did, use these features and make another one out of it.

PROBLEM: To draw a landscape by viewing objects in unlimited space as opposed to the limited space of a portrait or interior

TEACHER: Have you ever worked outside from something you see outside? What do you call that?

CHILD: Landscape.

TEACHER: How many of you have seen paintings of landscapes? What do they look like?

CHILD: Usually look like trees or sea. . . .

CHILD: Or mountains.

CHILD: They're usually spread out—trees and mountains spread out.

TEACHER: Why do you think that is?

CHILD: So you know it's a landscape.

TEACHER: We'll come back to the idea of "spread-outness." Everyone's been talking about trees, sea, sky, mountains. Imagine two hundred years ago what paintings of landscape looked like—maybe mountains, trees, cows, horses. But if we walk outside now what do we see?

CHILD: Smog, cars, people, buildings.

TEACHER: Yes, our landscape is really the city. So it's different from what we usually think of. Think of the idea of "spread-outness"—what's the difference between working inside and outside in terms of "spread"? In this room no matter how far you get from something, the greatest distance is only from one wall to another. So the space is pretty close between you and an object. But outside it's like looking up in the sky, how do you show space between you and it? There seems like a hundred miles of horizon between the land and the sky. So the sense of space is enormously different working outside.

CHILD: Outside things are moving or happening.

CHILD: Like when you're drawing a car and someone gets in it and moves away.

TEACHER: So there are two things that are different—space and movement.

CHILD: Scale.

TEACHER: What does that mean?

CHILD: Size.

TEACHER: Yes. The relationship between the largest and the smallest is different on the outside than on the inside. What is different between what is close and what is far away?

CHILD: Perspective.

TEACHER: Not really. Perspective is only one way of making space. In the room you don't get the same sense of difference in size. What else is different?

CHILD: Light and dark.

CHILD: Shadows.

TEACHER: What's different about the light?

CHILD: Sunlight can be softer or stronger.

TEACHER: What else is different between the light in the room and the light outside?

CHILD: There's all kind of light inside because of near, regular light bulbs.

TEACHER: Yes, but there's still something different.

CHILD: Outside light can be showing on one object so part of it looks bright on one side and dark on the other.

TEACHER: Yes, but that can happen in the room too, depending on how light hits an object. Light outside is constantly changing and shifting. Light in the room is the same because it's electric light, so we could stay here twenty-four hours and it wouldn't change.

Colors change because of change in the light. A painter named Monet stayed in one place all day and found he couldn't paint the same scene all day because the light changed and the color changed. So he painted lots of different paintings of the same thing.

There are several ways to approach painting on the outside. Because the space is so vast, you have to decide what to leave in and what to take out. Since we're near the beach we're going to walk to the park by the ocean and draw there.

PROCEDURE

TEACHER: There are three different ways you can make your drawing: (1) Focus on a special object, for example, a tree, and spend the whole time on it really looking hard, seeing how the shapes of the branches grow out of the trunk, the texture of the bark, the shapes of the leaves, and so forth. (2) Sit in a place and decide to draw pretty much what you see—that is, some things that are close to you, some at a middle distance, and some far away. (3) Select different objects from different places and put them together in some new way, like a boat, the dock, the sea—in other words, make your own composition.

You can decide to work very fast and make several drawings or to work more slowly on one drawing. We'll have an hour to work. Here are three kinds of pencils you can work with: (1) soft—it will never get as black as a compressed lead because it's softer; (2) compressed—it can be smudged but still keep a strong, distinct line; (3) pastel—you can use it like a pencil or piece of charcoal where you simply draw lines, or you can use it on its side. It's nice because you can build up colors one on top of each other so the underneath colors come through and you can see variations. If you draw with pencil first, it seems easier, but it's because you're afraid to experiment and see what happens. If you use pastel, use it directly as a line or shape. With charcoal don't draw a line and fill it in like a coloring book. How many of you have used coloring books and gone outside the lines? And how many have been told, "Don't go outside the lines"?

CHILDREN: *(Laugh.)*

DISCUSSION

TEACHER: Someone made a marvelous observation. Would you repeat it, please?

CHILD: Outside the pictures look so much better from far away than here in the room.

TEACHER: She's saying that having done these drawings outside, they look different when you bring them inside. When you're out there you see things like the sand, water, fence, and everything is moving horizontally. But when you're drawing you don't necessarily see them that way; things are not necessarily flat. If we had drawn a picture of a landscape in the room and then gone outside, you would see that the horizon is not a straight line. You almost get a sense of the roundness of the earth because your horizon line is round.

I want to talk to you about color. The water isn't really the color in this picture, is it?

CHILDREN: No.

TEACHER: Because the artist makes an interpretation when he paints it. Although your pictures deal with sea, sky, and mountains, the variations among them are completely different. What's different?

CHILD: She flattened the color out—there are no markings with the pastel.

TEACHER: Some of you used color just as it comes out of the box; that one has many colors in it; some used one color with textures in it.

Look at some of the objects in these drawings. Some of you put things in from your memory—things you've seen or done come into the drawing. For example, there are no red flowers on the grass but she put them in anyway. In terms of the picture itself, what do these red spots do?

CHILD: Pop around.

TEACHER: Yes, they tend to pop out of the picture. Hold your finger up in the air over them and see what happens.

CHILD: You see other colors in the picture.

CHILD: You see the grass as a whole shape.

TEACHER: Several of you got interested in people who are always around the beach. The problem is when you have a person sitting or leaning and you don't show what they're sitting or leaning against, it gives an uneasy feeling.

CHILD: Like they're floating.

TEACHER: But in this picture you get the feeling the people are really sitting

solidly because there are benches behind them. Does it bother you that the lines of the benches go across the figures?

CHILDREN: No.

TEACHER: It's interesting that he noticed everything about the people.

CHILD: All the hats are different. . . .

CHILD: . . . and two guys are wearing glasses and only one is reading.

TEACHER: Look at the way he's drawn the objects in this picture of the boats on the ocean. He starts you looking for an object in front and as you move from one thing to another he pushes your eye back in space. That's the kind of distance we were talking about.

CHILD: If he had used the blue to cover the whole paper it would just go on and on.

5
SCULPTURE

Definition and Description

As an art form, a sculpture is a three-dimensional object which sits in actual physical space. It is given tangible shape by its mass and volume. *Mass* refers to the material that displaces space. *Volume* is the space contained within an object. Although it may be likened to the space in a box, this is not to imply a square or rectangular shape. Volume is more than bulk. It includes not only the area an object actually occupies, but also the empty space around it which is essential in completing its "wholeness." That is, although we "read" the solid mass as the basic shape, a figure or object has continuity with the emptiness of the space around it.

When we refer to the form in sculpture as a "functional whole" (even though it has no function in a utilitarian sense), we mean that all of its parts must work together in making up a complete whole. The space that surrounds it and the space contained within it exist as forms vital in creating the total image. Thus, space in sculpture may be defined as *sculptural volume,* which includes more than the conventional notions of height, depth, and breadth. It is space which not only is visual, but is vitalized by an internal quality of movement. The uniqueness in the making and responding to sculpture is that it provokes both a visual and kinesthetic image.

A child working in volumes is not faced with the problem of creating three-dimensional objects in two-dimensional media, such as in painting. Nevertheless, a lump of clay is three-dimensional only in its materiality. It remains for the child to acquire a conception of three-dimensional organization by working with a vocabulary such as "up and around" and "from the inside out." In so doing, he becomes aware that forms take shape as volumes, mass, and planes which must flow cohesively out of the material itself. A concept of space as sculptural volume means that one is involved with creating *one* image, not many images. Whatever idea or feeling evolves is concentrated into one statement rather than a sequence of statements. Sculpture may thus be considered as a three-dimensional, shaped feeling. Different images may emerge in the process of exploration, but there is really one image created—the one a child finds at a given moment.

Sculpture, then, becomes a tangible expression of a conscious effort to use form in its unique spatiality. The intent for children, therefore, is not merely to manipulate materials, but to explore the possibilities of transforming and changing space so that they discover a new spatial concept. Given this description, we need to reconsider designations applied to children's work, such as "modeling," which tend to reduce the importance and elegance involved in sculptural form. Such a term does not describe the essential nature of this art form, but refers to a procedure which is in itself misleading. Modeling a lump of clay (usually the size of an orange) all too frequently results in "snakes," "snowmen," or handprints in the early years, and in ashtrays and Easter baskets in the middle years. The outcome of modeling is not a "model"—that is, something made that is considered worthy of imitation—but at best a uniquely conceived piece of sculpture. With a vocabulary that illuminates the symbolic possibilities of sculptural form, children can begin to perceive their work not only as *having* expressive form, but as *being* one.

Distinguishing Characteristics

SPACE

Of the aesthetic elements pervading the arts in various ways, space and force function qualitatively in sculpture. Particularly, it is the nature of *space* by which we distinguish its primary image. Space which is enclosed or unoccupied has no visual aspects, but appears as a void. Even young children can perceive in their own immediate environment that if space is not "filled" with something, it is empty. We see this in a child's expression of "emptiness" as, "This room is a hole." When asked to visualize what it is that defines space in a room, descriptions range from abstractions such as, "It's sealed in," to specifics of "the ceiling . . . floor . . . tables." Thus, there is an initial awareness that space is defined by objects.

Drawing from their own experience, children can more readily understand that sculpture, as a physical object, exists as volumes occupying space. The association is made even clearer in recognizing that just as their bodies define the space around them, so does a piece of sculpture become the center of three-dimensional space. The difference is that individuals occupy space in a generalized, objective atmosphere, but a piece of sculpture is a center of space all of its own. As an image having both visual and kinesthetic characteristics, it both dominates and gives definition to the surrounding space. That is, the area in which it exists takes its shape from the relationships and proportions derived from the object in terms of its outer contours and its inner shapes.

Seen in this way, sculpture involves organizing the space displaced by the material volume and also the external space essential to its appearance. Children must be made aware not only of the physical presence of an object, but of the tension and movement between it and the empty space around it. In this way, external space may be understood as being part of the sculptural volume.

Plasticity and Movement. Sculpture has been described as a visual–kinesthetic image to include its special characteristics of plasticity and movement. In general, plasticity implies something that can be molded or shaped. Its properties are experienced by children as pulling, pushing, twisting, stretching in the process of making forms that are developing, growing, changing. It is used here to denote forms that seem to flow organically to create the "wholeness" discussed earlier.

Plasticity can perhaps best be understood as it relates to painting as well as sculpture. When we say that a painting is plastic, we are perceiving space as moving in and out almost as if it were physical. We know, however, that what we are seeing is merely an appearance of space shaped by colors, lines, textures that exist on a flat surface. Thus, although we experience the space in a physical way, it does not emerge from the physicality of the object itself. In sculpture, however, plasticity depends upon the three-dimensional nature of the volumes and is always physical.

Movement may seem to present a contradiction because we usually think of a sculpture as being a static object. Aside from kinetic sculpture or mobiles which actually move, sculpture merely creates an illusion or appearance of movement. It is this quality, however, that gives an object or figure an inner vitality, whether the image is abstract or realistic. Although children do not initially set out to create movement, they become aware of it in examining those qualities that make a particular piece of work "come alive." Movement may be perceived in various ways:

- In the *rhythmical pattern* of the forms contained within an object itself. For example, in a figure of a mother holding a baby in her lap, we may see shapes such as the "rounds" of the mother's head, breasts, encircling arms repeated in the roundness of the baby's head and body. Thus, the repetition of the forms evokes a sense of rhythm.

- In the *thrust of a volume* as it moves "from the inside out" to displace the space around it, such as the soaring neck of a giraffe or the extension of a body stretching backward.

- In the *sequential rhythmic flow of the contours* so that as the eye follows these along, a sensation of movement is aroused. These outermost shapes are frequently referred to as "lines," but the edge of a three-dimensional form is not a line, it is the surface of a volume. A textured surface, for example, such as the fur of an animal, the hair on a head, the groupings of lines on a relief, gives an accentuated effect of movement and creates its own rhythm. In all cases, our eyes first pick up the elements of movement which we then perceive as visual–kinesthetic sensations.

Movement is not an "extra" element abstracted from or added to the form itself. It does not become a part of the sculpture simply by pulling out arms or legs or tail from a body, or showing a figure in action or in some type of gesture. It has an expressive function in that it gives a sense of vitality to the organization of the total form. Thus, movement becomes part of the aesthetic element of *force* in that the very mass and weight of the material becomes a visualization of intensity. The plasticity of the contours and the self-contained rhythms of the shapes give the impression of movement. And it is in this sense that we describe sculpture as a plastic form.

Difference Between Painting and Sculpture.   There is a frequent misconception in education that the aims of sculpture and painting are the same and that it is only the means that differ. Both are visual arts, yet sculpture cannot simply be distinguished from painting by categorizing it as a three-dimensional rather than a two-dimensional image. An art form owes its special characteristics to the particular sense organs by which it is created and perceived. Although both appeal to our visual senses, sculpture involves both visual and tactile sensations. That is, it calls upon us to look visually and feel tactually.

It is interesting to note that when children describe the differences between sculpture and painting, they speak a sensory language such as,

- Clay is some sort of a blob, things come out; painting is flat.
- In painting you can make something look thick when it really isn't.
- When you make a sculpture you don't make it skinny, it's fat.
- It's thick—you can feel lumps.
- You show a figure all the way around.

What is reflected is a beginning awareness of sculpture as physical shapes that "come out" into actual space, and painting as a projection of space on a flat surface. The observation that "something can look thick when it really isn't" expresses the difference between an image that gives the illusion or appearance of occupying space and one that actually does. The difference in the use of space, for example, is between painting a nose as if it were really "coming out" of a head, and actually shaping a nose in space by pulling out a volume of clay.

In conceptual terms, painting involves transforming three-dimensional experience into a two-dimensional image. On an experiential level, children can relate to the difference in the organization of space if we begin with them as the point of reference. They can become aware, for example, that they exist as three-dimensional objects in a world of three-dimensional space. Even very young children can translate the dimensions of sculpture to themselves as "so high, so wide, so deep." And they know, too, that in real life they can walk all around another person and see him from different views. In painting a picture of a person, however, a child must abstract elements from the experience of seeing him "in the round" to present only one point of view. (Or he may fragment it as the Cubists did in presenting one image from many different views.) The composition of a painting, in terms of its physical presence, requires that we look at it frontally, as if it were a scene on a stage. What is composed then is a single vision existing in an illusory space.

Sculptural space does not require our direct vision, for the volume is originally created by touch. It is its inherent "aroundness" that makes the difference, for each side has its own shape. In sculpting a figure, for example, a child is concerned with many different views, not just a front view. The concept of "aroundness" may be communicated through the vocabulary of working "up and around" to convey the idea that it is not just a question of fitting together the sides, front, and back, but of working all around it. In addition, working "from the inside out" may also release children from conceiving the different parts of a body as flat surfaces to be added together, to imagining them as projections of inside volumes, and even becoming aware of bones and muscles that lie below the skin. This kind of language may help children to perceive surfaces as thicknesses and to conceive of form as volume. Thus, the problem in sculpture is to create a shape wherein every contour "reads" three-dimensionally and projects a different form.

In children's early efforts with sculpture, their perceptions tend to be totally frontal. This may be due partly to a lack of experience with this particular medium, but also to a lack of general experience in looking at sculpture and other objects in the environment in all their spatial fullness. We come to realize that children's knowledge of space is not instinctive, but can be acquired by developing their sensibilities through consciously guided experiences. When children are encouraged to conceive of a sculptural shape as volume and to use the medium so that all parts are integral to the whole, they begin to understand that all points of view are important. What they discover in the process is that they must continually move the piece as they are working or they must move themselves around it.

The basic concept, therefore, is that sculpture does not deal with one static system of relationships but with a series of interlocking relationships—that is, with forms connected in such a way that any one part is dependent upon all the others. The means of creating a unified feeling in the material forms involves similar elements to those of painting—movement, texture, shape, rhythm—but it is the multiple qualities of these relationships in relation to space that distinguishes sculpture as a three-dimensional form.

A confusion in the difference between painting and sculpture also arises because no clear separation is made between the modes of seeing and touching. As has been stated, painting creates a space that is viewed directly and frontally, whereas the volume in sculpture is originally created through a sense of touch. For this reason Langer defines the problem of sculpture as one of making "tactual space visible." [1] In more immediate, experiential terms, a child expresses the difference as, "In sculpture, if you close your eyes you could feel it and see it; in

[1] Suzanne K. Langer, *Feeling and Form* (New York: Scribner, 1953), p. 90.

painting, if you close your eyes you could not see it." Thus, the uniqueness of this art form lies in the intimate relationship between touch and sight.

The distinction is perhaps most clearly made by Read, who suggests that sculpture is primarily an art of "touch-space" whereas painting is the art of "sight-space," [2] his premise being that the tangible "feel" of a thing and the "look" of it are distinctly different. "If sculpture has any particularity," he writes, "it is to be distinguished from painting as the plastic art that gives preference to tactile sensations as against visual sensations. . . . This peculiarity does not mean, of course, that we can discount our visual reactions to sculpture; nor does it mean that we refuse any aesthetic value to sculpture that is visually conceived. We are seeking the basic principles of this art, and these . . . involve tactile sensations." [3]

FORCE

Force is usually associated with active things, yet sculpture has been defined as a static object in space. How do we account for this? As an aesthetic quality, we perceive it as *forces in opposition* such as the tension between opposing volumes, the *differences in textures* which produce "active" rather than less active surfaces, and the oppositions created by *differences in light and dark.*

Volumes in Opposition. As has been said, force is also the *intensity* of the material itself. In painting, intensity is more easily identified because we can refer directly to the vividness of color or the energy of line. In sculpture, however, clay itself has no energy. It is clay shaped which has intensity and therefore its force. When we observe, for example, that an animal a child sculpts has a sense of force about it, we are not referring to the storytelling or literal aspects which tell us what a particular animal is, but to the energy of the forms.

In this same expressive context we refer to force as the *thrust* of a form in opposition to a related form. A sense of thrust comes from the physical projection of a volume in space, yet it is more than the materiality of the thrust. It is what happens to the space around it as a result of the shape of the volumes. For example, if a sculpture, whether abstract or realistic, has a long, thin form which moves against a much smaller, squat, solid form, these are two elements that are not necessarily equal but that seem to have the same amount of force so that they balance. As an inherent aspect of the total image, the shape of the long, attenuated form bisects an area of space in such a way that space becomes part of the sense of balance. Thus, in addition to the physical nature of the thrust, the space around it becomes enlivened in the sense that it is "pulled away" or "pushed toward" a particular volume. What we perceive is that surrounding space becomes activated, depending on what the forces of the volumes are doing, and therefore we may say that space becomes an element of force.

Part of our feeling that a piece of sculpture has energy has to do with *scale*— that is, with the relationship between the sizes of the elements within it. We see this most dramatically when children are encouraged to sculpt nude figures. For

[2] Herbert Read, *The Art of Sculpture* (New York: Pantheon, 1956), p. 48.
[3] Ibid., p. 70.

example, in a class of nine- to twelve-year-olds the problem was presented for the first time. A ten-year-old girl produced a female figure with breasts thrust forward standing on huge, rounded legs which give the appearance of a hoop skirt except for the appropriately placed genital area. Although the breasts have an immediate frontal thrust, they become small in relation to the vast, horizontal scale of the hips and legs. In this particular image, a sense of force comes through the exaggeration of the thrust of the breasts but also through the opposition between the two accentuated parts of the body. We can grasp the notion of scale more clearly if we consider a similar nude figure with more realistic proportions. In this case, there would be a very different sense of scale because the legs (or any other body part) would be more naturalistic and would not appear so enormous. We perceive force, then, as an expressive element of exaggeration and distortion given tangible shape by the opposition of volumes.

Texture.   Just as *texture* animates a surface and provides a sense of rhythm, so does it give a feeling of force. Whether it is deliberately smooth or varied, it appears as contrasts in the pattern of lines, shapes, and arrangements of forms as a means of giving further expression to a volume. As such, it is not a decorative feature to be added on, but an aesthetic element that gives intensity to the form itself. A highly accentuated texture draws our attention to a particular area within a given piece by creating opposition such as smooth against rough, refined against coarse, between a tactile or visual surface. At the same time, too much texture has less force because it can detract from the inner strength of the volume. It is the intent that determines the quality, for a smooth as well as an active surface produces a quality of force.

Light and Dark.   Light and dark is an ingredient of all of our perceptions. Whenever we look at anything in space, there is always a light playing upon it through which we see the differences in the surface. Without light we would be unable to see them, for the object would appear flat. If we put a very bright light on something, for example, its effect is to flatten it out. We may experience this on a bright, sunny day when we look at a face in front of us which is directly in the sun and we see it as flat.

In sculpture, light and dark function as contrasting shadows which are created by the volumes. Although we conceive of shaping forms in terms of volumes, we might also be aware that those volumes are expressed as relationships between light and dark. Just as spatial relationships change as we walk around a sculpture or turn it with our hands, so do light and dark appear to shift, yet the relationship remains the same because of the volumes underneath. Thus, in the very process of making a statue, dark and light become inherent to the volume and we perceive it as part of the total form.

When we touch or hold a statue, we do not see it in terms of light and dark; we "see it through our hands." As we look at it, however, we see it as a volume that finds one of its expressions through changes we observe on the surface. One of the primary ways in which we see that surface is through differences in light and dark. Because sources of light may change, light and dark have a relational quality, but even in relief sculpture, which is the least dimensional, this relationship always exists.

It is interesting to observe, for example, that very young children frequently make "dimples" in the shells on "skins" of animals. Initially, they are not conscious of creating darks and lights, for they see a surface as being purely decorative. Experientially, however, they may make these or similar indentations, because they are unable to perceive a mass without some kind of feeling of light and dark. In the process of perceiving and responding to the volumes they are making (either through their hands or eyes or both), they begin to see volumes as variations in a surface. They may come to recognize them not only as textures, expressed as raised or lowered surfaces, but as variations in light and dark which give force to those surfaces. Thus, as an aesthetic quality, the nature of light and dark impressions is not independent of the volumes, but is expressive of those volumes.

TIME

The process in sculpture is one of creating presences, not activities. It shares with painting a static form. Thus, time does not function as an inherent aesthetic element within the sculptural image. Characteristically, sculpture does not deal with time, even in its distortion of size. Rather, its strength lies in its timelessness —its stillness. Regardless of how much energy we feel is within a piece in terms of its force or plasticity, it never really "takes off" in a temporal sense. (Only kinetic sculpture or mobiles actually move in time.) Its power is in its compression rather than in its activity. That is, we are dealing with the compression of an image perceived as a whole. Although it is three-dimensional and we may be looking at one particular view, we perceive it all in one piece. A statue may even dictate how our eyes or hands move through it, in terms of its shapes and spaces, yet all the while we are perceiving it as a unified form.

We may attribute time by extending its forms in our own minds, such as continuing the action of a gesture or the thrust of a member in space, but in this case time is experiential. The time it takes for the eye to follow the contours or profiles or to walk around a piece is actual physical time invested by an observer. It is not aesthetic time through which the form itself finds expression.

Experiential Approach

The experience in sculpture is one of shaping a plastic form in its essential mass so that it occupies and defines space. As children become more deeply involved in the process, they become aware that what they are experiencing are sensations of relative weight, volume, and mass. Whether the forms they are creating are abstract or realistic—that is, whether they are making an object which is its own form and looks like nothing else, or whether it resembles something in the real world—the experience is the same.

PLASTIC SENSIBILITY

Sculpture derives its distinctiveness from its unique plastic qualities and from a special kind of sensibility. The sculptural process evokes a type of consciousness which Read called a "plastic sensibility" involving three factors: *a sensation of the tactile qualities of surfaces*—through textures, and in some cases, movement caused by light and dark shadows; *a sensation of volume*—through working in the round so that form is conceived not as illustration, which is flat, but as volume, which is thick; and *a realization of the mass or ponderability,* which is experienced by touching or lifting an object.[4] His description of sculpture as an "art of palpation"[5] seems particularly fitting for children as an art form which gives satisfaction through the touching and holding of objects. Thus, we may consider the experience of making and perceiving sculpture as one of "seeing it through your hands." Only by running their hands over an object and tracing the direction of the contours around it can children have a direct sensation of its three-dimensional shape. In so doing, they are experiencing "pure dimension" in the sense that they are not "reading" a shape as flat as any point but are sensing it in terms of its volume.

Seeing in sculpture is a complex phenomenon, for it involves not only what is being seen, but what was seen from another view, and also the memory of sensations of touch. From their earliest years, children sense the properties of weight, volume, and shape through touching before they understand them through their sense of sight. Tactile qualities are the modes by which a child first perceives his immediate environment, and they remain a means of discriminating between rounds and squares, sizes and shapes. Even as a child expands his sensory apparatus, he augments his visual knowledge of things with knowledge through touching. But as with space, his awareness of these sensations is learned, not "given" at birth. What must be "given" are experiences to deepen his visual–tactile sensibilities through an understanding of three-dimensional form.

A Touching Experience. Within the whole sculptural process, then, touch is essential to the perceiving and making of shapes (and to the subtler contrasts between shape and texture). We see this in a child's description of the experience as "feeling it through your hands." It has also been likened to a haptic experience wherein one tends to favor or rely on the sense of touch. In sculpture, it is a dual sensation of a touch and muscle sense involved in taking an object in one's hand and moving a finger over it to experience its shape.

This concept was initially introduced by Lowenfeld,[6] who observed in working with blind children that their approach to sculptural form emerged from a sense of feeling "from the inside out"—that is, feelings that come from an awareness of internal bodily sensations of swallowing, stretching, lifting. He noted that the general form of their sculpture was built up from many tactile impressions reflected in features such as wrinkles, dimples, and the stretch of muscles.

Lowenfeld's work with blind and sighted children led him to distinguish two types of art experience based on the nature of their products and on their ways of perceiving and responding to the world of experience. Those with *visual* ten-

---

[4] Herbert Read, *The Art of Sculpture* (New York: Pantheon, Bollingen Series, 1956), p. 71.

[5] Ibid., p. 49.

[6] Viktor Lowenfeld, *Creative and Mental Growth* (New York: Macmillan, 1964), p. 234.

dencies he characterized as individuals who draw their stimuli from the external environment and who orient themselves to it primarily through their eyes. Those with *haptic* tendencies are primarily concerned with their own bodily sensations and draw their impressions from subjective experiences with which they are emotionally involved.

These modes of perception do not exist in absolute terms, for most children reflect both tendencies. Yet it is interesting that some children produce forms that have greater tactility than others and can be "read" as easily by touching as by seeing. The notion of haptic experience has important implications for young children, for it explains the quality of perceiving and responding to something internally while trying to externalize its form as they feel it. The difference is that it is not externalized through sight, as with visually oriented individuals, but through touch and feeling. This is not to suggest that one mode produces a greater reality than the other. It is simply to recognize that although both are searching for their own reality, the haptic experience is one of groping toward a feeling rather than a visual reality. Both modes produce expressive forms, but a haptic experience is a different way of achieving expression. Its form is not constructed in terms of an externally conceived design (which may or may not look like something) but is internally shaped from within itself.

Haptic experience, then, may be appropriate in describing the nature of the encounter between a child and the type of "felt" meaning involved in the act of sculpting. In describing the tactual experience as, "It feels squizzy," "squooshy," "oozy," "slippery," children sense that as they move through clay, for example, their own movements becomes slowed and sustained with an intensity almost equal to the resistance of the medium. In so doing, they become engrossed in literally feeling their way through a piece. In relation to the emotional experience, the expressionist world of sculpture involves giving form to creations of the imagination that do not depend on the capacity to see things. Thus, a child's use of elements such as space, size, and shape is determined by the emotional importance he attaches to them, rather than by a consideration of what is "real." In this sense, they become expressive values more significant than the images or objects a child actually sees or remembers.

If we follow the logic of haptic experience, we can begin to understand how children of all ages frequently begin with no preconceived problem to solve but with only a generalized notion of exploring the qualities of the material. Such random exploration is to be encouraged, for children tend to approach sculpture with a two-dimensional picture in their heads. The suggestion to "let the material speak to you and help you decide what to make" implies that the properties of clay, wood, stone, paper, and so on, may themselves enter in and help direct ideas. It thus opens possibilities for children to play back and forth from the material to the idea and from the idea to the material.

Submitting to Materials.　Children's search for sculptural form reveals that different materials have characteristics they have to discover, which both lend and limit themselves to different ways of working. They discover that some materials, such as clay, are pliable, making it possible to add on sections as well as to take away, whereas other materials, such as wood or stone, require cutting away.

Whether they are involved with "hard" or "soft" materials, they need to become aware that they are working with mass as a whole form, rather than focusing on small parts or on a surface finish. A supportive vocabulary of working "up and down" and "in and around" conveys a sense of getting inside the material and working out. The response may be less a tendency to "take it apart" than to "take it all in," which helps them to perceive that volumes can grow from all directions.

As children begin to conceptualize a problem, a moment arrives at which an idea becomes conscious and the process of controlling and shaping it takes place. In this instance the process of sculpture works from material to image, wherein a child may discover the meaning of his forms only after he has created them. At this point a teacher must be especially sensitive in helping a child to recognize and appreciate forms of whose significance he was not previously aware. On the other hand, a child may begin with a subject or idea suggested by the teacher. In this case the process, although still exploratory, becomes an attempt to build a relationship of forms that will express that idea or subject. In either case the work does not proceed by logical, ordered steps. There are always inexplicable leaps in the process, given impulse by each child's imagination. For this reason we need to understand the process as well as focus on the product. In one session, for example, some children may work on one object only, others may finish one and begin another, and others may explore, destroy, rebuild, and realize a form only at the very end.

Organizing Volumes.   In general, the experience is one of simplifying and shaping a solid, uncluttered statement by capturing its essential qualities in terms such as, "How big does it feel?" "How forceful?" "Are the inside spaces important to the outside shape?" In concentrating on the volumes emerging in front of them, they discover the beginning of form. In making a figure of a person, for example, children tend to begin with the details by making the head separately, putting on eyes, nose, and mouth, and then forming the body. In response to questions such as, "Which is the biggest part of the figure?" "Will it stand—will the legs support it?" children may redirect their efforts so that parts or members emerge from the larger mass.

The human figure is the most personal statement if children are encouraged to look to themselves as the center of reference. Yet even a child's image of himself is not built up solely by sight, for even if he were to stand in front of multiple mirrors, he could only look in one direction at a time. He also comes to know his body through a sense of touch by which he can actually feel the shapes in space which make up its forms. For example, he experiences by touching the spaces that "go in" (such as the eye sockets, nostrils, inside of the ear, cavity of the mouth) and those that "come out" (such as the nose, cheek bones, lips, ears, breasts, hips, and muscles in tension).

In expressing a figure in movement, children can get a sense of their own gestures by feeling the ways in which body parts flow into another, instead of conceiving of them as separate units "stuck" together. For example, they begin to understand how the joints function by touching an elbow as it bends and by observing what happens to the body in twisting and bending poses taken by others. It is in assembling and comparing all these different impressions and sensations that children are able to create an image. In relation to the figure, sculpture calls forth two types of body images. The first is in response to a child's immediate experience with his own body in terms of what he can see of it and what he can feel of it. The second is the result of his observations of others, based primarily on sight but also to some extent on tactile sensations. And it is interesting to note the kinds of detailed observations that emerge when children are offered the problem of sculpting a human figure.

Thus, the nature of the sculptural experience is that children neither are given a "model" to copy nor are expected to "model" a reproduction of what exists in nature. Rather, the process is one of shaping from the imagination some object or series of objects which have attracted their interest, whether it be realistic, such as an animal or a mother and child, or abstract. Whatever a child creates from his imagination is drawn from many memories of the object and depends on both visual and tactile sensations. Regardless of the subject, the forms that he produces are marked by exaggeration—that is, by enlarging some or omitting or minimizing others, he projects those aspects that are of special importance to him. Although the subject may derive from an actual object in the environment, it is merely a theme to be utilized rather than to be imitated. Although this is not to imply an arbitrary division between subject and form, children's sculpture finds its power primarily from subject matter expressed through its arrangement of plastic forms in terms of its volumes, curves, and thrust and by its balancing of mass. Sculpture cannot be judged in terms of its resemblance to the "real" thing, for each piece is first of all a piece of sculpture, an entity unto itself, reflective of "real" feelings.

Elements of Sculpture

Turning to the specific elements involved in sculpture allows us to develop a working vocabulary and to identify further those properties which lend themselves to plastic form. In the process of exploring clay, as the most commonly used material, children become kinesthetically aware that it is *solid, malleable,* and *heavy*. Through random manipulation, they discover that it can be pulled, pushed, twisted, curled, curved, cut, torn, bent, flattened, hollowed out, and that through all of these means, it has the potential for retaining a shape.

Children first begin to experience the elements of clay when its *plasticity* yields to continuous changes in *shapes* and *textures*. Perhaps most important in working with shape as volume is an awareness that the edge of a three-dimensional object is not a line, but a surface which encloses a volume. The way in which they treat with a surface depends, as has been discussed, upon their understanding of texture and light and dark as expressive qualities.

Another element which functions as an aspect of shape is *size*. Too often restrictions are imposed because of insufficient materials. For the most part, however, teachers have yet to understand that size and shape are not arbitrary factors, but may reflect a child's emotional intent. Moore expresses this subjective relationship in the best metaphoric sense: "There is a right physical size for every idea." [7] In the same spirit, we extend this to poetry by suggesting that every thought has its own shape on a line.

Recalling our underlying premise that children see themselves as the center of reference in perceiving phenomena, Moore's observation of adult sculptors seems particularly fitting. He writes, "We relate everything to our own size and our emotional response to size is controlled by the fact that we men on the average are between five and six feet high." [8] The implication for children is that when given the freedom of a quantitative amount within a qualitative structure, shape, size, and scale take on emotionally charged meanings. If such a relationship does exist, it seems appropriate that teachers re-evaluate the conventional practice of presenting children with a fist-sized ball of clay. If we accept the expressive nature of children's sculpture, it seems reasonable that they be given a suitable amount of clay at the outset or be given the opportunity to select whatever amount seems to suit their needs. Each art form has its own economy and each artist imposes his own limitations. As children gradually become comfortable with a medium, they also become aware of its limitations and potentials.

PROBLEM: To explore the physical properties of sculpture

TEACHER: What would you say sculpture is, compared to painting?
CHILD: It has *texture,* like you can feel lumps.
CHILD: More *depth.*
CHILD: You can make it *three-dimensional.*
CHILD: Any *shape* you want.
CHILD: In painting, you can make it three-dimensional when it really isn't.
TEACHER: If you were painting a picture of a person, you know the person is three-dimensional and you can walk all around him, but you would be painting it from the front. You know that it has a back and that it has sides, but you couldn't see them; whereas when you're making a sculpture, what happens?
CHILD: You've got to paint the back and everything.
CHILD: But you can't paint the back.
TEACHER: Right, so in making a sculpture, it's not a question of painting it. What are you doing to it?
CHILD: You're making the whole thing instead of just the front of it.
TEACHER: So you really have to think about the sculpture as you're working on it all the way around; you can't just work on one part and suddenly say, "Oh, I forgot, let's see what happens around on the other side," because the minute you start to turn it, what happens?
CHILD: It's another shape.

[7] Henry Moore, "Notes on Sculpture," in *The Creative Process,* Brewster Ghiselin (ed.) (New York: New American Library, 1952), p. 75.
[8] Ibid., p. 76.

TEACHER: It is not just a question of front, back, and side; it's maybe fifty million different views, depending on how much you turn it. I want to show you a few pictures of sculptures and then we're going to talk about them.

CHILD: Are they very famous ones?

TEACHER: Not particularly; they're just to illustrate what we're discussing. What can you say about these sculptures? [Jacques Schnier, *Sculpture in Modern America* (Berkeley, Calif.: University of California Press, 1948).]

CHILD: They're animals.

TEACHER: Yes, you can see how they look like animals, don't they?

CHILD: The bird, it's so smooth, it looks like it's *moving*. [Dove, p. 83.]

CHILD: Yeah, and this one's *rough*. [Porcupine, p. 82.]

CHILD: And this is *solid,* no holes in it. [Setting Hen, p. 84.]

CHILD: Yeah, it looks like it's made out of some kind of granite that's glued together. [P. 84.]

TEACHER: You've noticed two basic things. You noticed that the sculpture, besides being sculpture, looks like other things like birds or animals, things you see in the real world; you talked about the *texture,* the kind of *materials* they're made of, and Kevin said something that's very important in the art of sculpture. Would you repeat it, please?

CHILD: It's solid, there's no holes going through it; no air passes through.

TEACHER: This is a completely solid form, isn't it? [Bear, p. 80.] Now let me show you one that isn't. What about these two? [Duo, p. 125; Spring, p. 126.]

CHILD: They have negative and positive space.

TEACHER: Would you explain what you mean by negative and positive space?

CHILD: The positive is where the clay is and the negative is where the air passes through it.

TEACHER: This one is all positive space; this is all "stuff," it's the material the sculpture is made out of. In this one, you have the spaces that go in between which are negative; they're the air, they're not the material. What happens to these spaces when they get surrounded by the material? [Pp. 125, 126.]

CHILD: They become just like positive space.

TEACHER: They become almost like positive space in the sense that they become part of the sculpture; this is completely enclosed by bronze and it becomes a very important shape in the sculpture, just as important as the outside. [P. 125.]

CHILD: It looks like a metal figure, not a sculpture.

TEACHER: Is that not a sculpture?

CHILD: I thought sculpture was just made out of clay.

TEACHER: Sculpture doesn't have to be just made out of clay. What are some of the things it can be made of?

CHILDREN: Glass, plastic, fiberglass.

TEACHER: Look at this picture again. Besides the fact that this one is solid and this has space going through it, what else is different about these two? [Bear, p. 83, and Duo, p. 125.]

CHILD: Different materials.

TEACHER: Yes.

CHILD: It's cutlike, so that the pieces stick out.

TEACHER: Yes, it's more three-dimensional than this one.

CHILD: That's not real life, there's nothing like that.

CHILD: That's more real.

TEACHER: Yes, this is the form of a sculpture and also looks like a bear; this one is in the form of a sculpture, but it doesn't look like anything that you recognize in the real world.

I want to show you some other things that sculpture can look like. We were talking about what sculpture is made of. When you're working with a material (this bear happens to be sandstone, which is a relatively soft rock) you can carve fairly easily. In most of the pictures I showed you sculptors have used the same materials for thousands of years. What kinds of material do you think they are?

CHILDREN: Clay, wood, marble, plaster, bronze.

TEACHER: Sometimes they cast in bronze. Today sculptors are using other materials, for example, the use of welding today makes it possible to extend forms into space that they couldn't do in clay. Do you know what welding is?

CHILD: Bringing it together with heat.

TEACHER: How?

CHILD: Like if you have two pieces of metal you can melt them and then just put the other together and they'll dry together.

TEACHER: Here's a piece of sculpture that's welded and, because it's welded you can get very long skinny arms sticking out into space that will support themselves. If you were making this out of clay, would these pieces hold? [*American Sculpture of the 60's* (Los Angeles: County Museum of Art, 1967), p. 165.]

CHILD: No, they'd fall down.

TEACHER: So you see that the form of the sculpture changes because of the materials that are used. Look at the negative space in this one. [P. 235.] Does this sculpture have more negative or positive space?

CHILD: Negative, because of all the air in it and around it.

TEACHER: Yes, paper maché is something you can make sculpture out of. This is not paper maché, it's called mixed media—means a lot of different things used together. This happens to be made out of fabric—it is material on the outside that is stuffed, like pillows (soft sculpture). So aside from things like metal, rock, bronze, and welding, there are other materials. Now imagine feeling all those things and imagine feeling a clay sculpture. When it's dry—like metal, bronze, and rock—what would it feel like when you touch it?

CHILD: Hard.

TEACHER: Hard, it wouldn't "give" like this fabric. But here is sculpture that you can push and it will push in. There's such things now as "soft" sculpture too because of what they're made of. [Pp. 172, 178.]

Another thing you'll see around is sculpture that is colored. A thousand years ago all statues were painted; in other periods the color was in the material itself, like bronze, stone, or marble. Today a lot of sculpture is colored, either painted after it is used or sprayed before, or the color is in the material like this plastic. These are layers of plastic. [P. 228.] This is made of colored plastic; it looks like pieces that are made out of Jello because they have that kind of color in them. [P. 204.]

CHILD: It's like when you take wax and put it into water and it just hardens.

CHILD: That one looks like wax. [P. 228.]

CHILD: That one's made out of driftwood, right? [P. 226.]

TEACHER: No, it's made out of laminated wood. Do you know what laminating means?

CHILD: Soft? Rotten?

TEACHER: No, it means gluing together.

CHILD: It's layers of wood glued on top of each other.

TEACHER: Do you see all these lines? They are all pieces of wood just piled up high and glued together; then this form was carved out of it so you see all the layers. That's very different from taking a hunk of wood and carving it—it's a very different use of wood. [P. 226.]

CHILD: That must take a long time.

TEACHER: Here's an interesting one. I've seen this piece and you really can't get a sense of the size by this picture; there are telephone poles and railroad ties and. . . . [P. 99.]

CHILD: Telephone poles?

CHILD: How did they get them up there?

TEACHER: If you look very carefully, you'll see these very, very thin lines that are wires holding the whole thing together, and they're all suspended from a point here; if it sat in the middle of this room, it would almost touch all the walls, that's how big it is. When I was standing there someone pushed on it, and all of the people standing around kind of pushed it and the whole thing spun around very slowly, all suspended from this one tiny point. It was a very strange feeling to see these massive telephone poles and railroad ties swinging around in space.

Now, this one is the opposite of it in feeling in that it's very, very polished and elegant and it's not made out of lost, left-over materials. It moves, too, but very slowly. If you were walking past it, you wouldn't notice that it was moving unless you really stopped and looked at it. What happens to these shapes as it moves? [P. 98.]

CHILD: They change.

CHILD: Maybe this one pulls out.

TEACHER: No, the metal doesn't move; the whole thing spins around on one point so that all these shapes in between. . . .

CHILD: Go into another. . . .

TEACHER: Change and keep spinning around. How would you describe the difference between this kinetic sculpture by Rivera and this construction-type sculpture by De Suvero?

CHILD: That one is so much more polished . . . that one looks like it was made by a king [p. 98] and that one looks like it was made by a garbage man. [P. 98.]

CHILD: That one has bends in it [p. 99], but this one doesn't have any bends in it [p. 98].

CHILD: Yeah, that one's sharp cut and this one isn't.

TEACHER: What does it have?

CHILD: Triangular ones put together.

TEACHER: Which is called what?

CHILD: That one has circles and bends.

CHILD: That one has angles, doesn't it?

TEACHER: So in this one [p. 99] you have sharp lines and sharp angles and in this one you have curves [p. 98].

CHILD: It's a mess of rectangles, one there and one there and. . . .

TEACHER: Could you make this out of clay?

CHILD: No.

TEACHER: Try it when you get your hunk of clay; try making a long, skinny shape spin around like that and see what happens.

CHILD: Why is that sculpture so good?

TEACHER: A lot of things that look very simple are not simple; it's having the idea and doing it that's important in sculpture. There are some sculptors who take common objects and make "things" out of them or take ordinary things and make sculpture out of them.

PROCEDURE

Let me put the books away and show you something about clay itself. Come and stand around the table (*cuts off 4-lb. pieces of clay from a 25-lb. bag*).

CHILD: Such a big hunk!

TEACHER: Does that scare you, such a big hunk? Somebody was saying that in clay it's easy to change things [*as opposed to painting*]. You really have to kind of play around with it, push it, let the clay talk to you; if you don't like the way it's going, you can turn it upside down or on its side and it will change. You'll get different planes. What's a *plane*?

CHILD: It's a flat surface.

TEACHER: Yes it is. Can you imagine that it could continue out into space like this. (*She pulls a form into space.*) Suppose you want a piece that is very thin. (*She pushes and squeezes vertically until the top falls off.*) What happened. . .? If I want it to stand up I can make a base down here that I can attach it to . . . . or if you want to support a form that is very thin, like an animal's neck or legs (*she makes a long, thin form*), take some paper towel, crumple it up, and tuck it in the curve; when the clay dries, you can take it out and it will stand by itself. What happens to the clay when it dries?

CHILD: It gets hard.

TEACHER: Why is that?

CHILD: The water disappears.

TEACHER: And when the water disappears the clay shrinks a little bit. So when you put two pieces of clay together, you can't just squeeze them, you have to push from one side, then the other, to make sure those pieces become one. If you're joining two little pieces, the best way is to take a third piece and put it in the middle and work it back and forth. Now here's the problem we're going to work with today:

PROBLEM: To experiment with solid or open spaces in abstract or realistic forms

TEACHER: You're going to make a piece of sculpture in the round. It can either look like something you know or look only like itself. It has to have at least one negative space that goes completely through the sculpture. When you're working, try not to start with a picture in your head; play with it, push it, punch it, tear it, and see what comes out.

CHILD: Can it be nothing?

TEACHER: There is no such thing as nothing; it can be a sculpture.

CHILD: Can it be a sculpture of nothing in particular?

TEACHER: It can be a sculpture of itself! It can be a sculpture that looks like a real object or it can be its own form and nothing else, but it has to have a space going through it.

CHILD: Can I make a belly button?

TEACHER: If it's a hole in the belly button you have to decide whether you want it to go all the way through the figure, which is perfectly acceptable in a sculptural form. You have to recognize that sculpture is sculpture; it's not a real thing. If you're making a sculpture of a person and you want to put a hole through its head. . . .

CHILD: Or through its leg. . . .

TEACHER: . . . or whatever. There are sculptors who do that, who make the form of a head or a body that's like an outside shell and it's open on the inside. If you've been to the Los Angeles County Art Museum, there are sculptures in the front, before you go into the building, which are like reclining nude ladies that have spaces that go through them.

CHILD: What is the sculptor's name?

TEACHER: Henry Moore.

CHILD: Can we make anything—even a real-life thing like a machine?

TEACHER: You can make anything as long as it's three-dimensional sculpture in the round with a space that goes all the way through it.

CHILD: Three-dimensional?

TEACHER: All of it is going to be three-dimensional; it's going to be *so high, so wide,* and *so deep*—that's what sculpture is.

OBSERVATIONS WHILE CHILDREN ARE WORKING

CHILD: Look at this, I can make it like a brick. *(Dropping the clay on each side, it assumes a square shape.)*

CHILD: *(Pokes fist through clay, gets a circle shape.)*

CHILD: *(Working from one volume, folds a piece over to make a negative space.)* I'm through.

TEACHER: Does it work all the way around? If you can't move it, move yourself. Does it look as good from the back as it does from the front?

(Observing two children at table) You're too close together, it's hard to work with your elbows against your sides.

(Observing a child's piece) You don't want to see where it's connected because if you can see it, it won't hold.

Do you think this space is an important part of your sculpture? What would happen if you tilted that part up so it reads as a shape? *(To class)* You really have to think about what is the important idea that you want to work with.

(To a child) Instead of sculpting with little spaces, make the space more important; make it bigger so that it reads like a sculpture with space.

The shape of that space can be more important than it is in your piece. A hole is a "shaped space" in sculpture.

DISCUSSION (THE FOLLOWING WEEK)

TEACHER: Let's review the idea that we were working on.

CHILD: To make a thing with a positive and negative space.

TEACHER: How can you describe the difference between a hole and a negative space? What is different?

CHILD: The shape of the space is different.

TEACHER: What does a hole look like if you poked your finger through it?

CHILD: It would be round all around.

TEACHER: But when you talk about negative space—look at the shapes of space *(looks at child's work)*—what changes?

CHILD: Space—the shapes of space.

TEACHER: Look at this piece. There's a hole going in there surrounded by the shape of this space—the space starts small, then opens out like a flower. It's quite different from poking a hole in the clay.

What does making sculpture "in the round" mean?

CHILD: Like you can turn it around.

TEACHER: Yes, but you must be aware of what's happening not just on one side, but in a complete going-around form.

CHILD: You mean it's like—if you make a beautiful side on one side and nothing on the other, it's great on one side and terrible on the other?

TEACHER: Some of you were more successful with the idea than others. I mean successful in terms of working toward the problem. Some of you took other ideas and worked toward them. Negative space hasn't to do with whether the piece resembles something or not; it works in either case.

TEACHER: *(Pointing to child's piece)* This one is more interested in textures than in shapes. In this piece you have a sense of the shapes helping to form the solid mass.

(To group) Can you look at the piece of sculpture and ask yourself, "Was this piece formed by the inner shapes or did the solids make the spacing?"

(To a child) This piece is very massive and very solid but the question is, "Are the spaces important to the problem?" Were they important to you?

(To another child) Here's one that really has the feel of a sculpture in the round. As you turn it it shifts and changes—it's constantly moving and becoming.

CHILD: Yes, from here you can see one hole; from here it looks like it's going all the way through.

TEACHER: Could this piece exist without its spaces?

CHILD: No.

TEACHER: No, the space is really part of it.

PROBLEM: To explore three-dimensional form in shaping volume and space by sculpting an animal

TEACHER: We have pictures of animals on our board and we've been to the zoo; now I want to show you some pictures of animals in this book. [Jacques Schnier, *Sculpture in Modern America* (Berkeley, Calif.: University of California Press, 1948).]

TEACHER: In this sculpture of the bear, the legs are separated. What happens with the legs on this tiger? [Pp. 79, 98.]

CHILD: The two front legs are pushed together and the two back legs are apart.

TEACHER: If someone were making an elephant, instead of having the trunk way out with a skinny piece of clay, how else could they make it?

CHILD: Trunk comes down.

TEACHER: Yes, and you can make it thick so it doesn't fall off. Suppose you make a giraffe or a camel, what about the neck?

CHILD: Bend it.

TEACHER: Bend it where?

CHILD: Down to the ground.

TEACHER: Where else can you bend it?

CHILD: So it's drinking water.

CHILD: Put it on its shoulder.

TEACHER: If you're going to have a long, skinny neck, you need to attach it strongly to the body. As you look at these pictures, what's the difference between sculpture and painting?

CHILD: When you make a sculpture, you don't just make a skinny thing; it's flat.

CHILD: It's thick.

CHILD: It takes up room.

TEACHER: In painting, how would you show a person—all the way around?

CHILD: No.

TEACHER: But in sculpture, you can show it all the way around. One thing I want to show you about clay. . . .

CHILD: Do you have tools?

TEACHER: We have tools but the best tools to use are your hands. Don't start out with a picture in your mind of what the sculpture is going to look like; I want you to play. I want you to "gush" it around and "squoosh" it around, pound it and pull it and let it half-decide what it's going to look like. (*Teacher is manipulating clay. Children are gathered around the table.*)

TEACHER: Suppose I start it and it reminds me of something and I think that the form is going to do such and such and then I don't like what's happening. . . .

CHILD: You can tear it apart.

TEACHER: Well, I can change it by pushing it onto a different side; I can drop it, tear it. I can start doing all sorts of things that will change it. Now look at this *edge* that I just tore.

CHILD: It's not smooth.

CHILD: It doesn't look like you made it that way.

CHILD: It's got more points and edges.

TEACHER: Look at this edge here; it's smooth.

You really have to have the *edge* of a thing and the *surface* of a thing become part of the sculpture right as you're working; in other words, rather than make a whole sculpture and then say, "Okay, now I want it to be rough or smooth," it should really happen as you're working. (*Teacher begins to pull a long, cylindrical form out of the block of clay.*)

CHILD: It's not gonna stay.

TEACHER: You don't think it's going to stay?

CHILD: No, try to make that stay.

TEACHER: It goes out something like this and let's say it just keeps going. . . .

CHILD: It wouldn't hold.

CHILD: I know what you can do; you can put it on a ruler.

TEACHER: You could do that. You could have something that would support it, except that when it dries, it would very likely crack. I want to show you something you can do to get thin members of things. (*Pounds clay on board and flattens it out like dough.*)

CHILD: Air bubbles.

CHILD: Air pockets.

TEACHER: If I make something fairly thin like this. . . .

CHILD: It's gonna collapse.

TEACHER: It will collapse unless I put something down here (*adds pieces of clay underneath*) . . . but now it will stand. When you pound it really thin, instead of pulling it out, supposing you wanted something here, with this hollow in here and you're afraid of it collapsing, then you can get some paper towels or brown paper and crumple it up and it will keep it up while it dries. Then when it dries, you just pull the paper out and it will stay like that. Now if you're joining two pieces of clay together. . . .

CHILD: You go like that (*sticks one piece onto another*).

TEACHER: But if you just do that, what's going to happen?

CHILDREN: They're gonna come apart.

TEACHER: But why?

CHILD: Because they're not even stuck together.

CHILD: You have to take a tool. . . .

TEACHER: First of all, what makes the clay mushy? What's in it that makes it soft?

CHILD: Water.

TEACHER: What happens to the water when the clay dries?

CHILD: It evaporates.

TEACHER: It evaporates; it's not there anymore. If this hunk of clay doesn't have water in it anymore. . . .

CHILD: It will come off; it will crack.

TEACHER: Because it is smaller than it was when it had water in it. So if this piece shrinks and this piece shrinks, they fall apart; so you have to push from one to another and really make sure that they're not just stuck together, but. . . .

CHILD: That they're part of each other.

TEACHER: Exactly. And sometimes if you can't get your finger in between them, you can use one of the tools. Now look at these different tools. (You'll have to share them because there's not enough for everybody.) For example, if you wanted to scoop something out and you can't get your hand into a small place, you can use the. . . .

CHILD: Scooper.

TEACHER: Wire tool for scooping inside. You can use all these others for cutting different kinds of edges.

So when you put two pieces together and it shrinks, it will come apart unless you attach it strongly. If I take this hunk of clay and make an arch as if it were a giraffe eating with its head and neck down, what's different from the way it would be if the neck were sticking straight up? What's different now?

CHILD: The stomach is way up.

TEACHER: Yes, I'm making the stomach way up high. As a shape, what happens to the space under the stomach?

CHILD: The legs support it.

TEACHER: The space under the stomach and under the neck are part of the sculpture. If the neck is down and the head is on the ground, this space is part of the sculpture. Whenever you have a space with a fairly skinny bridge and you're afraid that the weight will push it down, take some paper towel and crumple it up and stuff it in or under. You can do this if you want a skinny part or something like elephant ears.

CHILD: When you make the lion's mane and you make the hair, it falls off.

TEACHER: It's easier if you make the texture right into the sculpture by using a tool.

Now, I'm going to give each of you a big hunk of clay. You can make any animal you like, just remember that the space around it and through it is just as important as the shape you're making.

Okay, everyone find a place, there's enough clay for everyone. Work from the large piece and pull out the shapes. Work from the inside out. Start with the body and pull the head out.

PROCEDURE

CHILD: Can we pound?

TEACHER: Yes, if you pound for a reason. You don't want it to get thinner than this.

CHILD: If you get it thinner and it dries. . . .

TEACHER: Suppose you want to put the ears on this. You've pounded it already really thin, but because you've pounded it so hard on the other piece it will hold, so you've got a really thin piece of clay that will hold itself.

Everyone look here for a minute. Let me show you something about fitting things together. You can start from the whole piece and pull things out, but you can never take two pieces and push them together because they won't hold. [*Teacher demonstrates to the class using adult sculpture tools.*] If I want to connect two pieces and I can't get my finger into the space, I can push from one piece to another with this tool. It's very hard to use your fingers in some places—that's what tools are for. You can also use this wire tool to shape something. If you want to put two pieces of clay together that are very small and there isn't enough to make

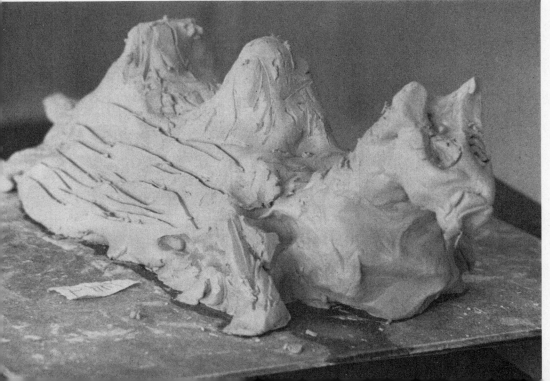

it hold, you can use a third piece to connect the two outside pieces. What sculpture looks like in the end depends upon how you want it to look—like texture. What is *texture?*

CHILD: How it feels.

CHILD: Like if it's rough or smooth.

TEACHER: You can get a texture by using your finger or using a tool; if you want an *edge,* you can get a very sharp edge by cutting. What kind of an edge is this?

CHILD: Rough.

TEACHER: Yes, what animal would have a really rough *surface?*

CHILD: An elephant, a crocodile.

TEACHER: What would have a fuzzy surface?

CHILD: Sheep, bears.

TEACHER: You have to decide what your surface has to look like and you have to decide that while you're working. It's easier to work the whole thing all together. Do you know what slip is?

CHILD: Clay and water. Can we have some?

TEACHER: If you really want a smooth surface, it's better to wet your hands. You can use slip to join pieces together but it's really better to use water on your hands.

PROBLEM: To explore the characteristic qualities of clay in forming an animal

TEACHER: We are going to work with a new medium today; do you know what this is?

CHILD: It's clay.

TEACHER: Each of you come and get your clay and put it on your board. It's right here in the pail. *(Children choose their own size. Most choose two fistfuls.)*

Close your eyes and let your fingers feel the clay. How does it feel in your hands? *(Children sitting around table with teacher.)*

CHILDREN: It feels cold, slippery, oozy, squooshy, squizzy.

TEACHER: Experiment and let your fingers see what they can feel with the clay.

CHILDREN: Make balls, roll it.

CHILD: It's not play dough; it doesn't feel like play dough.

TEACHER: What is Jaime doing?

CHILD: He's pinching.

TEACHER: What happened when you pinched it? Yes, forms come out. What else can you do?

CHILD: Squeeze it; that's fun.

TEACHER: Look at Wendy for a minute. What are you doing with your clay, Wendy?

CHILD: I'm stretching it.

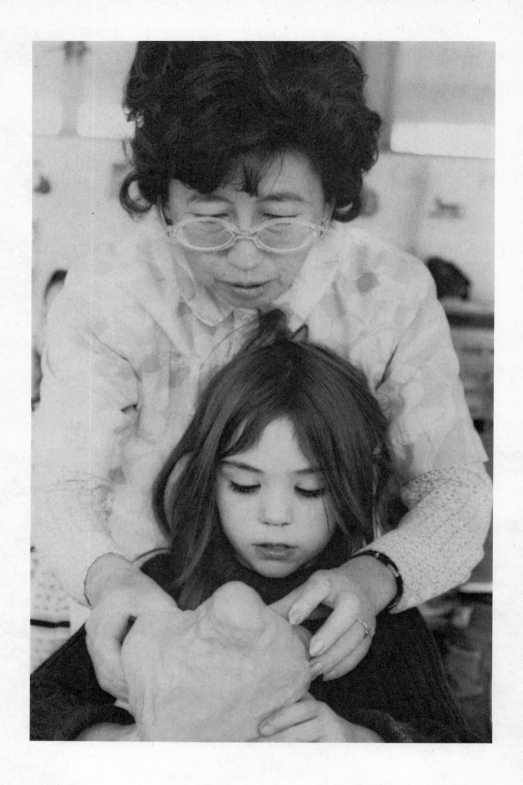

TEACHER: What other parts of your body can you stretch?

CHILDREN: You can stretch your neck, hands, arms, feet; your stomach when you stand on tiptoes.

TEACHER: How does the clay feel when you pick it up?

CHILD: Heavy.

TEACHER: What other things can you think of that are heavy?

CHILDREN: *(Shouting)* The school, the house, the table.

CHILD: Me. I'm heavy!

CHILD: Toothpaste when it dries.

TEACHER: We've been to the zoo. Today we're going to sculpt animals. Think of the things you saw that make an animal very special, like how it looks when it moves.

OBSERVATIONS WHILE CHILDREN ARE WORKING

CHILD: I'm making a rabbit. Here's his eyes. He's a kitty . . . no I mean he's a bunny.

TEACHER: Do a kitty and a bunny have the same *body shape*? What can you remember about the fur of a bunny? What is different? Think about the special things about a bunny.

CHILD: It's soft.

TEACHER: Make the bunny's fur look soft. How did you get this *texture*?

CHILD: I scraped it with my nails.

TEACHER: *(To the group)* When you look at a piece of sculpture, you should be able to see it from the front and the back and both sides. Let's look at Doree. Doree, stand over here and turn around slowly. Can you see her from the back? What can you see?

CHILD: Her hair, the back of her neck, her bottom.

TEACHER: Can you see her from the right side? The left side? Keep turning your board around as you make your animals and see if you can see them "in the round."

CHILD: My ear fell off!

TEACHER: What can you do that the ears won't fall off?

CHILD: Make them bigger.

TEACHER: Yes, since it's not a real animal, you can make them any size you wish. Do you think the ear that fell off was very strong?

CHILD: No.

TEACHER: How do you think you can make it stronger?

CHILD: Can I use more clay?

TEACHER: Yes, take what you need from the pail. Take an extra piece and work back and forth from the ear to the body so it will be strong.

CHILD: Look at my bear.

TEACHER: Does a bear have fur?

CHILD: Yes.

TEACHER: How do you think the fur looks and feels?

CHILD: It's hairy, I think.

TEACHER: How can you get a "hairy" texture in clay?

CHILD: Teacher, I'm through; it's an angry lion.

TEACHER: How does an angry lion's fur look when he's angry?

CHILD: I think it stands up when he screams.

TEACHER: Can you work on the *surface* and give him some fur.

CHILD: My turtle is carrying his house up on his back. See, I made him a funny house. I hope he doesn't get cold in his house.

TEACHER: Does a turtle have a smooth shell?

CHILD: No, he has a bumpy shell. *(Pushes "dimples" into surface of shell for a "bumpy" texture.)*

TEACHER: You're doing something interesting, Jody. What are you doing?

CHILD: Making finger holes. I'm also making it smooth.

TEACHER: So you have a smooth and rough texture in the same piece. Look at Cheri's elephant, please. Will those legs hold up the elephant's body?

CHILD: Its body is too big.

TEACHER: Then that presents a sculptural problem. What do you think it is?

CHILD: The legs aren't straight; it will fall.

CHILD: The elephant won't stand up; it has only three legs.

TEACHER: Let's see why it won't stand up. David, please stand on one foot. What happens?

CHILD: I will fall; I lost my *balance.*

TEACHER: Do you think the elephant will lose his balance?

CHILD: Yes, but David you need to add another leg.

CHILD: My head is falling off.

TEACHER: Let me show you how to make the form stay together. Let's mix some clay with a little bit of water in a dish. This isn't muddy water; it's called slip. Dip your fingers in it and use it to make the forms strong where they come together.

CHILD: I am really dirty.

TEACHER: Don't worry, there's plenty of soap and water to wash with.

PROBLEM: To explore the three-dimensional nature of space and volume by sculpting a human figure

TEACHER: There are many ways to work with clay. We work with it in a whole *mass;* that means, don't begin by pulling off pieces, work with it in one piece. Work from the bottom up and around. *(Children are manipulating clay.)* Look around you at the different shapes of our bodies, our heads. Let's make people.

CHILD: Do you mean a face?

TEACHER: You can put a face on your person. If you do, make it out of one mass of clay; don't break it apart and stick it on. You can push, and pull, and stretch to make the head and body.

CHILD: I know what you mean—no breaking for the eyes.

CHILD: I'm making a flat face.

TEACHER: Feel your own faces. What shapes go in and what shapes come out?

CHILD: I'm not making a pot, I'm making a person.

CHILD: What do you think I'm making? First you have to rub it. *(Makes a ball-shaped face and smoothes surface to begin working on eyebrows.)*

CHILD: *(Talking to himself while pulling the head out by twisting the neck)* "Twist 'til it gets bigger."

CHILD: Teacher, look at mine.

TEACHER: It's fine, but is it going to balance?

CHILD: Look what happened. *(Head fell over.)*

TEACHER: You'll have to repair it. Why do you think that happened?

CHILD: There isn't enough clay to hold the neck. *(Adds clay to connect the neck to the rest of the body.)*

TEACHER: Make the head nice and strong.

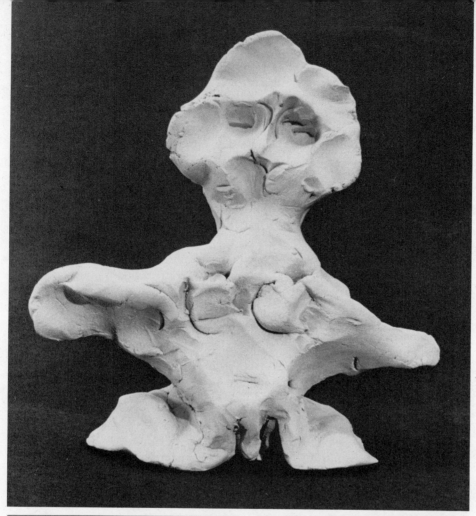

CHILD: How about smoothing this out (*connection of neck and head*) and making it flat?

TEACHER: Try it.

CHILD: It fell off.

TEACHER: Try again. This time put some water on your hands.

CHILD: How can we make the eyes?

TEACHER: Explore your own way by pushing in or pulling out.

CHILD: (*To another child*) You're making yours flat. (*Child is patting as if making a pancake between her hands.*)

CHILD: I want to make a mouth. It gets too fat or too thin (*making a standing figure*).

TEACHER: What gets too fat or too thin?

CHILD: The mouth.

TEACHER: It looks pretty good to me.

CHILD: I'm going to push it in.

TEACHER: Look at my mouth. When your mouth is closed, it doesn't go in; it comes out. Do you see that? Close your mouth, Jenny. Look at Jenny's mouth.

CHILD: (*Making a standing figure*) Here's the belly button. Mine is going to be funny. No, this person doesn't have legs, but he has a belly button on him. Here are the two tits and the stomach. Here's the "tee-tee." (*Makes figure with breasts.*)

(*To another child*) This is dirty, my mommy told me so.

CHILD: What are they?

TEACHER: These are not dirty; all ladies have them and you can make them on your sculpture.

CHILD: What about the ding-a-ling? Is that dirty too? Can I add it?

TEACHER: No, it's not dirty. What is the proper name for it?

CHILD: It's called a penis.

TEACHER: No part of the body is dirty.

(*To another child*) Look at the base of your sculpture. It is very strong.

CHILD: Mine stands up alone, too.

TEACHER: That means that the base of yours is strong; it can hold the weight of the rest of the sculpture.

(*To another child*) I thought you said you wanted to put legs on her.

CHILD: I do.

TEACHER: Well, you can make the body move into the legs.

CHILD: I'll have to cut it.

TEACHER: Yes, you've used too much clay in the body.

CHILD: Then I have to take some off.

TEACHER: Attach the clay back to the body and then shape the legs out of it.

CHILD: Oh! I get it.

CHILD: I started making the body and I really got into a flat shape and then I started making the legs go and the arms go.

TEACHER: And what did that look like?

CHILD: A gingerbread man.

TEACHER: Is that a sculpture in the round?

CHILD: No, it's flat.

TEACHER: So how can you work on it?

CHILD: All the way around, so it's got bumps.

CHILD: See what I'm doing? It's sticking out. *(Head extends out from body.)*

CHILD: This is what girls have, don't they? *(Pinches two small breasts on figure.)*

TEACHER: Yes, you're right.

CHILD: What are they called?

TEACHER: They're called breasts.

CHILD: This is a big tummy.

CHILD: This is the belly button; this is the waist.

CHILD: This is my belly button—it's deep. *(Pushes finger through to the back of the figure.)*

CHILD: This is his ding-a-ling.

TEACHER: Do you know what it is called?

CHILD: Yes, a penis. Can I make one?

TEACHER: Sure, you can make anything you want.

CHILD: Can you make a leg for me?

TEACHER: I can help you, but if I make it it will be my sculpture.

CHILD: Okay, I'll try it.

PROBLEM: To investigate the characteristics of sculptural volume by sculpting a human figure

TEACHER: Here are some pictures of sculpture. How do they look? Do they have a lot of details in them? [*Jacques Lipchitz* (Los Angeles: UCLA Art

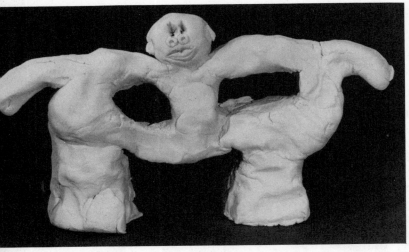

Council, 1963), Fig. 87.] What do these look like? Are they all of one piece? [Lipchitz, Figs. 48, 63.]

CHILD: No.

TEACHER: Why?

CHILD: They have less parts.

TEACHER: They have fewer parts than the first ones I showed you. What about this one? [Jacques Schnier, *Sculpture in Modern America* (Berkeley, Calif.: University of California Press, 1948), Fig. 68.]

CHILD: That's like one big piece.

TEACHER: That's right. It really looks like one big, smooth lump. It doesn't have any face in the sense of features—it doesn't have a nose or eyes; the face

146

is just one solid lump that grows out of the neck, that grows out of the body.

CHILD: You wouldn't need any face cause you wouldn't be seeing it if the head is pointing down. [Schnier, Fig. 68.]

TEACHER: Maybe that's why the sculptor who made this decided not to put in a face. Look at these two. Can you tell me one main difference that you see between these two sculptures? [Lipchitz, Fig. 42; Schnier, Fig. 28.]

CHILD: On one, the skinny one is like a lotta bones. . . .

CHILD: And the other one is a super ball.

TEACHER: Right, this one looks like a big lump that's made out of others, and this one has a lot of skinny parts like snake parts. Because this one has a lot of very thin parts, what is happening here that is not happening in the other one? [Lipchitz, Fig. 42.]

CHILD: That one has a baby. [Lipchitz, Fig. 4.]

TEACHER: Forget about whether there's a baby or not, or whether it's a lady or a man.

CHILD: That one's all put together and this one has big openings. [Lipchitz, Figs. 2, 4.]

TEACHER: Yes, because this one is like one solid lump. Look at the space—the space is all around it. [Lipchitz, Fig. 2.]

CHILD: But in that one it goes in and out.

TEACHER: It's as if you were the sculpture and your arms were tucked close to your body; there's space all around you but no space goes through you. *(Gestures with arms, as in photograph of sculpture.)* Now put your hands on your hips or touch your shoulders. What happens?

CHILD: It comes through you.

TEACHER: What happens to the space between your head and your arms? *(No response.)* Is the space between your arms and body different from the space around you? *(Children make gestures and look at each other.)*

CHILD: Yes.

TEACHER: What's the difference?

CHILD: It's trapped it.

CHILD: It's not round; it's oval.

TEACHER: Yes, the space gets a different shape because it's surrounded by your arms and it's surrounded by your head and shoulders. If my arms are here *(holds them above head with elbows bent, hands clasped)*, the space gets a different shape.

CHILD: A triangle.

TEACHER: Yes, so the space becomes part of the picture, too. It has shapes just like the clay has shapes. Let me show you some other pictures. Some of these are very simple and some get very complicated. [Daniel H. Kahnweiler, *Les Sculptures de Picasso* (Paris: Les Editions du Chêne, 1948).] Are these all open or are they all rounded?

CHILD: Some are open and some are rounded.

TEACHER: Look at the difference between this one and this one. [Kahnweiler, Figs. 45, 63.]

CHILD: The big one has more spaces.

TEACHER: Right. Here's one like the first one I showed you where it's broken up into very smooth kinds of shapes. [Picasso, Fig. 8.]

CHILD: Are those wood?

TEACHER: These are now metal. They started out being either clay or plaster, not wood. Do you know what plaster is?

CHILDREN: Yes.

TEACHER: They are metal and the metal piece is made from a clay or plaster model; it's moulded. Look at what's happening in this one [Lipchitz, Fig. 47.]

CHILD: Two eyes, no nose, no legs.

CHILD: You can see the face and the eyes, nothing else.

TEACHER: I'm just showing you these to show you different ideas, different ways that sculpture can look. I want to show you one thing that happens all the time in painting and sculpture—look at this one. [Picasso, Fig. 45.]

CHILD: It's got bumps.

TEACHER: Besides bumps, what else do you see in it?

CHILD: It's got a little head.

TEACHER: Yes, look at that little, tiny head on a big body. Now, supposing you

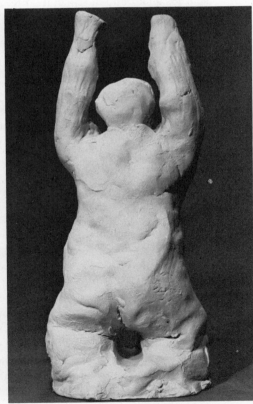

started making a piece of sculpture and you wanted it standing on two legs and you were thinking about making them long, skinny legs but the clay just wouldn't hold them?

CHILD: You could make a platform.

CHILD: You could make them fatter.

TEACHER: You can make a platform but you can also change the legs. You can make them fatter than they really are because a sculpture isn't really a person; a sculpture is a sculpture.

CHILD: A sculpture is something you make up.

TEACHER: If you have to make the legs fat for them to hold up the body because of the material you're using, that's what you have to do.

PROCEDURE

TEACHER: I want to show you something with this lump of clay. When you start working, you shouldn't have a picture in your head of what the sculpture is going to look like. Just start mooshing the clay around—*squeeze* it, and *pull* it, and *push* it and *stretch* it and let the clay begin to help you decide what the sculpture is going to look like. For example, when you start making a figure, don't think about what it's going to be wearing, or about fingers or toes or noses.

CHILD: You're pulling out everything.

TEACHER: *I'm* pulling everything out; you don't have to pull everything out.

OBSERVATIONS WHILE CHILDREN ARE WORKING

CHILD: I made a person.

TEACHER: Okay. You made a person. Now, you're making long, skinny legs. Do you think it's going to fall down?

CHILD: Maybe.

TEACHER: Maybe by the way it falls down, interesting things will begin to happen. You might say, "Hey, that's not so bad," and maybe this arm is going to be holding the leg.

CHILD: *(Begin pulling out clay.)*

TEACHER: You can take this leg and make it even longer now because it's supporting the body, so you can make it as long as you want. . . .

CHILD: What is that?

CHILD: A person.

TEACHER: (*To another child*) You can lift this whole side of the body up and even lift the head up. You can have this person flopping over the other way if you can't make it work this way.

CHILD: Wow, it looks like a spider.

CHILD: I'm going to move this arm back over to this side.

CHILD: That looks like a turtle now.

TEACHER: What's this person doing?

CHILD: Looks like she's ready to do a hand stand.

CHILD: Looks like she's going to make a back bend.

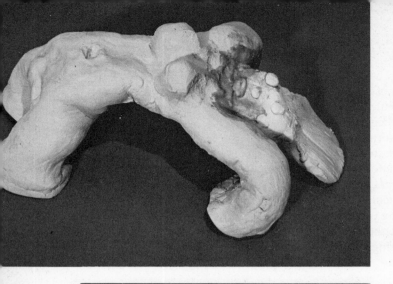

TEACHER: Exactly, she's doing a back bend.

(*To another child*) What's your person doing?

CHILD: Reading a paper.

TEACHER: He's really too flat, like a gingerbread man. If you want him sitting up, take part of his arm and part of his leg and give him a seat.

(*To the class*) Suppose you like this position and someone asks, "Where's the nose and mouth and so on?" Once you get the position the way you really want it, you can decide whether you want to put in a nose, or face, etc. So if you just push the clay around in the beginning, it's much more fun to let the clay help you decide what it's going to be than to have a picture in your head and keep working for that.

Remember, when you're working, either move yourself around or move the board around.

(*To another child*). Pull the clay down from here and get it fatter. When you're attaching two pieces, take a bit of clay and put it in the middle and push it from this side to this side so that it will become like one piece.

CHILD: I have to take some clay off the body to make the arms.

TEACHER: Put your arm on your stomach and see what happens. What's it attached to?

CHILD: My stomach.

TEACHER: Yes, and then it goes around to here.

(*To another child*) Work from the whole body, forget about the head; now pull from the body into the arms.

(*To another child*) If those are the legs, then put the body on. Start attaching it and shaping it.

(*To another child*) Those legs are awfully thin; pull some more clay from the body, because they may break off when they dry.

(*To another child*) Take some clay and strengthen the way the back of the chair is attached to the body, because it's got a lot of weight to support.

CHILD: What do you mean?

TEACHER: Do you see this little crack where you attached the back to the legs? Make that stronger.

(*To another child*) The clay is too smooth; the nose is not going to attach. You have to make the part that you are sticking in rough. When you attach it, you can shape it. Do you like that nose?

CHILD: No.

TEACHER: Then change it!

PROBLEM: To explore the difference between sculpture in the round and sculpture with limited space by making a relief plaque

TEACHER: Today we're going to explore the opposite kind of space from what we worked with last time, which was to make a sculpture in the round.

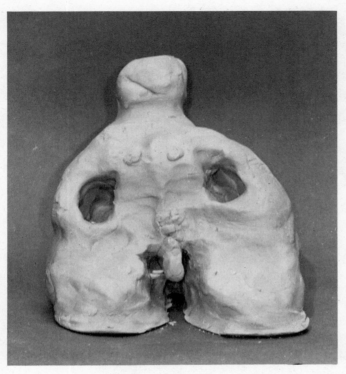

Look at these pictures. [Herbert Read, *Arp* (New York: Harry N. Abrams, Inc., 1968), No. 51, Constellation; No. 60, Torso; No. 61, Bird Mask; No. 62, Paolo and Francesa I.] What is the name of this type of sculpture?

CHILDREN: *(No response.)*

TEACHER: It's called relief sculpture or bas-relief. It pushes out or in from the surface, but we can't go completely around it; it usually comes out of the wall or building but some things we carry around are reliefs. What are they?

CHILDREN: *(No response.)*

TEACHER: Coins and metals are reliefs. Sometimes relief is quite shallow; that means there's not much space between the parts that push out and the parts that push in. Sometimes relief follows the outside edge of whatever forms are within it (the subject matter); sometimes it's within a rectangle or square. What do you notice about this? [No. 15, Figure]

CHILD: Part of it is pushed back in and the other part is pushed back out.

TEACHER: This artist named Arp did a lot of reliefs. Here's one that is very shallow, the yellow shapes are cut out of paper. [No. 33, Configuration.] He also did a lot with pieces of wood placing one on top of another. [Nos. 39–44.] Sometimes someone takes something like a stone and carves into it, and that's relief carving. Masks are relief if you think of them as something coming out and something going in from a surface. [No. 28, Mask]

CHILD: A mask is just showing the front part of a face not the back. . . .

TEACHER: . . . and therefore, it is not in the round. What's the difference between a relief and a sculpture in the round? Look at these solid sculptures. [No. 104, Growth; No. 113, Ptolemy I.]

CHILD: "In the round" is something you can turn around and get different angles.

CHILD: Relief is almost like a painting 'cause you can hang it on the wall except that it pushes out in the air.

TEACHER: Relief is something between sculpture and painting; it's like a three-dimensional painting except that a painting is flat. Relief starts with a flat surface and pushes back; you can cut into the surface. If you cut with a tool, you might get some nice shapes left over. These may be "accidents" but it is up to the artist to decide to use them or not. When you're working with something that is not recognizable as a "real thing," you can turn it around on both sides and see which way it works best.

PROCEDURE

TEACHER: You're going to make a relief sculpture which may look like something in the real world or look like its own form; it may have space or spaces that go all the way through, or it may be solid. I want to show you one thing about making a relief; you have to be careful not to start it too thin. I would not get it thinner than a half-inch, or it will crack. You can start with a flat surface and build forms on top of it or you can start with a round one and pull your forms out of it so that the surface is moving in and out.

CHILD: It has space but it isn't in the round.
TEACHER: Right, that's a relief.

DISCUSSION

TEACHER: What is the problem you were working with in your piece?
CHILD: How to create negative spaces in a relief.
TEACHER: Where are the negative spaces in this piece?
CHILD: Right there. *(He points to empty spaces.)*
TEACHER: There's another name that doesn't have to do with sculpture, but what are these called in general?
CHILD: Holes.
CHILD: An air pocket.
TEACHER: But if a hole is not defined by something, it's . . . .
CHILD: Empty . . . .
CHILD: This room is a hole.
TEACHER: What defines the shapes in this room?
CHILD: It's sealed in . . . the walls.
CHILDREN: The ceiling, the floor, the table.
TEACHER: The tables define the shape within the room. Now in Donna's piece, what defines these shapes?
CHILD: The positive shape.
CHILD: Curves.
TEACHER: Donna, what are the positive spaces? Are the positive spaces the holes?
CHILD: The clay.
CHILD: The light.
TEACHER: Are they all the same shapes?
CHILD: No, they're not all the same thickness.
TEACHER: No, they're not. How is that possible?
CHILD: The clay divides them—the form of it.
CHILD: It's shaped in different forms.
TEACHER: Yes, you can shape them—the form of what?
CHILD: The clay—the sculpture.

156

CHILD: The way that she felt at the time.

TEACHER: So how did she form them? What's the general feeling of this piece when you think in terms of shapes?

CHILD: It's round.

CHILD: It's curved.

TEACHER: It's curved—it's really not round in the sense that a circle is round.

CHILD: It's just like one thing curving up.

TEACHER: Yes, there's a "curveness" about it. What's the difference when you look at it this way and when you look at it this way? *(Teacher first stands sculpture up on its base; then lies it flat on back as a relief.)*

CHILD: It changes its form.

CHILD: Because there's that thing that sticks out and it's only on one side.

TEACHER: And what does that do to this curveness?

CHILD: It changes the shadows and stuff.

CHILD: It pushes out.

TEACHER: Yes, it kind of thrusts forward. And if you look at it this way, what is within that thrust?

CHILD: It's a thrust upward.

TEACHER: So there's another shape. Look what happens here—the thrust forward creates one shape it's repeated here, and there's another shape; repeated here, there's another shape of a very different dimension. Donna, did you work from one very long roll of clay and make this like a loaf of bread like a challah? Have you ever seen a challah?

CHILD: Yes, I've seen a challah.

TEACHER: It's twisted and twisted from one long loaf of dough.

CHILD: I took a big blob of clay and I started making it into different shapes; then I got it into a long shape and I made it into a square.

TEACHER: Was it a long, cylindrical shape like one long roll to begin with?

CHILD: I started from the bottom then I curved over like that *(traces contours with fingers)*, then I kept on building it like that. . . .

TEACHER: With pieces of the same roll?

CHILD: Yeah.

TEACHER: In other words, she started with a sort of spaghetti form or snake form, a rounded form, whatever you want to call it, then she flattened it so that it was like an elongated cube; it was like a rectangle—it had sharp edges or a square that was long and she flattened it; then she took it and started blending it. Did you mean to make this a relief, Donna?

CHILD: No, in the round.

TEACHER: But it's really more related to a relief; you can see the long, flat forms in this; it's a relatively flat relief. When you start getting a relief that's very three-dimensional like this one *(holds up piece by another child)*, then it functions in either way. I could see this hanging up on a wall as a relief, or lying down horizontally as a sculpture in the round; I think it is more interesting as a relief because you have relatively large, low shapes.

CHILD: Can't all sculpture in the round really be relief?

TEACHER: Well, it could in an absolute sense, except that supposing you had a piece of sculpture that was of three figures so that you saw a complete figure standing up and maybe they have their arms encircling each other; if you have them up on the wall so that their heads were coming out at you, it really wouldn't be the same kind of thing at all.

CHILD: But if it was a sculpture in the round, like Kevin's, that had a flat surface on the bottom that could go against the wall. . . .

TEACHER: The difference is also in the way you read each piece. This one, for example, works well as a sculpture in the round and also as a relief.

CHILD: Is it a relief because it has a flat bottom?

TEACHER: All sculpture has a flat bottom in a sense; it becomes more sculptural, that is, three-dimensional, when it has more *mass,* more *volume,* and more *projection.* Part of the difference is that you have made abstract forms that are not related to things in the real world, so that you're not reading a mother, father, a child sitting in an armchair. . . .

For the same reason, Jill's head is much clearer as a piece of sculpture in relief than in the round; I'm not saying that it wouldn't work this way, except that it's very different looking down on it flat this way, and looking at it this way.

In Molly's mask the outside shape is an integral part of the relief and it is important; notice also that the outside repeats the shape of the eyes. Leslie started out with cut out shapes which she added on to a flat round pancake; what's the difference between this one and the mask?

CHILD: The mask is much more sharp and clearer; these edges are fuzzy.

TEACHER: We talk about really flat ones and very three-dimensional ones, Leslie's is sort of in between. It could almost read as a sculpture in the round because you have such a variety of where the forms are in space; there are some that push out very far, some that are very flat against the back surface, and a lot of spaces in between . . . and there also are a lot of variations in the shapes themselves.

CHILD: It looks like bridges that you go up and down and curve all around.

CHILD: It was meant to be a park with sort of a river there.

CHILD: Ecology!

TEACHER: Were you thinking about in the round or as a relief?

CHILD: I was thinking about it both ways. I wanted a lake and I wanted different shapes and forms in the middle and how it ended up was it sort of had scenery to it.

TEACHER: Well, things happen that way in sculpture. You start out with one idea and other things happen as you're working on them, and it kind of becomes something else and it becomes a combination of ideas.

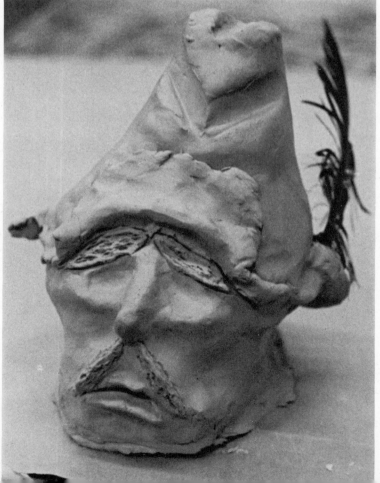

PROBLEM: To sculpt three figures in a spatial relationship either in the round or in a relief

TEACHER: Today I want you to do a sculpture that should be its own form, and also be representative of a group of at least three people.

I don't want you to make three separate people and stick them on a hunk of clay. Think about the sculpture as a group of people who have a relationship with each other—they could be dancing, for example; they must have a form where they are interrelated; so they're not completely isolated.

CHILD: Can we put the people in something like a boat or something?

TEACHER: You can make the people surrounded by something; you can show the place where they are (environment), either a boat, or by pieces of furniture, or by indications of trees; the people can be very complicated in the sense that they can have all kinds of details, like eyes, nose, hair, whatever, or they can be very simplified; a person could simply be a rounded form for a head and a cylindrical form for a body; it's up to you; make it as simple or complex in form as you wish.

CHILD: Do we have to make three things?

TEACHER: It can be more than three but not less.

CHILD: Can we have animals?

TEACHER: You can put animals in if you want to; you can put as many things in as you want; you can make a sculpture out of ten people and five animals and three mountains. . . .

CHILD: Do the people have to be with something else?

TEACHER: No, it can be the three people by themselves; three animals by themselves; three people and animals by themselves; it can be more than three people by themselves or it can be three people and three animals in an environment, surrounded by other things; that's up to you, but the people are really the important part of the sculpture.

CHILD: You mean we can just make people?

TEACHER: Just as in your relief, your sculpture is made up of curved or rectangular forms or, let's say, of curved planes. Here you have one plane that curves down, one plane that curves over (*demonstrating with blob of clay*); the sculpture in this problem is going to use all these things but they're also going to look like people. For example, in your relief you may have a figure bending this way and another figure over it, and maybe the beginning of a figure that's creeping out this way.

Put your arms on the shoulders of the people on either side of you— suppose these three [children] are the figures in your sculpture, you have to think of it not only as this head and this body and this head and this body but. . . .

CHILD: Relationship.

TEACHER: Exactly, you have to think about this arm not only connected to this body, but what happens when it becomes part of this figure? What happens to this face?

CHILD: Like if I had my arm around her, I'd make the arm longer than it really is.

TEACHER: Yes, you can exaggerate, but the figure should look enough like a person, so we can see it's a person; it doesn't have to have all the features and all the details in it. Someone should be able to look at your sculpture and say, "Oh! Three people."

CHILD: Can we make a big square with three people and an animal sticking on?

TEACHER: That's up to you, but the three people should have some relationship to each other.

CHILD: Can I make people on sleds?

TEACHER: Why not? But it's better to make it than talk about it.

DISCUSSION

TEACHER: What was the problem you worked with?

CHILD: To make three people, build them out of clay in the round or in relief, and anything else you wanted, animals, architecture. . . .

TEACHER: Let's look at these; I'd like you to describe what you think about them. *(All are placed together on the table. The children gather around.)*

CHILD: It's just three people—mother, father, sitting with a child.

TEACHER: That's the *subject*—what do the rest of you think of the sculpture?

CHILD: There's no nose or eyes, there's just the figure.

CHILD: No detail.

CHILD: It's abstract because there's no faces.

TEACHER: It's simplified.

CHILD: You can tell the difference between the woman and the man.

TEACHER: How?

CHILD: The mother has something different *(embarrassed)*.

TEACHER: What? From the back both figures look alike.

CHILD: The mother is holding a baby.

TEACHER: Yes, but what else is different?

CHILD: Mother has breasts.

TEACHER: From a sculptural point of view, the father's right arm pulls your eye into the center of the piece.

CHILD: You can tell there's something going on—that they're sitting somewhere.

TEACHER: How do you know?

CHILD: That's supposed to be my mom, and that's my brother and me. My mom is just praying and we're staying there.

TEACHER: What about the pond? It helps relate to other rounds. Notice the

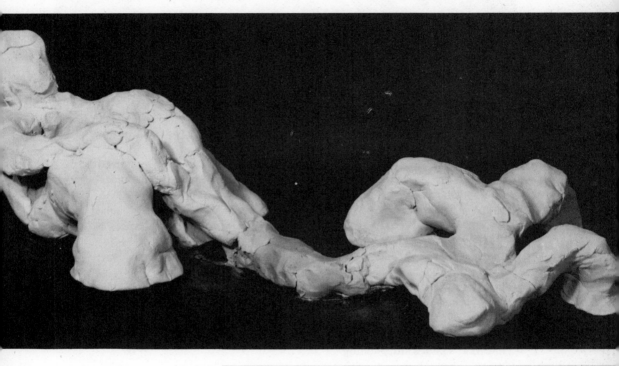

slight variations in body position—if they were not that way, they would all look like they're doing the same thing.

CHILD: They're all doing the same thing—with Scott's it wouldn't look good but with this one it does.

TEACHER: Notice how they're sitting—some leaning sideways, backwards; also he has started to make the face—a nose that pushes out and eyes that push back—very simple. What about this one?

CHILD: The people aren't detailed but the things around them are.

TEACHER: What would have happened without the table and chairs?

CHILD: We won't know where they are.

CHILD: Determines where they are and what they're doing.

CHILD: The dog is probably new, because he's sitting on a chair.

TEACHER: The heads are slightly tilted, like the other sculpture. Sculpturally, what are they doing? As a piece of sculpture, what do the chair and table do as a form?

CHILDREN: (*Story-telling about family and dog.*)

TEACHER: That's story-telling.

CHILD: They take up space that would be empty without them.

TEACHER: They help to pull you around the whole piece. Instead of more people, she's used chairs and a table to vary the size—so the figures are squares, circles, rectangles. She has used the idea of a circle but has varied the forms within them.

CHILD: Mine is one main piece and another one that you can place anywhere.

TEACHER: It's different from Molly's because it takes one sculptural form and repeats it. What do you think of the outside shape?

CHILD: Most of them are round; this one follows around from the place of the figures.

TEACHER: We have several reliefs—let's look. What are these figures doing in sculpture? Don't tell stories about it.

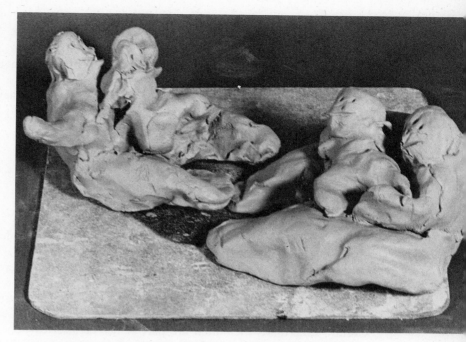

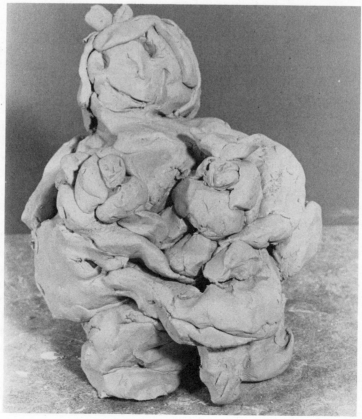

CHILD: He's pushed the figures in.

TEACHER: Are his forms individual people—all doing individual things?

CHILD: No.

TEACHER: They're really one simplified form repeated. Are they specific people —mother, father, child?

CHILD: No, they could be anyone.

TEACHER: What about the way he made his forms?

CHILD: They're pushed in, like a texture.

CHILD: The people aren't detailed, which is okay, but they're not detailed enough.

TEACHER: Is this relief the same as the other two?

CHILD: More detailed—it has a face.

TEACHER: What's different about the forms on this one, besides that the forms are pushed out? Look at the three figures.

CHILD: In the other pieces, the figures are the same size. Here the two babies get littler and littler.

TEACHER: The outside shape repeats the roundness of the figures—look at these figures.

CHILD: Like the two children are part of her themselves—one solid form with variations the way the arms and head grow out of the whole.

TEACHER: Yes, you read it like one form.

CHILD: The arms lead you up to the breast and up to the head.

TEACHER: You can look at it not just as breasts, but as forms that *push out,* repeat in the arms which push out, and in the feet and head—you get a feeling of repetition.

Aside from the body, what do you think of it as a sculptural form?

CHILD: It's eating.

TEACHER: Aside from the story-telling, what else about the forms of the baby?

CHILD: It's like a passage from arms to breast.

TEACHER: What else does it do as a form? Aren't they repeating each other? So all the forms repeat themselves.

We're going to paint all the sculpture we've been saving, but I want you to discuss with me which ones you're going to paint because some are better not painted. Why?

CHILD: 'Cause some of them have parts you can see better without painting, but if you put paint then it would change the shape completely.

TEACHER: When you paint sculpture you can make it more sculptural or flatten it out completely. Three-dimensional form has shadows which help to define the form; when you paint it, you sometimes lose the form; also, little things like ridges or overlapping planes where one plane goes over another would get lost. Some that aren't clear may become clearer with painting, like defining the flat reliefs. It really has to do with the kind of form it is—it's a question of whether painting it will make it look better or not.

DANCE

Definition and Description

Rhythmic movement as it relates to dance is closest to a child in that his body is the medium of expression yet in the schools it is the least practiced of any of the art forms. Perhaps this is because it requires a reorientation of the way the body moves through space and also demands a restructuring of the physical space itself. With little precedent for dance in the classroom, the question for teachers with no previous background is where to begin? It seems simple to suggest that to begin is to move, but from what frame of reference?

Within an educational context, we are dealing with forms of movement associated with modern dance which, as a tradition, have departed from ballet and classical forms developed in Europe. In this country its greatest contribution has been to give importance to the personal expression of the individual. In relation to children, dance is considered here as the interpretation of a child's ideas, feelings, and sensory impressions expressed symbolically in movement forms through the unique use of his body.

Because each child is different, the forms of modern dance can be easily adapted for movement experiences in the classroom. Perhaps a beginning lies in the recognition that experiences in dance are fundamental and accessible to all children because a child's body and its expression are one. This means that the body is not an external instrument or a "thing" which a child manipulates. It is his very self, in that psychologically and kinesthetically it is a direct agent of his feelings. In dance we do not conceive of a child's body as an instrument which is foreign or outside of himself; dance is an experience which involves the body completely. Thus, in bringing his own body under control, a child is controlling the most immediate part of himself.

In observing children from early childhood through the elementary years, we come to the realization that what is common to all is their propensity for movement. Such observations are supported from studies in psychology and kinesiology which suggest that from an activity point of view, movement is basic in children's learning. It may even be that movement is the initial way in which a child begins the creative process, and that within a motivating educational environment, he may be inspired to release that creative potential through dance. No one can determine the extent of children's imaginative or creative abilities. Children know about rhythm because they have already experienced it in their normal, everyday movements. They have yet to discover creative rhythmic movement, however, by learning ways in which they can use their bodies for creative expression. To do this, they must have actual experience in being *consciously rhythmical.* [1]

Dance as an Expressive Language

We are concerned with introducing children to dance as yet another language for expressing ideas and emotions. In order for a child to explore his own sensory responses in terms of what his body can do, he must experience a variety and range of movements so that he can develop a dance vocabulary which bears his own imprint. Educational dance involves control of the body, but it differs from sports or gymnastics in that it is not task-oriented in the same way. Both include problem solving, but a child's projection of the qualitative elements in dance is not geared toward the refinement of skills as ends in themselves. Whatever skills a child needs in his search for a particular form arise inherently as a means to the expression of that form. The mastery of skills alone does not guarantee that dance is imaginative or creative, but they are necessary as instruments which serve the expression of movement. Thus, the importance of dance for children is that it helps them to develop a kinesthetic awareness of their ability to use their bodies expressively. By *kinesthetic awareness* we are referring to a child's bodily reactions or "muscle memory," but also to a conscious perception of his body's ability to "feel" movement. Because dance is an art form and not simply a physical activity, his perception is based on his own sensibility. That is, it is made perceptible through his senses and involves him in the total process of perceiving, feeling, expressing.

With children, as well as adults, dance finds its image through movements which are not realistic but which are created and shaped. Langer attributes much

---

[1] Geraldine Dimondstein, *A Conceptual Model of the Arts as Sensuous Expression in the Education of Young Children,* unpublished dissertation. UCLA, 1967, p. 76.

of the confusion as to what dance is to the fact that "its space is plastic, its time musical, its themes are fantasy, its actions symbolic. . . ." [2] But dance is not a purely visual art, like painting; it is not plastic in the same sense as sculpture, nor is the presentation of fantasy the same as in poetry. Its similarity to other arts is that feelings and ideas are expressed in symbolic forms. Its primary distinction is that it is a *kinesthetic–visual* image made tangible by means of the body.

Although all movements are important in that they reflect a child's personal experience, temperament, and emotional needs, all movements or gestures that occur in daily living are not art. In everyday actions, movements are used to convey intentions, desires, and expectations and are conditioned by social customs. A side-to-side shake of the head is clearly understood as "no," just as a shaking of hands implies a gesture of friendship or at least a social amenity. Within a child's general behavior, movements become an aspect of self-expression, because they are immediately reflective of how he feels at the moment. Within the dance experience, however, gestures become transformed only when they are executed apart from the momentary situation or emotional impulse which prompted them. As such, they are neither conventionally confined nor uncontrolled. Rather, they are responses evoked in relation to aesthetic elements, in this case, to *space–time–force,* which are explored for their qualitative, emotional, dimensions.

For example, a child may enter the dance experience in a state of rage or pent-up anger because of something that has occurred elsewhere. A teacher's well-intentioned suggestion that he make "angry" movements is unlikely to produce anything beyond random, flailing gestures, for he is too close to his own feelings to control his body. Although a child needs to feel a certain commitment to the dance experience, there must also be a sense of detachment, and it is the search for a form which allows this interplay of emotions to happen. If, in noting his emotional state, a teacher presents a dance problem which involves him in consciously exploring the difference between sustained and percussive movement by "punching" the air and slowly "pushing" it away, he may begin to organize those diffuse feelings through forms which speak not only to himself, but to others. It is this twofold approach to experience to which we referred earlier as the difference between giving vent to self-expression and giving form to feeling.

ORGANIZING EMOTIONS

Our approach to dance as an art form, therefore, is in helping children become aware of the importance of organizing their emotions and of communicating them through forms of movement. In emphasizing the expression of a movement quality rather than a literal idea, they gradually become aware of how emotions function. For example, some sixth-graders decide to choreograph a dance about a Voodoo witch and her tribe. The story line is one in which the witch is "scary" and "mysterious" in compelling her people to follow certain actions. In an initial presentation to the class, it becomes apparent that facial grimaces and stylized hand gestures (which seem to derive from TV images) convey neither the magical feeling nor the course of events. In turning away from the narrative

[2] Suzanne Langer, *Feeling and Form* (New York: Scribner, 1953), p. 204.

aspects to the tension and contrast within the movements themselves, they discover that their "message" can best be expressed through the vocabulary of dance. This example applies equally well to a dramatization of a familiar story or a nursery rhyme.

Organizing and expressing emotions also involves a kinesthetic awareness which makes it possible for a child to go beyond the mere "making" of movements to a consciousness of how they take form. In so doing, children begin to perceive the relationship between the body and its capacity for expression. Because each child has a unique body structure and is motivated by his own interests and needs, it is a process which always permits experimentation from both the teacher and the child, with the ever-present realization that there may be other alternatives.

ORGANIZING MOVEMENT

We conceive of dance as a problem-solving process which opens possibilities for differing qualitative levels of performance within it. In relation to educational dance, they may range from explorations of movement fundamentals, to improvisations, to more organized dance studies. All problems are designed as explorations, which imply a kind of sensing and experimenting with what the body can do in its encounter with dance elements. Initially, explorations are random, as a child literally "feels his way" in testing what his muscles can do and how he can bring his body under control. For example, all children explore movement fundamentals because they are basic to the development of more complicated patterns. That is, they explore the differences in the use of space–time–force in locomotor movement (walking, running, leaping, skipping, crawling) and in non-locomotor movements (swinging, rocking, swaying, bending). Although such activities are presented to an entire group, each child experiences them in his own manner, "educating" his muscles in ways that are unique to him.

Improvisation.   Although there is no precise division in terms of sequence or time, children gradually move from explorations into improvisations. As children begin to combine ideas and feelings with new combinations of movement, improvisations evolve in the very act of moving. For each child it is a continuous search for forms which emerge, recur, take on new dimensions, and may or may not be repeated. For the most part, development follows a back-and-forth, zigzag pattern, depending on the nature of the problem, a child's interest, and his ability to bridge the gap between execution and intention. Improvisation usually moves beyond exploration in that it may not arise from random, fragmented ideas, but relationships may be formed from within the structure of a problem which a teacher presents, or which a child defines for himself.

Improvisations may be built around a concept, an element, or a specific image. For example, in exploring the difference between whole notes, half notes, and quarter notes in metrical time, children work in groups of three. Using a clock as an image, each child must evolve movements which not only correspond to a "countable" number of beats, but relate those movements in some continuous pattern to other members of the clock. In the process of making it "work," each child has improvised his own movements which flow into the improvisation of the whole group. Although improvisation may or may not be limited to one theme, it is intended to engage children in capturing and refining the qualitative aspects of a particular problem.

The structure for improvisational experiences is open-ended, and, as we have seen, lends itself to both individual and group participation. Whether the problem is set by the teacher or is suggested by a child, those who choose to work together must relate their efforts to the needs of the group. Here again, exploration yields to improvisation. Although a child may initially explore his own movements according to his interpretation of a problem, he must ultimately adapt his needs to the interests of group expression. Because dance is nonverbal, the challenge is to communicate and relate kinesthetically to the movements of others.

For the teacher, the value of such a structure is that it allows her to support and reinforce the expressive qualities of a child's innovative movement of which he might otherwise be unaware. To do so she must be able to accept a child's ideas, perceive an exciting movement, and make it known to him so that he can elaborate upon it if he so desires. In this way, teachers can develop their own sensitivity in designing problems which continuously draw upon children's movement cues. By emphasizing a conceptual rather than a technical approach, they can elicit responses which lead to spontaneous, inventive solutions.

Dance Studies.   Just as explorations lead to improvisations, so improvisations serve as preparations for dance studies. Although it is usually older children who have the interest and sustained drive to develop an idea into a more structured form, children at the primary levels may also be inspired by an experience they have shared as a group, a topical theme, or a special celebration. Dance studies may evolve from improvisations which have been repeated and refined as successful expressions of a particular problem or series of problems. As children improvise, whether in response to an abstract concept, specific movement elements, or a particular image, they find that certain movements appear which are satisfying to both their kinesthetic and visual sense. It is these movements which tend to be repeated and which, with subtle guidance from the teacher, become part of each child's unique movement vocabulary.

DEVELOPING A DANCE VOCABULARY

A dance vocabulary does not imply a stringing together of loosely connected movements, any more than a verbal vocabulary is composed of separate words which are mechanically put together. One motion does not make a rhythmic statement any more than one word makes a sentence. To draw an analogy between these two types of language, basic locomotor and nonlocomotor movements make up the grammar of movement, improvisations are the syntax, dance studies are the presented metaphors. To speak of an individualized movement vocabulary means that each child takes the fundamentals of movement and combines them in varying dimensions of space–time–force to produce his unique style. As with the other art forms, style does not imply skill in the sense of technique or a skillful device. A child's style reflects the qualitative or sensuous aspects that he imparts to movement, which emerges from the interrelationship of ideas, moods, or emotions through the manner in which they are given form by the body.

Although improvisations are built upon explorations of basic movement elements, dance studies are purposefully conceived and designed. Through conscious repetition, certain improvisational forms become elaborated and extended into fixed patterns which express a particular theme. Unlike improvisations, which may begin and end at any point, dance studies usually have a beginning, middle, and end, so that there is a sense of development, elaboration, and closure. By way of definition, we may say that the process is one of inventing movements into structural dance forms which may be repeated.

Because we have come to depend so much upon the written word, it is important that teachers recognize that dance studies are neither stories that must accurately follow narrations in books nor dramatizations. Although there are dramatic aspects involved, dance is not storytelling. For example, a group of ten- and eleven-year-olds selects three Haikus as a motivating source for dance studies. The teacher reads them slowly several times with a cadence and intonation which heightens the emotional rather than the literal aspects. The intention is not that children follow the sequence of ideas (which are very meager and ethereal in this type of poetry), but that they form pictures in their minds out of which they can create "movement poems." The children work with as many people as they need, so that groups range from couples, to trios, to quartets. In the process of transforming a word picture into a kinesthetic–visual image, they discover that each movement does not have to represent a specific idea in the poem, but rather, the movement qualities of their feelings in response to it. It becomes, as we have stated earlier, a metaphoric presentation of qualities that are abstracted to symbolize objects or events. It is metaphoric in the sense that it is a connecting of diverse experience by means of symbolic forms or images.

The tendency to tie dance to subject matter, even in its exploratory stages, is as inhibiting for teachers as is their concern over whether children's movement is spontaneous or imitative. Again, it is a question of accepting standardized categories which serve to limit our perception of what is happening at the moment. The notion, for example, that a child "pretends" to be something rather than "being" it, in the sense of freshly experiencing it, conveys to children that they are simulating rather than formulating movement. In the same vein, we need to reconsider the implications of imitation.

INTERPRETATION VS. IMITATION

The relationship between interpretative and imitative movement is very subtle, yet is always subject to a teacher's judgment. Because, directly or indirectly, her attitudes and values become apparent, evaluations as to what is imitative cannot help affecting children's perceptions of themselves. In most instances, the quality of expression she elicits from children relates directly to the models and expectations she sets. By assuming that her role is to demonstrate movement in order to clarify it, she inadvertently creates an image of herself as a "model," and the unspoken message is, "Do as I do." Thus, children respond to the expectation of being judged in terms of how accurately they can follow a movement. We might consider that the physical intrusion of an adult is similar to making marks on a child's painting or shaping forms on a child's sculpture. In dance, this may be particularly diverting, because an adult's size, shape, and use of movement elements is unlike those of a child. Perhaps a more serious implication is that when a teacher does it, it must be "right." There are times when a teacher's presence is appropriate in guiding an observed movement or in taking a child's hand in moving with him for a few moments so that there is a transference of energy. In all cases, however, the intent should be suggestive rather than prescriptive—that is, suggestive of ideas which help a child find forms of movement within his own body structure.

The differences between imitation and interpretation must be viewed in the light of our knowledge that a child's physical coordination, past experiences, and personality condition his responses. Whatever feelings are aroused as a result of the interaction of the teacher, content, and classroom environment can only be satisfactorily expressed through a child's own perceptions, through the medium of his body. A child may admire what another child is doing and want to try it. Imitation is sometimes necessary for a child who feels initially self-conscious in moving out on the floor. But imitation of another's movement is never an exact duplication, any more than a child is capable of repeating his own movement when called upon to perform it a second time. Some movements may be consciously investigated or may come about by an initial understanding of purpose, some will be found by seeming imitation, some will be "learned" or "taught." What is important is that continuous encouragement by a teacher of the momentary fragments or interesting movements she observes will help children appreciate their own efforts toward individual exploration. Ultimately, children can only express creatively what is natural and comfortable for them.

No matter how the process unfolds, we need to recognize that dance movement is an essentially individual, emotionally formed response to a stimulating experience. Two children may respond almost the same and their movements may contain elements of imitation, but this is part of the process. Because a child can never duplicate a movement or impression exactly as he perceives it in nature, or as executed by someone else, he must search for his own forms. We are concerned that a child become more sensitive in his feelings and in his use of the body to interpret them. If he is able to express ideas and feelings with a different insight or understanding than he had before, this is what may be expected in terms of developing interpretative responses. Each exploration, improvisation, or dance study is an experience that is of value in and of itself and that, over an indeterminate period of time, forms the qualitative steppingstones in the creative dance process.

Distinguishing Characteristics

A definition of children's dance within an educational setting is helpful in distinguishing it from other dance forms. In order to make it come alive, however, we must turn to its own immediate context, and to those qualities by which it takes shape as a living experience. Dance is distinguished from the other arts in that all the elements of *space, time,* and *force* are essential in forming the dynamic image. To say that a movement is created only in space–time–force means that it must be considered in relation to the *space* which it occupies, the time which it uses, and the *energy* which gives it *force*. It is the interrelationships of these elements which produce the endless variety of movement combinations and determine the outward form of expression. Basically, they serve as the generating factors that are motivated by each child's emotions and ideas. As aesthetic qualities, they are transformed from conventional gestures to dance movements and become the connective tissue from which a personal movement vocabulary unfolds.

SPACE

A child's awareness of space begins with his own body and involves two conditions: (1) that the body is the center of reference and determines the way he uses space, and (2) that movement is focal in the way he perceives space. Although a child himself is three-dimensional, in that his movements have not only length and breadth but depth and thickness, he still needs to discover how to use space. When we speak metaphorically of a line that the body makes in space, we may well speak of a volume in sculpture which fills or displaces space. But as a concept, space does not become meaningful for children unless it becomes functional for them. Through movement explorations with the elements of space, they come to realize that in order to cope with it, it must be occupied, contained, and defined.

For example, as a child walks around the room observing the others in various positions on the floor, he becomes aware that a body defines space by its very presence. That is, the area in which he exists becomes occupied. Even if he stands perfectly still, he designs space, for we can see around him, follow the plastic lines of his body, and know that he has volume. If he extends a leg or swings around the axis of his own body, he defines both his immediate (internal) body space and the outer (external) space around him. As soon as he moves from "here to there" in any locomotor movement, he is designing the space between himself as a body in motion and the walls or perimeter of the dance area. But most important, it is the feeling of exhilaration of covering space and of experiencing the full use of all dimensions available to us. Whereas painting is two-dimensional and sculpture is three-dimensional, dance adds the dynamic of the fourth dimension—time.

In dance, space is perceived in relation to the body and to the surrounding space. We can help children use it expressively by presenting problems which allow them to organize space in relation to themselves, and to find their own ways of relating spatially to objects and other individuals. Stated simply, it is the difference between telling children to "take space" when they are out on the floor and physically placing them in position. The first makes them kinesthetically aware of their own spatial needs, because they must "find" space; the second makes them passive recipients of someone else's awareness.

Whether children work alone or together, they must be conscious of one another. This awareness does not come about intellectually, but kinesthetically, in the sense of "knowing" it through the body. Depending upon the nature of the problem, even a very young child should be able to determine whether others who are moving are simply like other objects in his environment, or whether his movement should relate to theirs. This holds when a child works as part of a small group or when he is working individually amidst the entire group. What we are suggesting is that spatial awareness also includes knowing who shares the space and how.

Directions in Space.   Space is further defined through exploration of its basic elements of *direction, level,* and *range. Direction* is the line of motion made by the body moving *through* space (forward, backward, sideward, diagonally). In daily behavior, children are continually called upon to respond to directions such as forward, backward, sideward, around. In dance, they have yet to discover how they function in relation to the position of their own bodies as well as to the surrounding space. Directions move up and down, in and out from the center of the body as the point of reference. Because of the way our bodies are constructed, we move with greatest ease in a frontal position, and thus, in a forward direction. Because both sides of our body are identical, it is more difficult to perceive lateral space involved in moving from one side or the other or in discriminating between left and right. Children are frequently confused by the difference between moving from a side position (such as sliding) and moving in a diagonal direction. When the impulse is from the side, all parts of the body— head, shoulders, torso, legs, feet—must express the same feeling. In carving a diagonal line through space, one may take any body position as long as the movement is in that direction.

Children are unaccustomed to moving in lateral space and therefore it is a developmental phenomenon which must be learned through consciously guided experiences. For this reason, a teacher must be particularly aware of her body position vis-à-vis the children in giving instructions which require a left–right orientation. For example, asking children to extend their left arm while facing them is disorientating, for they would tend to respond with the same side of their body, which would be their right arm. In the early years, it is not absolutely necessary that children define "left–right," but exploring laterality in many different ways significantly affects the way a child organizes his space.

A movement *through* space is defined when all parts of the body follow the same directional line. For example, an awareness of how the body moves through space comes through an exploration of the function of different body parts. In response to the suggestion, "Let your head pull you through space," children recognize that in a forward movement, it is the front of their body which leads them—that is, forehead, head, chest, stomach, knees, feet. To the problem, "What parts lead you backward in space?" children discover that when they tilt their head, round their back, or extend their buttocks, that it is the weight from the back of their body which propels them in a backward direction. To the suggestion, "Let your elbow take you for a walk," children experience that a strong sideward pull by the elbow is followed by the thrust shoulder and the incline of the head and that the feet follow in a crossing pattern to carry through the sideward movement. It is always a surprise to discover that turning is not a separate direction, but is a combination of the three which can be sensed by slowly rotating the body, taking one step in each direction. It is a simple way of making clear to children that the position or plane of the body remains frontal even though directions change, and that a turn may be executed in any spatial direction. Focusing on the directions of the body in space helps children come to know the planes of their body (front, back, side) and to become acquainted with another facet of how the body functions in locomotor and nonlocomotor movement.

Levels of Space.   As well as moving through space, the body also moves *in* space on *levels,* which is sensed as a transfer of weight from the center of gravity. Because each child has a unique body structure, the exact center varies with each individual. In any case, levels are expressed in relation to the body in terms of three dimensions: *High* begins when the center of the body is shifted above its normal position. Children typically reach "high" by simply raising their hands over their heads. But if encouraged to "reach for space," there must be enough tension in the body so that the heels leave the floor, as in tip-toeing, leaping, and jumping. Extending the arms may represent a stretch but there is no shift in body weight. *Middle* exists when the trunk is in an aligned or upright position, as in walking, running, or turning; or when the upper torso is bent or extended at the waist in a forward stretch of the back, or in a lateral stretch of the arms. *Low* begins below the center of gravity in whatever direction is taken, as in walking with flexed knees, rolling, or any collapsing movement.

Understanding these spatial elements expressed through direction and level also reinforces learnings in other areas. Abstractions such as, "How high is high?" "How low is low?" "How wide is wide?" can be translated into concrete experiences as children investigate these dimensions in relation to their own body size, shape, and organization of energy. Even such common terms as *over, under, around, through* take tangible forms when children experience the feeling of moving through a body shape created by another child, around and over an object, or under one of his own body parts.

Range in Space.   Although a directional movement may be expressed as a line, it also has a *size* and *shape*. *Size* describes the *range,* which is the amount of space the body occupies (e.g., large–small, narrow–wide). Because a child moves in space three-dimensionally, range applies not only to the space filled by the total body in motion, but also to the distance covered by the movement of any body part. As children explore range by deliberately varying the size of a movement, they discover that the quality of that movement changes by using more or less space. In investigating the contrast between "big" and "little," expansive or confined, they become informed through their muscles that this element functions as an ingredient of what they are trying to express. They also become aware in the very process of moving that no single element of space can be controlled in isolation, but that changes in the range of a movement inevitably involve variations in time and force.

Body Shape.   Whether in a state of stillness or as a form-in-the-making, the body has volume and creates its own shape. Because dance is a visual–kinesthetic image which "shapes space," we include the notion of *body shape* here even though it draws upon time and force as well. *Body shape* is not determined by a child's natural structure such as his height, width, or breadth, but refers to the shape that his body makes in space in forming expressive movements. Again, with the body as the center of reference, children must become aware of two aspects of spatial orientation—the internal space, which is shaped by the way a child uses different parts of the body in relation to the torso (circular, angular, linear), and the external space (around, above, below), which is occupied by the shape made by the total body.

In the process of exploration, children's excitement is apparent when they realize that they can create many different qualities and types of shapes (round, flat, heavy, filled, empty), that using body parts in various positions makes particular shapes, and that the actual shapes of their bodies are not necessarily the shape they are attempting to describe in dance forms. For example, squares, rectangles, triangles, and circles are shapes which make up a child's environment. Although the problem is not one of translating geometric forms literally in movement, children can begin to sense "roundness," "squareness," "pointiness" in both visual and kinesthetic terms. In so doing, they create interesting shapes which involve both internal and external space by working out spatial relationship with others, either in harmony or in opposition to another body shape.

As a child becomes increasingly aware of the dimensions of his body, he also becomes aware of the dimensions of other people and objects. For example, in response to the problem of creating the shape of a box with a partner, the space which is designed is not judged by metrical standards, but in terms of the way each child relates to the other's body shape in creating a new space. The same applies when children work in groups of fours. Similarly, a child's response to "How high can you be?" is not measured by a yardstick, but in relation to how and what he selects (level, direction, range) to extend his body in space. It is the difference between geometric space as defined by objects and the space his body defines. What is important is that teachers realize that in dance a child's use of space is not rational or logical as it must be in everyday living, but is expressionist and kinesthetic. As in painting and sculpture, it is "felt" space.

Searching into the properties of space leads children to appreciate their bodies as a medium of creative movement, rather than simply as an instrument of functional action. They learn that dance is not the shaping of the body for movement, such as bending to lift something up, or raising the foot to climb a stair, but that it is using the body to shape movement expressively. As children experience the shifting relationships through changes in direction, level, and range, space becomes known to them not merely as something to "get through," but as something they can control as an expressive quality. Although each may be explored as separate problems, the nature of the unity of movement is such that all these elements function together. Yet each lends a different and more developed aspect to a dance experience.

TIME

Children cannot grasp the concept of space unless it is limited and defined; similarly, time as a concept must be divided and made relative in order for them to deal with it. That is, it must be arranged in groupings which have a beginning and an end.

Time is expressed in the body as *rhythm,* which penetrates through those functions which are recurrent, such as pulse, heartbeat, breath. Each child has his own inherent rhythm, which can sometimes be noted by observing him walk across the floor without accompaniment. Frequently the beat that he establishes will relate to his own heartbeat or energy level. This tells us that a child's response to rhythm is essentially a kinesthetic awareness of his underlying pulse, but is also experienced as a phenomenon of force–time. Through dance explorations, children learn that time is an element that they can control and is more than simply making a movement faster or slower. They discover that it is deeply connected to the way they express movement, for it gives meanings which may change its entire characteristic.

Rhythm is movement; there can be no body motion without rhythm. Yet mere repetition of a movement does not produce rhythm. We distinguish a rhythmic pattern more easily when we recognize repetition, but it does not of itself make a movement aesthetically rhythmical. For example, repeating a single movement or a movement sequence may lend emphasis and intensity, but so may prolonged repetition make a movement tedious or overextended. Because there is no absolute rule, a child can only sense this relationship in terms of how it expresses the quality he is trying to achieve. As an expressive function of rhythm, repetition cannot be used mechanically, for it is creatively composed. In order to awaken a consciousness of rhythm in children, they need to sense that all the muscles in their bodies "cooperate" regardless of the particular movement. That is, they come to realize that although an impulse may begin in one part of the body, it affects the action of all the muscles. An awareness that no part of the body is inert helps children understand how their bodies move as a totality in both space and time.

Rhythmic Awareness.　Rhythm may be characterized as giving *continuity* and *repetition* to movement. At the same time, kinesthetic response depends upon the feelings and emotions which initiate the impulse. We are suggesting, therefore, that rhythm gives structure to the emotions and is a means by which a child organizes and interprets them through movement. In a physical sense, the body experiences rhythm through a varied succession of muscular tensions, relaxations, and rests. Just as children need to discover how to use space expressively, so do they need to internalize ways in which they can use time for contrast, accentuation, and physical balance. It is a common misconception that children are inherently rhythmical or that they have an instinct for time or time values. All children have an inherent bodily rhythm, but they do not all have the same motor faculties and therefore do not necessarily have rhythmic awareness. Although the ability to perceive and respond to rhythmic patterns varies, such rhythmic perception is heightened, because rhythm is the very heart of the dance experience.

The extent to which children learn to develop a rhythmic sense depends largely upon the sensitivity of the teacher, perhaps more in this area than in any other. Children find it difficult to move rhythmically under the guidance of a teacher who does not respond kinesthetically—that is, feel pulse, duration, and tempo in her own body. If she can neither "keep time" in terms of setting a beat for children to follow nor discern the rhythmic patterns which they create, she is unable to recognize a similar lack of perception in their own performance. Unintentionally, she not only fails to stimulate their rhythmic acuity, but impedes their development. For teachers new to dance, the use of a drum or other percussive instrument, such as a tambourine or tone block, may reinforce their sense of rhythm. Whether such accompaniment clarifies or confuses will soon become apparent in observing children's responses.

Rhythmic Patterns.   As an aesthetic component of dance, rhythm plays an important role in organizing movements and in giving coherence to the total form. It does so by providing a time structure or grouping of beats, which determines the relative duration and stress of the movements within it. Thus, just as movements create visual patterns in space, so do they create observable patterns in time. We need to understand that these time patterns derive from two sources: from music, where rhythm is produced through sounds; and from dance, where rhythm is created from movements. Thus, time, in dance, is experienced through both *metric* and *rhythmic patterns. Metric patterns* come from music and are more familiarly known to us as *tempo, beat, measure, phrasing; rhythmic patterns* are evoked from internal bodily rhythms and are defined in terms of *pace, pulse,* and *duration.* Although there is a similarity between the two structures and they are sometimes described interchangeably, dance has its own vocabulary which needs to be clarified.

Perhaps the notion of an "internal" and "external" rhythm can help us to distinguish between rhythmic and metric time. Internal rhythm is a combination of pulse, heartbeat, and breath which is brought to bear on the elements of dance whether in response to a specific or abstract movement problem. It is internal in the sense that it is self-imposed, and functions only in relation to the experience of the movement itself. This means that for however long it lasts, it is continuous and all-inclusive. The difference is in the feeling between, "Take a deep breath so that your chest becomes a balloon filled with air," and, "Take a deep breath for six counts."

We may also consider the difference as a contrast between "free rhythm" and "keeping time." In the latter, we are not concerned with being "on time," but "in time," in the sense of responding to a grouping of beats that is based on a mathematically organized structure. Therefore, a response to an external rhythm can be accurately followed by counting. We are not suggesting that a child become involved in counting verbally while moving, for this frequently produces movements which are mechanical and unfluid. We are concerned that he become kinesthetically responsive, so that even though the beats come from an external source, he "feels" them in his body. Metrical time is a means of explaining that one movement may last half as long as another, or may be twice, three times, or four times as long. We begin to understand, then, that a metric pattern reflects the relationship between the duration of one movement and that of another.

Thus, time is divided into rhythmic and metric patterns which is made functional, but they must also be seen in terms of their aesthetic relationship to the expressiveness of dance. Although children must experience rhythm as organized groupings, they do not always respond to a regular rhythmic pattern, but may improvise patterns of their own. Even with folk music, which children especially enjoy for its simple repetitions and familiar content, the rhythm does not always follow in regular measures, but may change from 3/4 to 4/4 in the middle of a song. We need to be sensitive to the possibility that a child may not respond to the rhythm that he hears at a given moment, but to the rhythm that he feels.

Developing rhythmic awareness does not rest solely upon a child's ability to follow a rhythmic or metric pattern. A more subtle but necessary observation is, in getting from one movement to another, what happens with the body between the beats. It is this kind of awareness that gives children a feeling for the flow and continuity of movement. This sense of transition or "betweenness" is the sensuous connective tissue which gives movement its organic quality, which we observe as the difference between being fluid and continuous, or jerky and mechanical. We may draw the parallel that, as in painting, children do not dance "by the numbers." Whether a child responds to a metrical pattern or to his own rhythm, he is involved in exploring and improvising movement qualities. Therefore, it is the unified feeling that his body is able to express which determines whether he is merely executing isolated gestures or is engaged in the total process of dance. In offering opportunities to move in response to both rhythmic and metric patterns, we present alternatives through which he can control his body and broaden his scope of rhythmic expression.

In exploring these basic rhythms, children become aware of how time functions as an element that they both create and use. For example, every child has a time sense with which he is most comfortable. Changes and contrasts in time are defined in terms of *tempo* and *pace*. To distinguish between rhythmic and metric patterns, we may say that tempo is to music as pace is to dance.

Pace.   *Pace* is determined by the amount of time it takes to execute a movement from its beginning impulse to the end. It refers not only to the rate of speed of a single movement, but to the general tempo level that a child establishes for an entire movement sequence. Because it is totally subjective, it has much to do with the expression of "movement color," or mood. For example, successive slow movements tend to produce a sedate quality, whereas vigorous, percussive movements may suggest a more vibrant feeling. Whatever mood or emotion a child wishes to express is underlined by changes in pace which lend more or less intensity. Although we are accustomed to thinking of simple contrasts of fast and slow, there are variations along this continuum which create subtlety and interest. For example, the pace may be steady and constant, or it may be changing and irregular. A simple locomotor or body movement, a brief improvisation, or a dance study takes on one appearance if it is executed in a thoroughly unrelieved tempo, but takes on quite another with contrasts which involve changes in force as well as time. Thus, children can explore dynamics such as fast–slow–fast, slow–fast–slow, or the entire range from slow to fast and fast to slow.

The ability to control their own pace also becomes known to children as they discover that different parts of their bodies function differently in time. Partly because of the structure of their muscles and partly because of the placement on the body, the head, legs, arms, feet, torso can move at different rates of speed. By varying the pace at which each body part moves (alone or in combination), children can see as well as feel that such changes affect the total time pattern. At this point, the rhythmic elements of pulse and duration also come into play as the other essential components of rhythmic patterns.

Tempo.   In metric patterns, *tempo* is the rate of speed of a movement, or the rate at which one movement follows another. The tempo of any movement depends upon *beat,* which is the pulse of music, just as the heartbeat is the pulse of internal rhythm. The difference is that metric patterns derive from an external source of rhythm, which is *meter.* Whether the structure is 3/4, 4/4, 6/8, or some other tempo, it is a grouping of beats in mathematical relationships which determines the duration of each beat. In performing movements, children's response may correspond to the number of beats in a measure, the number of measures, or the groupings of measures into phrases.

Tempo, like pace, is continuous and repetitive and defines the intervals of the unit by which time is measured. In rhythmic patterns, the interval is sensed as pulse; in metric patterns it is established by beat. Tempo may be fast, slow, or moderate, but in all cases, it acts as the steady underlying line against which the beats form a pattern.

Because rhythm is produced by sounds in music as well as by movements in dance, we need to understand the difference between these two units of time. Stated simply, *beat* in music is an aspect of time; *pulse* in dance functions in both time and force. Beat in itself can be subdivided, but there must be at least two beats to define an interval in time. Beyond this, we can explore equal intervals of 3, 4, 6, or uneven beats such as 5, 7, 9. Children have to listen "hard" in order to respond to the latter grouping, because it departs from traditional metric standards. The results usually produce less symmetrical movement and frequently more interesting inventions.

Children can experience these relative durations through simple locomotor movements. For example, the walk as our basic motor activity corresponds to the time unit of the quarter note. For this reason, we use the walk as a beginning of movement exploration because it is a comfortable, everyday experience and requires less control than other steps. In order to "feel" a quarter beat, the children may begin by walking in a steady 4/4 time to the accompaniment of a drum, claves, or tone gourd. When asked to move twice as fast to the same beat, they find themselves running or stepping on tiptoes in a tempo which corresponds to eighth notes. To the suggestion that they move only on the first and third beat, they sense that they must execute more control, because they are "slowed down," and that a half note has a different feeling. Supported by the resonance of a gong or cymbals, children discover further that they can express the duration of a whole note through sustained movements which shift from locomotor to body movements, and do not take them through space.

Pulse.   In rhythmic patterns, *pulse* also represents an amount of time but as dance is a kinesthetic experience, it is expressed by the body as greater or lesser force. That is, each pulse in movement is projected as an extension of force in a moment of time. It is the continuous flow of impulses, one growing out of another, to which we referred earlier as that quality of "betweenness." In establishing a rhythmic pattern, every movement represents an alternation of degrees of force, and the greatest amount of force given to a particular movement is felt as a beat.

Just as pulse may be regular or irregular, so are *beats* both *accented* and *unaccented.* An *accent* is an emphasis which is given to certain beats in a series which we hear as louder or softer sounds. There may be any number of beats, depending upon the pattern of movement, but there must be at least two for an accent to have meaning. A series of beats without accents is difficult to respond to (whether in music or sound), as are groupings of words without inflection. In any rhythmic activity, including speech, we sense the need to give a continuous grouping of beats differing degrees of emphasis. Thus, an accented beat gives coherence to music as it gives impulse to rhythm. Each accented beat in music and each impulse in dance is a force which produces motion suddenly and immediately. Without them movement would be aimless and monotonous.

As an expression of time–force, *pulse* is a regular, recurrent wave of movements which may be likened to the throbbing or rhythmic beat in poetry. It is that poetry most characteristic of children which departs from a standard meter and has an open form composed only to give emphasis to the emotional intent of the words. In pulse, such emphasis is observed as *stress,* which is the degree of force or intensity expended in a movement. Although each child's pulse reflects his own internal rhythmic continuity, he applies stress to a movement for emphasis or clarity. He may give stress to what he considers important beats, measures, or phrases, but given to any particular movement at a specific time, it serves to intensify the quality of that movement.

Thus, whether a pulse is regular or irregular depends upon the stress of a movement. For example, in exploring the rhythmic quality of animals, one child expresses the ponderous feeling of a bear in a swaying movement of the body, with heavy, plodding, equally paced steps. Because each movement is of equal duration in time and equal in weight (or force), we observe a regular and steady pulse. As we follow him through space, we see a pattern developing in which each movement appears as long as any other. On the other hand, a child whose "monkey" rocks and gallops around in uneven, jerky, up-and-down movements gives each impulse an unequal time–force value, establishing an irregular pattern. By experiencing these time elements in various combinations, children come to realize that a rhythmic structure is made up of certain groupings of beats and accents which they can impose over an underlying pulse. In responding kinesthetically to different groupings, they become aware that accents or stress are created out of movement itself, and that it is these elements which bind a movement sequence together and give it a unified feeling.

Measure.   Once we are involved with any grouping of beats around an accent we are defining *measure.* Grouping beats into measures permits us to create more complex and extended movement patterns. It is comparable to linking sentences together to embrace a larger, more elaborate thought. Children can easily understand that a measure is a sentence of beats, just as a spoken sentence is a line of words. In terms of movement, they must first discover the underlying pulse, which they can do by responding to the steady beat, and then to each beat which forms the melody or "words." For example, a class may divide into two groups seated on the floor, alternately clapping the tempo and the beats, and then one rhythm against the other. Although clapping serves as a "warm-up," an awareness of measure comes not only through hearing, but through feeling change and contrast. They can, therefore, extend the exploration into movement.

Once having established the beat, changes in measure can be expressed by changes in direction or levels, in the contrast of larger and smaller movements, and by introducing dynamics of loud and soft. In any case, searching for appropriate movements in which to express the relationship in time is a richer kinesthetic experience than merely beating with the hands. Regardless of what elements children select to demonstrate these changes, they will inevitably alter the space (direction, level, range, body shape) and force (heavy–light) of their movement.

Phrasing. When measures are formed into larger rhythmic structures, we refer to *phrasing.* As a measure is a rhythmic sentence, so may a phrase be considered a paragraph. Just as we speak in sentences and need to stop for breath, so do we group time in music or movement to give the same "rounding off" feeling to our ideas before starting again. Thus, phrasing is a rhythmic sequence of movement which develops and diminishes in the same way that a flowing inflection of the voice gives us a feeling of partial or total completion at the end of a paragraph. A phrase is longer than a measure and elicits children's responses to larger groupings of time. Although there must be at least two measures, each phrase does not necessarily have to be equal in length. Because its function is to express a continuous movement theme, we are not concerned with merely adding measures together. As an expressive quality, phrasing is that element of time that is organized to give a sense of fluidity and continuity from the beginning to the end of a movement sequence.

DURATION

In the language of dance, divisions of time are known to us as *duration,* which is the span or interval of time from the beginning of a movement to its end. In order to help children understand the nature of their own rhythmic inventions, we need again to distinguish between metrical and rhythmic pattern. Because of the consistent, repetitive structure of metrical time, the groupings to which children respond must relate to an underlying beat or meter; that is, the basic rhythm is "given" and it is left to the children to design movement within it. Although it is not the same as "real" or clock time, it is structured in the sense that each beat or movement must be given its appropriate time value.

Relative Duration. In establishing their own rhythm, children are dealing with *relative duration* in which the underlying pulse emerges from the form of the movement itself. It is the child who imparts a particular length of time to a movement, which lasts only in relation to other movements. Actual or clock time is of no import, for duration is not bounded by physical time. Rather, the duration of a movement or series of movements depends upon the force necessary for its expression and the amount of space necessary for its execution. Thus, it comes into being through a combination of aesthetic qualities; that is, although it exists in *time,* it is also a *force* which is directed and released, and which extends in *space.*

Children seem to have a need to give some organization to the internal rhythms of their body, for even when there is no external metrical structure, they inevitably produce an underlying pulse. Even when they evolve a rhythmic pattern of which they are not consciously aware, we can "pick up" the beat, and frequently the measures and phrasing. Once a child establishes a unit of time in whatever exploration or improvisation he is engaged, we can determine the duration of a movement. In terms of children's sensibility, it is their own feeling for duration which largely determines their awareness of time patterns.

FORCE

In the chapters on painting and sculpture we referred to force as the tension or opposition of one part working against another. In dance, it is the actual physical energy of the body which gives a sense of stress or tension to a movement. Force deals with the opposition of energies in terms of contrast and dynamics. Fundamentally, it involves the rhythm of a movement from beginning to end, and is the essential factor in expressing different relationships in space–time.

In everyday movement, the amount of force necessary to perform a certain action affects the accuracy of that movement; in dance, the amount of force serves only to enhance its expressive intent. Children sense these qualities as greater or lesser tension, heaviness or lightness, resistance or acquiescence to the pull of gravity. By expending and releasing energy in various ways, children become aware that movements appear and feel differently when given different amounts of force. Just as the child is the center of reference in his perception of space and time, so his own body weight becomes the reference point in his relationship to other weights, both internal and external. A child perceives weight through the existence of a force which he creates (tension) or which works upon his body (gravity).

Although all of our movements are affected by the force of gravity, children are not usually conscious of its influence until they experience the range of qualities from tension to relaxation. By exploring sustained, percussive, swinging, and collapsing movement, they discover that various states of tension enable them to resist gravity, just as relaxation causes them to "give in" or submit to it. We can reinforce children's awareness of the "pulls" they experience through a vocabulary which speaks of tension as "feeling the strength in your muscles" and relaxation as "letting the energy flow out of your toes or fingers."

In the same way, childen can understand how their own body weight functions by exploring gradations of force. For example, children can feel the contrast in contracting and releasing (which they understand as "bending and stretching") by responding to such instructions as, "Quickly pull all parts of you into your middle so that no air can get through; now slowly, slowly unfold into space and let the air push through your fingers." Whether they move in a sitting position or away from the floor, any response to gravity carries a feeling of heaviness or lightness. Similarly, in pushing or pulling, the energy is strongly controlled from the center of the body, which gives a feeling of solidity. The giddiness that frequently comes from circular movements, such as turning or twirling, arises from a sensation of lightness or loss of body weight. Resistance to gravity is experienced by the feeling of "taking off" through such movements as jumping or leaping, just as acquiescence is the feeling of being "earth-bound" as expressed in falling or collapsing.

Thus, movement is influenced by force in the following ways: (1) by the external forces of gravity and momentum, (2) by the control and flow of energy applied to the muscles, and (3) by the tempo and rate of a movement against a resistance which is real or imaginary.

Tension. Tension as a quality in dance does not imply an unhealthy disequilibrium as it might in general behavior. As in other art forms, tension is a necessary and exciting ingredient. Thus, when we speak of muscle tension, we are referring to the amount of tension an individual needs to yield to or overcome gravity, which he senses kinesthetically. There are many ways in which a child can increase the feeling or awareness of tension, but he is most immediately affected by how his own lines of gravity relate to the transference of his body weight.

The center of gravity is commonly misunderstood as a fixed place in the body which is the same for everyone. Children, especially, point to their belly buttons when asked to identify that particular area. Actually, it is made up of three planes —the vertical, horizontal, and diagonal—which come together somewhere in the center of the torso, between the shoulders and the hips. It is that shifting "point" from which energy is expended or controlled. Each child has a unique body structure and each plane, because of its special relation to gravity, lends different qualities to movement.

Children can be made aware of how the muscles in the center of their bodies affect their ability to control different types of movement. A child can locate his "middle," for example, when his weight is placed equally over both legs in a standing position, or, in adult terms, when his body is in alignment. As soon as he shifts away from the center, either by moving in space with a part of his body or by taking a step, he senses a change in body weight. If he alternates his weight from one foot to the other in skipping, he has one sensation; if he extends his torso as far as he can in space, he has quite another. Thus, he begins to realize that body weight and balance are closely connected.

In our discussion of directions in space, we noted that the body moves most comfortably in a frontal position. Therefore, moving on a vertical or horizontal plane produces a greater feeling of stability than moving on the diagonal. When a child is standing still, as in the preceding example, balance is no problem as long as his body maintains a vertical position in relation to gravity. Moving on a horizontal plane elicits a sense of "pushing out" into space, in contrast to the contained feeling of being vertical. The greatest sense of imbalance comes in shifting the weight from the vertical to the diagonal plane, for it requires the most control. Again, using the center as the point of reference, we begin to understand that because diagonal movements are created further and further from the center, the amount of physical tension increases.

Balance. Achieving a sense of balance means really grappling with gravity. Children need to become consciously aware that as they produce different types of movement, their center of gravity must shift according to the weight necessary to support them. As an indication of the interrelationship of space–time–force, we return to the example of children's perception of levels in space. Because force is the focus here, we are concerned with what happens to the distribution of weight as children relate to different levels in the body. In response to the problem of "How tall can you be by stretching your whole self?" we observe that beyond raising their hands over their heads, they must sense the displacement of weight which pulls their heels off the floor and pushes their arms into space by shifting the center of gravity from the middle of the body to the rib cage. In exploring the contrasting feeling of "How small can you be?" a child may bend forward in a crouching position with his arms encircling his knees, in which case the center of gravity shifts to the muscles of the buttocks.

In addition to experiencing tension in the whole body, children can also control the amount of energy in different body parts. For example, while sitting on the floor, children can begin to feel the energy it takes slowly to lift one leg as high as they can. Even when concentrating on one part, however, they must become aware of what the other leg is doing and how their weight is shifting to support their bodies. Lifting one leg requires relatively little control, but lifting both legs (without tipping backward) means that they must center their weight firmly in the torso. And extending three limbs presents a further challenge.

Dynamics.   In both locomotor and body movement, force is expressed through the use of *dynamics* which are sensed as changes in the release or compression of energy. Dynamics involve changes and contrasts in the output of energy which are most familiarly known to children as heavy–light, strong–relaxed, fast–slow. The way a child expends or controls energy affects the dynamic quality of his movements. For example, a lack of dynamics reflects a lack of vitality, whereas too many sudden changes impart a frenetic, disorganized quality, in both a physical and emotional sense. Because it is not a question of mastering a technique, muscular effort alone will not create living, expressive forms. The dynamic power that a child gives to movement comes from within himself, charged by his emotional need for expression.

Explorations of Force.   Explorations of the qualities of force are found in movements described as *sustained, percussive, swinging,* and *collapsing.*

Sustained movement is expressed as a smooth, constant flow of energy, such as in responding to the vibrations of a gong, pushing the air away in a steady, even movement, or pulling an imaginary rope of a heavy bell. The degree of muscle tension may be great or light, depending on how fast or slow the tempo is. Sustained movements are not the same as the sense of suspension at the end of a swing or a "throw." The difference is that this type of movement has no accent and no sharp beginning or ending. Because the flow of energy must be continuous, children frequently find it more difficult to exert this kind of control.

Percussive movement involves a totally opposite feeling. It is a sudden, explosive release of energy in sharp, quick movements. It is similar in quality to the percussive beats of a drum, tambourine, and triangle or of maracas and wrist bells, and it varies in both tempo and range. When short, percussive movements occur very rapidly, they take on vibratory or "fluttery" effects. Even though a movement may be executed with more or less force, it always begins with a strong impulse, changes suddenly, and stops abruptly. Because it may begin and end at any point, it lacks continuity. Children find this a comfortable movement, for it suits their tempo level and requires less balance.

Swinging describes the rhythmical movement of a part of the body in an arc or circle around a stationary center (or axis of the body). Children sense a swing as a "giving in" to gravity, similar to the easy rise of sitting in a real swing. The action is initiated by a lack of force in the muscles, but as it picks up momentum there is an acceleration which gives it impulse. Whether consciously breathing in and releasing air, or moving out into space, the highest point of suspension is felt like the end of a deep breath that is released slowly. We may think of it as the slowing down of energy in the final phase of a swing.

Collapsing movements are too quickly identified by children as "falling down," but they discover that there are gradual ways in which their muscles can respond to the pull of gravity. When children engage in collapsing movements with complete loss of control, they are unable to sense that there are degrees of force expended in acquiescing to gravity. For example, if falling is a natural outgrowth of a movement sequence, the descent may involve some resistance at the start and then end in a sudden collapsing release. Or energy may be released instantly throughout the body, which would result in a collapsing·fall. In either case it is the difference between falling and "falling apart."

The excitement of dance for children lies partly in the realization that even though there is no apparent tension, their muscles are always in a state of activity and motion. They support the body against gravity, not only in sitting or standing still, but in expending energy in space and time. It is variations in force which also give quality to the action "between" movements and help a child maintain balance between the parts of his body. As children's awareness and control of tension develops, they perceive their bodies in a new way. They discover that their bodies can move in more or less space, in faster or slower tempos, with more or less intensity, to serve the function of expressive movement.

Experiential Approach

Children's experience in dance is a continuous process of selecting and simplifying significant aspects of their experience and of finding forms to express them in movement. It is through creative problem solving that this process comes into being. We can observe that a child is solving problems when he searches for ways that are new for him, at any phase in his development. Neither the fact that a movement has been done before nor that it is newly presented assures that it will be successful or creative. What is important is that it is a new discovery for that child, and that it becomes part of the process of selection and abstraction which he relates to his ever-changing needs for expression.

For this reason we engage children in the exploration of movement elements within the larger context of space–time–force. As we have seen in the previous section, each of these qualities has an objective identity. Yet in creating and observing movement, they do not function as separate factors. Depending upon what a child is trying to express, each exists in a greater or lesser degree, but they are experienced together as an on-going process with the body as the unifying center. Sheets suggests that the "lived experience" of dance moves beyond a consciousness of the body as a mere physical phenomenon, to an awareness of the body as a "form-in-the-making." [1] In the dance process, therefore, the child becomes the "moving center of a moving form." [2]

This tells us that when a child is involved in movement, he does not experience it as something apart from himself. Whatever he creates as a dynamic, expressive form, he is both physically and emotionally involved in the total act. Space–time–force do not exist apart from movement, and they do not exist apart from the child. In the previous section we noted particularly that although a movement appears to occur in one part of the body only, it is supported through a movement impulse throughout the entire body. Thus, although a movement impulse is the initial step, it extends through whatever muscles are necessary to bring that original impulse to fulfillment. Children understand this process on different levels, but they are actually experiencing these qualities all at once.

Through consciously guided experiences by the teacher, children gradually become aware of the "wholeness" of their body movement. They discover, for example, that the feeling of jumping on two feet changes when they alternate feet for leaping. At the point at which jumps become leaps, a child senses the need to change the distribution of his body weight, and to use different dimensions of space and time. In the example given earlier of using a body part to lead him through space, he senses in the doing that whatever part he selects will become the center of weight or tension. As he experiences the "pull" of moving in a certain direction, he becomes aware that his whole body must accommodate by changes in position, path, and even foot pattern.

DEVELOPING KINESTHETIC PERCEPTION

The essence of the dance experience is that it opens children's perceptions to another way of knowing and feeling about themselves. In this case, the perception is *kinesthetic,* which simply means that bodily movements are the result of muscular activity and that children can understand and appreciate these movements by developing a "muscle sense." To draw an analogy with the other arts, this would be comparable to a "visual sense" in painting, a "haptic sense" in sculpture, and a "metaphoric sense" in poetry.

Strictly speaking, kinesthetic perception results from an awareness of sensory data—that is, visual, auditory, tactile sensations; and the muscular system acts as an integrating center through which a child learns to orient himself in space–time. In a broader sense, a child's ability to move with fluency depends upon his feelings of "rightness" or "wrongness" in relation to how he can adjust and control his own body parts. The process is actually one of a combination of awareness and control, both of which function interactively. If dance is to be of value, a child must be able to express his way of feeling, moving, being, and he can do so only by developing a vocabulary of movement. Therefore, kinesthetic perception not only is related to motor learning, but depends on a consciousness of the feeling sensations of movement. This points again to the idea that

[1] Maxine Sheets, *The Phenomenology of Dance* (Madison, Wis.: University of Wisconsin Press, 1966), p. 27.
[2] Ibid., p. 28.

technique alone is not sufficient, for "doing" without feeling is an incomplete experience.

As with all art forms, we need to reconsider the notion of technique in relation to skills. Children inevitably develop certain skills as they strengthen and control their bodies, yet we are not concerned with a specific action or movement, but with the context in which that skill is demonstrated. Thus, we regard skills as overt changes in a child's perception which are recorded and produced in the muscles. As a process, skills evolve as part of the ongoing growth of a child and function as a means of increasing the range and depth of his expressive movement.

We present dance experiences which provide opportunities for a child to use skills already learned (for example, some of the basic locomotor movements) and those still being learned in ways which continuously challenge his level of ability. Although the material of dance is movement itself, dance derives from experiences, feelings, and ideas of children and finds sources in stories, poems, songs, images, and other content in the curriculum. Our introduction of new materials or techniques, however, does not always await the expressed needs of the child. Frequently the excitement of new ideas for modes of expression stimulates him to explore new solutions and to deal with previously felt experiences in new ways. As a child investigates the infinite uses of his body, he begins to create new movements (new in the sense of being new to himself and to the environment which nourishes such explorations).

Thus, the search in dance is for the sensations and qualities of expression that are brought to life as movement patterns develop. It is this kind of aesthetic awareness that gradually unfolds from experiencing and feeling. As children use various relationships of space–time–force, they come to realize that hands, feet, and head are capable of moving at different speeds with different intensity, that the torso can show heavy and light movement, and that the whole body can speak for them as an expressive medium. But although the combinations used in movement are transmitted through a muscle sense, a child's kinesthetic sensitivity depends upon the emotions or general feelings which stimulate the initial movement. Because the experience involves both objective and subjective factors, we must recognize that no two children move alike, any more than they talk with the same inflection, intonation, or use of language.

Dance is one art form through which children may achieve quality through group participation as well as by working alone. At the same time, the success of a movement experience depends upon a child's unique ability to conceive of space–time–force in relation to his own body, and to control these elements imaginatively. In so doing, he learns that he can impose an order upon his environment by speaking through emotional forms which have a larger scope than self-expression.

When we suggest that children "speak" through a movement vocabulary, we recognize the paradox that when children are in the act of moving, they are not concerned with conceptual forms, but with movement forms. Although we cannot "talk" dance, we can communicate concepts so that they understand the fundamental sources from which their movement takes shape. To do this we present a vocabulary which is translated from verbal to movement terms. It is a language which can be shared by teachers and children alike, because it is simple and direct, and completely in keeping with the lexicon of dance. For teachers, it is the difference in communicating meanings between, "Put your arms out as far as you can," and, "Reach for space," between, "Jump up high," and, "Feel the air push under your heels."

For teachers, using spoken language in eliciting responses to any art form requires a delicate balance: enough to set the problems as clearly and non-prescriptively as possible, yet not so many instructions that children become preoccupied with the words and lose the purpose of the experience. Because dance is so physically absorbing, an overemphasis on verbal preparation (e.g., "What animal are you going to be?" or, "What kind of movement are you going to do?") tends to reduce children's spontaneity and they are "talked out" before they even explore the possibilities of movement itself. At best, the vocabulary must lead children immediately into the dance experience with directions that are clear and concise.

Verbal cues can be very helpful, however, with comments such as, "We can't talk dance—your body will speak for you." When children tend to "explain" their movements either because of ambiguity on their part or because of the observations of their classmates, a comment such as, "Its not important that we understand every movement—it's the overall feeling that speaks to us," places the focus more appropriately. Helping children to develop a language which describes the inherent nature of a particular experience also offers them a vehicle for self-evaluation and for constructive criticism of others. As children learn to identify the internal aspects of a problem in terms of its concepts and elements, there is less tendency to rely on judgments such as, "I don't like the way he did it," which is enlightening neither to the dancer nor to his peers.

Once a child recognizes that as an individual he moves in ways that are unique to him, he can appreciate his ability to develop his own vocabulary of movements. What we begin to observe is that he uses space–force–time in forms which reflect his own individuality. When he becomes attuned to the fact that he can make his own statements through movement, he finds less need to imitate others. Exploring one's own repertoire gives a child opportunities to discover whether certain movements are harmonious with his body structure and whether they best serve to express his emotions, moods, or ideas. Because children tend to repeat the movement they enjoy, an observant teacher can readily identify and help children become aware of the feeling qualities of their movements. Thus, although we cannot reduce the lived experience of dance to verbal equivalents, we can help children give expression to both the knowing and feeling aspects of dance, which they mold and synthesize into tangible forms.

Elements

Children become aware of space–time–force as the essential components of dance through their initial explorations of movement fundamentals. It is these elements which make up the basic vocabulary from which dance forms come into being. All movement, regardless of the age of the child or the level of complexity, falls into three categories: (1) *Locomotor movements,* which propel the body from one place to another *through* space "from here to there" and include walking, running, leaping, jumping, hopping, galloping, skipping, sliding; (2) *body movements,* which project the body *in* space, emanate from a fixed base around the axis of the body from a sitting, standing, kneeling, or lying position and include bending, stretching, swinging, swaying, pushing, pulling, turning, twisting; and (3) *combinations of movements,* which may involve two or more locomotor movements (hopping and leaping), a series of body movements (bending and stretching), or a combination of locomotor and body movements (sliding and swinging, walking and stretching).

As we have noted, locomotor movements are most familiar and comfortable for children because they are used most frequently in covering space in everyday activities. Although we build on the "natural" movements of children, dance is the means by which such movements may be controlled, abstracted, and given new expressive shapes. The preceding examples are referred to as fundamental movements which vary in space and time, and most distinctively, in the use of force or energy. For example, in a walk, leap, or gallop, the weight is transferred from one foot to another; in a jump or hop, the weight is centered on both feet while the body is elevated. Most children engage in simple locomotor movements as part of their spontaneous bodily activity. When the emphasis is on the qualities of the individual movement, however, confusion arises over changes in body weight, such as the difference between a skip, a gallop, and a slide, or a jump and a leap.

If we are to help children become conscious of the alternatives offered by different movements, we must be able to observe the characteristics of each one. To release ourselves from focusing only on the mechanics, we must bear in mind that although these movements are executed primarily in the legs, the actual distribution of weight is controlled from the torso. Thus, if the muscles in the center of the body are allowed to "collapse," or if they are not engaged in the action, these movements tend to become mechanical and lack buoyancy.

LOCOMOTOR MOVEMENTS

Walking carries the body through space by transferring the weight from one foot to another in a smooth, even rhythm; as the weight shifts, one foot is always in contact with the floor.

Running is walking at an increased tempo, with more force to impel the body through space; the weight is transferred alternately so that for a moment both feet leave the floor at the same time.

Leaping transfers the weight from one leg to the other, which carries the body in an upward and forward direction; the feeling is of "pushing and reaching"— i.e., the back leg pushes off the floor, the front leg reaches forward, and each foot lands alternately; leaps cover a greater distance and range in space than a run.

Jumping propels the body in space by pushing off the floor with the weight equally distributed in both legs; at the highest point, the body is suspended and then submits to gravity by landing on both feet with knees slightly bent.

Hopping carries the body upward in space, pushing off and landing on the same foot; the weight is centered over the hopping leg but is also sustained in the torso; the knee of the opposite leg may also be flexed to aid in elevating the body.

Galloping takes the body through space in a forward and backward rocking motion; the weight is carried on the forward foot on the longer or accented beat while the backward foot steps on the shorted beat; it is the simplest of the uneven rhythmic patterns because the feet do not change their relationship.

Skipping is a combination of step–hop; the step gives impetus to the hop, which lifts the body upward in space; the higher the knees, the more buoyancy; it is similar to the gallop in that there is a transference of body weight, but it differs in that one foot always alternates with the other; this is the most difficult of the uneven rhythmic patterns because of the alternation of feet.

Sliding carries the body in a lateral position through space in a step-together motion; the weight may be equally distributed between the legs or additional force may be given to an accented step as in a sideward gallop; in a smooth, even rhythm there is increasing elevation; the knees are always relaxed and both feet are in continuous contact with the floor.

BODY MOVEMENTS

Body movements also derive from conventional activities in daily life, such as bending, pushing, pulling. Instead of traveling through space, however, the body shapes the space by moving in greater or lesser dimensions within it. Unlike locomotor movements which involved the whole body, these may be formed by the head, arms, legs, torso, alone or in combination. Movements radiate from the axis of the body, with the lower torso, legs, and feet acting as a fixed base. Children find these movements more difficult because they require a greater awareness of how energy is released and they demand more control of body weight or balance.

Bending and *stretching* both involve the extension or release of energy against a resistant force (real or imagined); *pushing* is a movement outward, away from the center of the body from a fixed base; *pulling* is a reversal of energy into the body, toward a fixed base.

Swinging and *swaying* have a similar quality, but it is the nature of the impulse that makes the difference; *swinging* is a circular or arclike movement which shifts the weight up and down, side to side, or around; it is a feeling of "reaching and dropping" like a pendulum motion in which the impulse comes not only from the arms but from the torso; swinging is more gravitational and uses more energy in that it may occur suddenly and then go downhill; *swaying* is a rocking movement from side to side, or forward and backward in a smooth, even tempo; it involves less energy than a swing, is more contained in the torso, and has a more limited range in space; there is less feeling of suspension than in a swing, in that the impulse is of easy relaxation and recovery.

Turning and *twisting* are both revolving movements around the axis of the body and tend to have a cyclic pattern; if in *turning,* the body rotates on one level, a complete circle is formed; if the impulse carries the body on different levels or planes, a spiral or open circular pattern occurs; *twisting* is a rotation of the upper part of the body while the lower part remains stationary. Although the weight is usually propelled from the torso, the arms can rotate from the shoulder, as can the legs from the hips. The impulse builds up a sequential rather than a simultaneous rotation in a rippling action. The amount of force affects both the tempo (fast–slow) and the quality of tension (relaxed or intense).

Although each of the movements described here are fundamental in developing a movement vocabulary, they should in no way be regarded as exercises. To do so would reduce movement to physical training and would divest it of its dynamic, creative qualities. Mastery of one "step" does not guarantee the successful execution of another. The problem in dance is not how well a child performs a movement in isolation, but how these movements relate qualitatively as a total visual–kinesthetic statement. That is, as children invent a new combination of movements, they come to understand how it looks as well as how it feels. The dance experience offers children endless possibilities of exploring space, of responding rhythmically and creating their own rhythms, and of sensing the excitement of controlling and releasing their energy. Perhaps most important, it presents an avenue wherein children can connect their ideas and feelings with their bodies. Even in developing a beginning movement repertoire, children discover that they can express themselves through still another language—"body talk"—through which they can give form to their impulses.

Explorations in Direction

Problem I: To explore the use of different body parts as the impulse for direction *through* space.

    A. *How do we get from "here to there" using different parts of the body? (The space from "here to there" must be initially defined for the children in relation to the dance area.)*

        1. When you walked into the room today, what parts of your body were leading you? (Children's responses: feet, toes, stomach, muscles.)

        2. You do not always have to walk with your feet leading you. For example, how would you get from "here to there" with your "behind" leading you?

        3. Let different parts of you take you on a walk through space, move freely around the room following in your own direction.

Problem II: To sense how qualities of force expended in different body parts give added impetus to direction.

    A. *Feel that there is a string attached to some part of your body and let that part pull you through space.*

        1. Let your forehead lead you; your nose; your chin (forward locomotion).

        2. Move with your ear leading you; your elbow; your shoulder (sideward locomotion).

3. Walk where your heels take you; now let your back lead you; shift the weight to your back (backward locomotion).

B. *Now let's divide into three groups; while one group moves at a time the others will watch, then take turns.*
   1. This time feel the difference between *pushing* that part with your body and letting it *pull* you in the direction in which it is facing.

Problem III: To establish a direction by coordinating the moving body with a fixed point in space.

A. *Just as we can walk with different parts of our bodies, so can we "point" to directions without using our fingers.*
   1. Look around the room; find three places to which you are going to move to, each one on a different level.
   2. Everyone take space on the floor; point to the first spot with some part of your body and keep moving in that direction until you touch it with your "pointing" part.
   3. From where you are point to the second spot with a different part of your body and approach it with a new part leading you.
   4. Now change the part of your body that will take you to the third spot. (If there are too many children for the space, a few may move at a time, beginning from different places; in the final exploration, children may be divided into small groups who are moving in the same direction, although with different body parts.)

B. *Different parts of your body took you in different directions* through *space, and on different levels* in *space.*
   1. How many different ways did you use your body to get to your three spots?
   2. What kinds of movements took you through space?
   3. What directions did you go in?
   4. Let's watch a few people at a time and notice how the *lines of their bodies* change as they move in different directions, and what *shapes* their bodies make as they point with different parts.

Problem IV: To explore the relationship between body plane and spatial direction.

A. *The way our bodies are shaped helps us move in many different ways; your body may face one way, but you can still move in a different direction.*

B. *Even when you are sitting perfectly still your body is a shape, just like any object in the room, and each side of you can use its own space differently.*
   1. You know that when rabbits hop forward they face frontward, but when frogs hop backward, they still face frontward.
   2. Let's explore to see whether being frontward and moving forward is the same thing.

3. Take two steps forward, turn two steps to the side, turn two steps backward, two steps to the other side, two steps forward.
4. In what direction did you move? Each time you changed direction, how was your body facing?

C. *Machines that work for us also move in different directions, and change their positions. Can you think of some? (Children's responses: steam shovel, snow plow.)*
   1. Find a place on the floor. How does a steam shovel work?
   2. Does it move in one direction?
   3. Does it always face the same way?

   ADDITIONAL ELEMENTS　*Awareness of immediate* space *around body and external space involved in locomotor movement; use of* force *as impulse for directions of body parts; changes in* range *and level; rhythmic pattern of movements.*

Problem V: To become aware of new coordinations of body parts in locomotor movements.

A. *How many ways can you get from here to there without using your feet?*
   1. What parts of your body did you use to get across the floor? (Children may move across the floor three or four at a time, depending on the amount of space.)

UNDERSTANDINGS FOR TEACHERS—PROBLEMS I–IV
How does a child move when an elbow or shoulder leads him in a sideward direction in space (as contrasted with conventional modes of locomotion)?
   What do his feet do? How do his arms help him move?
   How does he feel the different parts of his body "push" or "pull" him? What is the difference in the qualities of force (energy)? What happens to his sense of balance as he uses various body parts?
   What shapes do his body make when his head, back, or knee lead him?

UNDERSTANDINGS FOR TEACHERS—PROBLEM V
What do children sense in the coordination of body parts? Can they relate their kinesthetic experiences to a movement vocabulary of such action words as "walking on my hands, rocking on my back, turning in circles on my behind, rolling on my side; pulling with my hands, pushing with my knees?"
   Are children aware of the different types of locomotor movement they used?
   How do they sense the need for redistribution of body weight in coordinating new body parts?

Explorations in Levels

Problem I: To understand levels as the direction of the body *in* space, described as "high, medium, or low" in relation to the center of the body.

A. *When we move from here to there, we are moving in different directions* through *space, but we can also move on different levels* in *space.*

B. *Let's explore levels of space on your own body. Where are they in relation to the space around you?*
1. Stand perfectly still with your feet together and your head and body in a straight line. Where is the middle level on your body? Where is it in space? Move out into space with any kind of movement but keep your body on a middle level.
    a. The middle level is not just in the center of your stomach; it is the whole area between your shoulders and your hips. Can you move on a middle level in space by raising, lowering, or extending parts of your body in different ways?
    b. Put your weight on one knee and try all the possible ways of moving on a middle level. Now place your weight on both knees and see how many ways you can move in space.
2. Where is "high" on your body? Where is "high" in space? What direction are you moving in on this level?
    a. High is not just from the top of your shoulders to your raised finger tips; it starts from the moment that you lift the center of your body higher than usual.
    b. How high is high? How high can you walk without actually leaving the floor? How high can you go if you leave the floor? Can you reach for more space? What parts can help you reach higher?
3. Where is "low" on your body? How low is low in space?
    a. Can you find different low levels in space before you reach the floor? Your muscles will help you balance when you lower the center of your body.
    b. How low can you go if you keep your feet on the floor? How much space can you use with your whole body on the floor? How little space can you use?
    c. Now from some of these positions can you move *through* space on a low level?

Problem II: To explore levels in space with locomotor and body movements using different sources of imagery.

A. *Think of all the different levels we move on when we work and play.*
1. Imagine that you are going to paint the walls of your very own room. Decide where these four walls will be and stay within that space.
    a. Pick up the bucket of paint without bending your knees; stir the paint with a big stick; and put it down slowly.
    b. Take a brush in one hand; paint the walls from top to bottom, from bottom to top, and from side to side; take long, even strokes and feel the weight of the brush as it moves in space.
    c. Now paint the ceiling; stretch to reach it. What happens to your body

when you paint in that position? What parts of you are supporting your weight?

    d. On what levels in space are you working? In what directions are you painting? What parts of your body are you using in addition to your arms?

ADDITIONAL ELEMENTS   *Use of force in sustained movements redistributes body weight as directions change; creating a shape in space.*

2. What do you do with toys and blocks when you are finished playing with them? Put them away? Where? Yes, shelves are good places.
    a. Because there are no "real" toys lying around here, imagine that you are going to find a place and put your toys on the lowest, middle, or highest shelf.
    b. Remember, toys and blocks have different shapes, different sizes, and they do not all weigh the same. Your movements should show whether you are picking up something light, heavy, big, small, round, or square and on what shelf you are putting them.
    [If there are too many children for each to have his own place, two or three "shelves" (spaces) may be designated and children can move toward them singly or in small groups.]
3. Let's watch a few people at a time and see if their bodies tell us what kinds of toys they are carrying and at what level they are placing them.

B. *An elevator takes you up and down in space but may stop on many levels between high–medium–low.*
    1. You can be an elevator alone, with a partner, or with a group; if you work with someone, make sure that when you stop at different floors, you stop together.
    2. Elevators can go fast or slow. If you are alone you can work at your own speed; but if you are with others, you have to move and stop in the same rhythm.
    3. Now we have a new problem. Divide yourselves into small groups and decide who will be the "elevators" and who will be the "passengers." The "elevators" must find a shape that will hold the "passengers" so that you can all move up and down smoothly.
    4. How will you know at what floor someone wants to get out? (Children's responses: The "elevators" will announce the floor at each level, or the "passengers" will call out their floor as a signal to stop.)

ADDITIONAL ELEMENTS   *Creating an external space by relating body shapes; accommodating to tempo and rhythmic pattern; relating to another's movement on different levels.*

UNDERSTANDINGS FOR TEACHERS—PROBLEMS I–II
Both problems involve an awareness that force *is expended in various ways in moving in or through space (that is, weight must be shifted to different body parts to allow for movement in different directions).*

Children are shaping their outside space (walls, elevators) as well as designing their inside space by stopping at different levels.

The response to elements of size, shape, weight of imaginary objects requires the redistribution of body weight and affects the type of movement in and through space.

The imagery is simple and familiar and can be used as the basis of other activities suggested by the children.

Problem III: To relate levels in space to levels of tone on percussive instruments by responding to accompaniment cues.

A. *There are levels of tone on different instruments that sound high–medium–low just as there are levels in space.*
   1. Listen as I play clusters of notes up and down the keyboard; say "high," "medium," or "low" as you hear the levels change.
      [Piano is used as an example but a xylophone may be used, as well as a combination of drum (low), tone block or maracas (middle), and bells or triangles (high).]
   2. Move on the same levels that you hear on the piano. When I stop, you stop at the level you hear; when I play, you move again.
   3. I may play only at one level or the levels may move up and down; listen to the changes and use your whole body in space.
      (To stimulate a flow of movement from one level to another, chords, clusters, or melodic line are played in an up-and-down progression so that children are constantly changing levels.)

4. This time I'm going to play faster and slower; as you move, feel the rhythm in your muscles so that your bodies will know when the levels change.
[Accompaniment must have a steady beat with clearly defined measures (that is, 4/4 time in phrases of two or four measures).]
5. Now that you know how it feels to move in space, let your body reach out on different levels; listen to the tone and begin from that level (you may be starting from low, high, or medium).
6. Just as the levels change, the rhythm is going to change, so let your ears listen while your body moves.

Problem IV: To explore surrounding space on many changing levels in relation to each other.

A. *As you move* in *and* through *space, stop on a level that is different from someone near you.*
1. Let's work in small groups of three or four; move together and "pick up" the beat of the drum; when the drum stops, each of you "freeze" at a different level.
[Accompaniment must establish a clear rhythmic pattern (for example, walking, running, swinging, skipping, galloping) through the repetitive, uneven beat in skipping or galloping, the accented beat is 3/4 or 4/4 time, a consistent number of measures in a phrase, and the number of phrases.]
2. Take enough space for yourself but stay close enough together so that you can see whom you are near and at what level to "freeze."
3. If you find that you are on the same level as someone else in your group, quickly change and make your body shape relate to theirs.

UNDERSTANDINGS FOR TEACHERS—PROBLEMS III–IV

There are two elements of spatial awareness: children must be conscious of the changing levels within the group and they must respond individually by finding their own level and position distinct from any other child. How do children observe and relate to the group as a whole and still express their own quality of movement?

This problem extends an awareness of external and internal space (that is, the space around them formed by relating to other moving bodies and the space which a child creates in finding his own level).

Introduction of time (expressed through tone and rhythm) as well as space and force (that is, each group responds to the tempo and underlying beat but each child develops his own rhythmic pattern as he seeks a level in space).

Finding a level in relation to another body shape elicits increased use of arms, legs, and torso for greater range and differentiation of body parts.

Increased use of directional space (that is, toward, away, in, up, around).

Explorations in Range

Problem I: To explore the extent to which movement reaches out from the body into space.

A. *Any movements that you make in space can be wide or narrow, or large or small.*
   1. Let's begin with your own body; even when you breathe, parts of you get larger or smaller and use more or less space.
   2. Sit on the floor "Indian style" and rest your hands in your lap.
   3. The whole upper part of you is a balloon; start as a very small balloon and fill up with air until you feel your chest and stomach grow larger and larger; hold it until it almost bursts, then let the air out slowly.
   4. This time, let's hear the sound of the air going in as the balloon gets bigger, and let's hear it coming out as the balloon gets smaller.
   5. Let's make the balloon even bigger; fold your arms lightly across your stomach so that your elbows are touching your sides; as you fill up with air, fill your whole upper part (not just your chest) and see how far your arms are pushed forward. Do it several times and look at the shape of your body.
   6. The balloon can be wider and rounder; rest your hands in your lap but let your elbows touch your sides. When you blow up the balloon, try to make it so wide that it pushes your arms easily away from your sides; as the balloon goes down, let your arms come back slowly.
   7. The air in the balloon is going to push your arms out into space; let your arms rise slowly as the balloon gets bigger and bigger and feel how much space your body uses.

   ADDITIONAL ELEMENTS   *Rhythmic pattern is introduced by breathing; changes in range produce different body shapes; flow and control of energy affect range of body parts.*

B. *Just as you can change the size of parts of your body, so you can make your whole body bigger or smaller, skinny or wide.*
   1. Your whole body is a balloon; begin from any position (standing, sitting, kneeling) and fill up the balloon from the center of your body (that is, your belly button). As your balloon gets rounder and wider, what happens to your arms and legs and head?
   2. As you reach for space, can you feel the shape of a balloon? What shape are you?
   3. You know how a balloon crumples when all the air goes out? Feel the size of your balloon change as you let the air out; begin from where you are now and collapse very slowly.
   4. Now let the air out quickly and feel the difference between being big and small, wide and skinny.

Problem II: To explore how range of movement is affected by the amount of surrounding space.

    A. *When you have lots of space around you, you can make your bodies big or little, wide or narrow. Now explore your movements when you have only a little bit of space.*
1. This whole dance area is a forest. Some of you will be trees; some of you will move through the forest around the trees (two alternating groups).
2. The trees can arrange themselves in different places, with only a small amount of space between each other, but leave enough space for people to move through.
3. Remember that trees have different shapes and sizes, so find a level and shape and hold your position so that the people moving can see the spaces before they come in.
4. The range of your body in space should tell us whether your tree is tall, thick, skinny, small, gnarled, or leafy.

    B. *As you change groups, feel the difference between the amount of space you use when you do not move and when you move in a small space.*
1. Let us have the moving group start out from different directions and find ways of moving through the small spaces around the trees; start with an easy walk and make sure that you move around every tree.
2. Because the trees are so close together, this time walk between them, slowly stretching whatever part of your body you need to get through.
3. The size of your movements has changed from when you were just walking; what parts of your body are you using now in such little spaces?

    C. *Now feel the difference in your movements when you walk through more open spaces.*
1. Let's have the trees move out into space and take new positions so that the people can move more freely in different directions with wider and bigger movements.
2. Now let's make uneven spaces; some trees arrange themselves close together, some far apart.
3. In this new forest the moving group can use many different ways of getting through the spaces in as many directions and levels as possible.
4. Now slow down your movements and use more of your body (torso, arms) to move from tree to tree.

    D. *Each movement we make takes a different amount of space. Explore how much distance you can cover with different parts of your body.*
1. We are out of the forest and you are walking in a stream; some of the stones are very large, some are very small.
2. Step over the small stones across the whole stream. Is there much distance between your legs? What parts of your body are you using?
3. Now the stones are much larger. Can you just step over them or do you

need another kind of movement? (Children's responses: Jumping, leaping.)

4. Yes, jumping and leaping use more distance and take you further into space. What other parts of you help to get you across?
5. Now these big and little stones are all mixed up and they are not in a straight line; they are all over the stream; show by the way you move whether you are stepping over big or little stones and where they are in the stream.

UNDERSTANDINGS FOR TEACHERS—PROBLEMS I–II

How do children express verbally and kinesthetically the changes in their range of movements given more or less space? How do they become aware that different parts of the body have different ranges of movement?

The static group becomes part of the spatial environment as in a stage setting (that is, the moving group relates to them as "props" whose positions and shapes affect the amount of space available for movement).

Range as a dimension includes space, time, and force [for example, moving from bigger to smaller (or vice versa) involves changes in tempo as well as changes in the flow and control of energy].

Problem III: To explore contrasts in range using animals as imagery.

A. *Animals in the zoo are all sizes and their movements take different amounts of space. What are the largest animals you have seen? (Children's responses: Elephant, giraffe, hippopotamus.)*
   1. Choose your animal. Let your movements show whether you are wide and heavy, tall and thin, or tall and wide.
   2. Take space out on the floor. An elephant and hippopotamus are both big but they move very differently; feel the difference in the shape of your body and the way certain parts of you move in space.
   3. If you are a giraffe, how do you move on long, skinny legs and how does your neck stretch out from your body? Do you move faster or slower than an elephant? How far can your legs take you in space?

B. *What is the smallest animal you have seen in the zoo? (Children's responses: Snake, bird, bat, turtle.)*
   1. Whatever small animals you choose, move on different levels, at different speeds, and use different parts of the body.
   2. For example, how does a snake use its body when it moves? Do all parts move at once?
   3. Where do small animals live? On what do they move (air, earth, water)?

UNDERSTANDINGS FOR TEACHERS—PROBLEM III

Whereas imagery involves space, time, and forces, range is emphasized through the qualities of size, weight, and shape. (For example, does an elephant have the same range of movement as a snake?) How does the use of space differ in terms of direction, level, tempo? How does range of movement differ in animals who live on the ground, walk on the ground, or fly in the air?

Imagery such as this is familiar and easily adaptable to other sources which include all living and moving things.

Explorations in Body Shape

Problem I: To explore the body as a three-dimensional object made up of volumes in space.

A. *Your body is a shape that takes up space even when you are standing or sitting still.*
   1. Everyone find a place on the floor and sit down in a relaxed position; look at all the different shapes that your bodies make; walk around each other (in small, alternating groups) and see that we have one shape from the front, another from the side, the back, and still another from the top.
   2. The way you place your arms, legs, and head in relation to your body makes an "inside" shape; as soon as you move a part of you outward, your body makes a different shape in the outside space.
   3. Pull every part of you in toward the middle and see what happens to the "inside" space; now extend different parts into the "outside" space, from both a sitting and standing position.

B. *Let's explore different shapes that the body can make.*
   1. Make every part of your body as sharp (angular) as it can be. Where are the corners of your body?
   2. How does a circle feel? What is the shape of the space around you? How round can you be?
   3. Design the space inside and around you to make a triangle shape; you can be one big triangle or different parts of your body can make little triangles.

   ADDITIONAL ELEMENTS   *Level, range, force (tension).*

C. *Now feel the difference in the space as you change from one shape to an-other.*
   1. Begin from whatever shape you like; do not tell us, show it with your body; start from any position—standing, sitting, kneeling, lying, and so on.
   2. When you find a shape, change it slowly, slowly into a different shape; can you see that every part of you makes its own shape as you move from one to another?
   3. Those of you who are circular or curved, sharpen your corners and find a square shape; if your shape has angles, soften the movement into

a round shape; if you grow from a triangle into a rectangle, feel the stretch in your back, arms, and head.

4. What happens to the shape of the space under your arms when you change? What happens to the space between your legs as you change from a triangle or circle to a tall, skinny rectangle?

UNDERSTANDINGS FOR TEACHERS—PROBLEM I

Children become conscious of not only being a shape but of making a shape, both of which use internal and external space.

Creating different shapes and changing from one to another makes children aware of the ways different body parts move in space, and with distinctive qualities, for example, soft (round, curved) and sharp (angular, pointed). Beginning with geometric shapes helps to relate the body to shapes of objects in the environment.

Problem II: To explore the relationship of two bodies designing a shape.

A. *Your body can create shapes that have the qualities of objects; can you form the shape of a box?*
   1. Take space on the floor; you can work from any position and on any level.
   2. We should be able to tell whether it is tall or wide, big or small, flat or bulging, by the way you enclose the space.

B. *How do you make a box with another person?*
   1. Find a place with your partner. Make a box that has both an inside and an outside shape.
   2. You do not have to close all the corners or angles; we can see the shape from the spaces in between.

C. *This time make the shape of a box with four people working together.*
   1. Feel each other's weight so that you can hold the shape.
   2. Your box may be open or closed, and it may have a top; it can stand at any level in space.

   ADDITIONAL ELEMENTS   Body parts: *Use of body parts alone and in relation to torso, for example, legs and arms, arms and head, trunk, head and arms;* force: *distribution of body weight;* space: *levels, range.*

UNDERSTANDINGS FOR TEACHERS—PROBLEM II

Making a shape first in relation to their own bodies and then in relation to another's sharpens children's kinesthetic awareness of the body's position in space.

New elements of force are brought into being. That is, how does a child feel when he creates a box whose "sides" are supported by others? How does he control his body weight?

Through the simple image of a box children are exploring qualities of shapes (for example, heavy, light), and as they relate this visual–kinesthetic experience

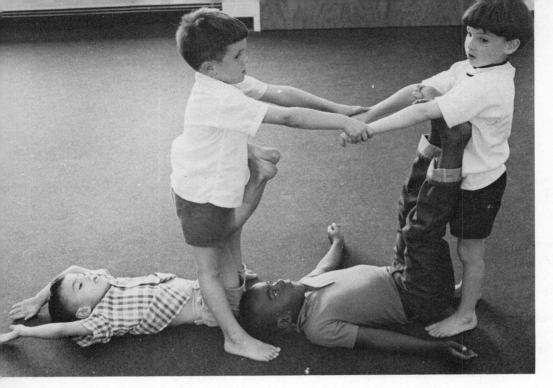

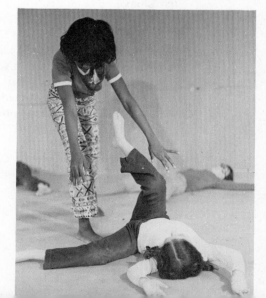

to their own body shape, they are abstracting a conventional, everyday object into movement terms.*

Problem III: To explore spatial relationships created by group shapes.

A. *Explore a shape where you are touching or connecting with each other.*
1. Even when you close the spaces in between, each body will have its own shape.
2. Work with partners or in small groups.
3. Feel the difference between leaning on someone and just touching them. What happens to your balance?
4. Work at different levels and fill in the space around, under, and over.
5. You will be meeting and staying together like "frozen" shapes.

B. *Each time you make a shape with another person or with a group, the space around you changes.*
1. Divide in small groups and explore movements that take you *over* and *under* each other.
2. Are you touching, or are there spaces between you?
3. Is everyone in your group on the same level in space?
4. Are you moving and staying together, or are you meeting and moving apart?

ADDITIONAL ELEMENTS   *Range of movement, spatial direction in relation to body plane, levels, balance and control of body weight.*

Problem IV: To form one group shape through the interrelationship of individual body shapes.

A. *You can make a large group shape if you design your own body in relation to others around you.*
1. Divide into groups of fives or sevens; find a place on the floor and work together to develop your shape; then we will look at them separately.
2. Let's have a person in each group create the first shape, and each of you, one at a time, find a shape that relates to it; take turns making the first shape.
3. Work in all levels and directions—below, above, around, behind, and in front of each other.
4. We should be able to see two kinds of space, the space around your own body shape and the space that you create between each other.
5. What was the shape of your group? (Children's responses: curved, circular, triangular, free-formed.)
6. What was the general shape of each person's body within it? Was it the same as the large group shape?

* These problems are shown in the film "Children Dance," produced and co-directed by the author and Naima Prevots (Berkeley, Calif.: University of Calfornia Extension Media Center), b/w, sound, 14 minutes.

7. This is not "follow the leader." You are meeting and surrounding each other using your bodies in different ways.

UNDERSTANDINGS FOR TEACHERS—PROBLEMS III–IV

Children discover that when they work in relation to others they are not only creating their own body shapes, but are becoming part of new spatial relationships.

Creating shapes involves various spatial dimension (up–down, in–out, under, around, far–near) and directional elements (in front of, behind, beside) allow children to explore the limitations and possibilities of each particular body shape.

Forming group shapes introduces new spatial relationships which emerge from meeting and moving together, meeting and moving apart, approaching and encircling or surounding.

Static or "frozen" shapes require greater control of body parts through the distribution of body weight (that is, the difference between interlocking or open shapes involves differences in the flow and control of energy).

Group shapes do not always remain static but may be used in explorations of locomotor movement.

Explorations in Rhythmic Patterns

Problem I: To explore rhythm by organizing it into long and short beats.

A. *Each of you uses time differently in dance, and the way you show it is through rhythm.*
   1. If-I-speak-to-you-with-out-chang-ing-my-voice-how-does-it-sound? What is missing? (Children's responses: Flat tone, no tone, all the same, no rhythm.)
   2. Sound and rhythm go together; let's explore the rhythms of your own name.
   3. What is your name? Clap it exactly as you say it; your feet will move to the rhythm your hands clap, and your whole body will move to your name. How are you going to move? (Each child responds in turn.)
   4. As you move across the floor, talk the movements you are making so that you can hear them as well as feel them; be sure to end your movement on the last syllable of your name.
   5. Let's have the whole group talk the movements with you. (Each child moves alone for the first phrase, then teacher or another child picks up the rhythm on the drum.)
      a. "Chris-to-pher An-tho-ny John-son" (Claps inaccurately.) Did he clap "John-son" or "John-on-son"? Take it again, Chris. (Chris claps and the group responds.) How will you move to it?

      run   run   run   jump   jump   jump   leap   leap
      —   —   —   —   —   —   ——   ——

      short   short   short   short   short   short   long   long

b. "Doug -las   Ee -yore   Vo -gel"
   (Eeyore, like in Winnie the Pooh?)
   skip and   skip and jump jump

   ——— —   ——— — ——— ———

   long short long short long long

c. "Jen- i - fer   Joyce   In - dic - tor"
   run run run   run   step leap leap

   —— — ———   —— ——— ———

   short short short   long   short long long

   Both legs come off the floor when you leap, don't they? If you take
   a big step on *Joyce,* it's not a run, it's a leap. Do it again and feel
   the difference between a long and a short step.*

6. How can you use your arms to get bigger movement?
7. Now come across the floor in groups of four, taking turns moving to
   each one's name. (Accompaniment follows each group's rhythmic pattern.)

B. *Every sentence that you speak has a rhythm of long and short beats; let's
   put the rhythm of the words and the movement together.*
   1. What street do you live on? Say the whole sentence, "I live on _____
      _____." When you feel the rhythm, clap it.
   2. As we listen to each person, we can hear that some of you have different
      streets but with the same rhythm.
   3. Listen to the drum speak your different rhythms and see if you can tell
      what street it is. (Teacher may call on children with streets of same and
      different rhythmic patterns to emphasize similarity and contrast.)
   4. Now tell us what street you live on by just clapping the rhythm. (Other
      children identify the rhythm; group can also create choral rhythms or
      diverse rhythmic sound patterns.)
   5. Come across the floor one at a time on the diagonal. First clap the
      sentence as you say it, then move to that rhythm.
   6. The drum will help you hear the long and short beats; you begin and
      the drum will follow you.

C. *Now let's put two rhythms together by moving to two names at the same
   time.*
   1. Work in partners; find a rhythmic pattern for each name and move first
      to one and then the other.
   2. Now put the two names together; explore different directions while you
      are moving in the same space.
   3. Repeat the pattern three times; change from one name to the other or
      use them both together.
   4. Use parts of your body other than your feet to "talk" the rhythm; let
      your arms help you move through space.

* These solutions are excerpted from the author's master's thesis, *Creative Rhythmic
Movement for Young Children, UCLA,* 1959, pp. 72–77.

ADDITIONAL ELEMENTS   *Direction, range, difference in energy expended on long and short beats.*

UNDERSTANDINGS FOR TEACHERS—PROBLEM I

Beginning with a personal reference such as his own name or street, a child becomes aware that the rhythm of his syllables corresponds to rhythmic units of longer or shorter time. Whether he moves accurately to his own sounds demonstrates his kinesthetic response to the pulse that he establishes.

Relating rhythmic patterns to verbal symbols emphasizes the association of sound and rhythm. Each child says his own name until it loses its immediate connotation and becomes a rhythmic pattern. In hearing and observing others, children discover that each name has its own peculiar rhythmic quality or inflection which can be translated in movement terms. When several children respond to the same pattern, each shows a different use of space and force.

The drum in this case serves only to emphasize and reinforce the sound–rhythm relationship established by each child.

Problem II: To explore the relationship of different rhythmic patterns using imagery.

A. *A clock tells time in three ways. What are they? (Children's responses: Hours, minutes, seconds.)*

1. Your torso is the face of a clock; use only your torso to show hours, minutes, or seconds.
2. Using your whole body, show how your clock moves from 12 o'clock, 3 o'clock, 6 o'clock, 9 o'clock, and back to 12 o'clock again.
3. Some of you are moving only on the hour; some are moving on every beat; and some are moving in one big circle from hour to hour.
4. Do it again and feel how many beats it takes you to get from one hour to another. Let's look at some of the clocks and hear their "tick-tock." (Teacher picks up each child's beat on some percussion instrument to emphasize different rhythmic patterns.)
5. Some of you are taking four beats, some three. Listen to the rhythm of the drum and change the hour each time you hear a strong beat. (Teacher alternates between 4/4 and 3/4 time to demonstrate different rhythmic patterns and to encourage response to accented beats.)
6. Your movement has a different quality when you use three beats or four beats. Can you feel the difference? What kinds of movements are you making?
7. Keep one hand on the hour and move the other hand on the minutes; you can move the minute hand anywhere in space. (Teacher alternates between 4/4 and 3/4 time, playing enough phrases of each so that children can sense the difference in movement.)
8. Now change the hour on every fifth beat; feel the five beats in your body as you hear them. (Teacher plays 5/4 time, accenting the first beat of every measure.)

B. *Let's explore the different rhythms of the minutes and seconds against the steady beat of the hours.*
   1. Divide into three groups—hours, minutes, seconds. "Hours," move with your whole body; "minutes," move with your arms; "seconds," use only your legs.
   2. Here are some instruments which have sounds like a clock; listen to each one and decide which sounds like hours, minutes, or seconds. (Teacher distributes instruments arbitrarily and children experiment with different sounds and rhythms; children alternate between playing and listening.)
   3. Now some of you from each group take the instruments and sit together so you can hear each other; watch your own group very carefully before you play, so that you can pick up your rhythm; let's have the hour establish the steady beat.
   4. Take a partner. When you have developed a rhythmic pattern, the people with instruments will pick up your rhythm. (After a period of free exploration, each group improvises before the class.)

Problem III: To explore, using imagery, underlying and divided beats.

A. *In a cuckoo clock, when does the cuckoo jump out? (Children's responses: Every hour, every fifteen minutes.)*
   1. Take a partner. One person move to the steady beat of the clock; one person move only on the cuckoo.
   2. Make your own sounds on the cuckoo's beat. Feel the beat as you move together. (After movements have been improvised, accompaniment may be used only for the cuckoo or to reinforce the accented and underlying beat.)

ADDITIONAL ELEMENTS   *Spatial relationships; body shape; range; difference in energy expended in the two rhythms.*

   3. Work in groups of threes. Two of you move to the ticking of the clock. One person moves only on the "cuckoo." Keep the rhythm going. (Teacher picks up underlying beat on drum for each group; plays accented beat with a higher-pitched instrument, for example, tone block. Children may also accompany each other.)

ADDITIONAL ELEMENTS   *Differences in body shape; range; level; direction; new spatial relationships created by three people.*

B. *Machines have different rhythms and sounds; let's explore some of them.*
   1. Work in partners. One of you start the rhythm of a machine part and make a sound as you move so that we can hear the beat.
   2. The other person should find a different movement with a different rhythm and attach himself to the moving part.
   3. Keep the rhythm going so that we can see which part is establishing the

steady beat and which part is dividing the beats. You can be in one place or you can move through space.

4. Both partners in the "pistons" and the "gears" are moving in the same rhythm. Try to find two different rhythms.
5. Now choose as many people as you need for your machine.

UNDERSTANDINGS FOR TEACHERS—PROBLEMS II–III

Through these explorations children become aware that rhythm is experienced as different groupings of beats. In rhythmic time the underlying pulse is established by the child, and divided beats must be sensed within his framework.

A clock is a familiar image and is easily adapted to a child's ability to establish his own "time." Working in partners gives children an opportunity to observe the relationship between different rhythms and to explore different possibilities with different body parts.

The association of sound and rhythm offers two sources for developing a "listening ear": (1) recognizing different tone qualities and rhythmic patterns made by various instruments playing together and (2) relating sounds to the movements of others.

In experiences with clocks and machines, children are combining an auditory (hearing) and kinesthetic (muscle) sense, which helps them understand that both sounds and movement form rhythmic patterns.

Problem IV: To explore the relationship between tempo and force.

A. *When you move fast or slow, you use different amounts of energy. Let's explore the feeling of* heavy *and* slow.
  1. Think of the biggest bell you've ever seen. Pull that big, heavy bell using your whole body. Feel the weight as you pull the rope.

  ADDITIONAL ELEMENTS   Force: *slow, sustained movement;* space: *range between legs, between arms and torso;* body shape; time: *rhythmic pattern of even beats.*

  2. How many beats did it take each of you to ring the bell? Do it again and feel the number of beats you use to move from high to low. (Teacher may accompany on drum or gong to make children more conscious of their own rhythm.)

B. *Now let's explore the difference between* light *and* fast. *What makes a small bell ring? (Children's response: Clapper.)*
  1. Work in twos. One of you move as the bell, one as the clapper.
  2. Are you both moving at the same time? What is the difference in your rhythm?
  3. Does the bell use the same kind of energy as the clapper when they move?
  4. Now put your movements together and each couple make a bell.
  5. Using machines again, make the parts move first loud and fast; then change the movements so that they are light and slow.

UNDERSTANDINGS FOR TEACHERS—PROBLEM IV

Although the focus is on time and force, all the elements of movement are involved. As in the problem of the clocks, there are spatial *relationships involving:* range *(space between the legs, between the arms, between the arms and torso);* direction *(up and down, side to side, in and out);* body shape *(relation of bell to clapper);* rhythmic *groupings (bell establishes underlying beat, clapper divides the beat). Distribution of* body weight *differs between slow and heavy (sustained movement) and light and fast (percussive movement).*

By combining these qualities children are able to experience contrasts in the dynamics of both force and time.

Explorations in Metric Pattern

Problem I: To explore groupings of beats within a metric structure.

A. *In certain rhythms everyone moves in the same amount of time.*
1. Jump to the beat of the drum. When the drum stops, you stop. (Teacher beats a given number of measures, using different groupings of beats, for example, 4, 5, 6, 8, 9.)
2. How many beats did you jump? (Initially, children's responses may differ because of lack of kinesthetic awareness of movement and timing.)
3. Listen again and jump one measure with the drum. When the drum stops, you jump the same number of beats alone. (Teacher establishes a steady beat in an even or uneven pattern.)
4. How many beats did you jump by yourselves?
5. Now let's take turns with the drum. Beat a measure of as many beats as you wish but keep them steady. Everyone else jump to the beat.
6. *(To the group)* How many beats did you jump? *(To the drummer)* How many beats did you play?

B. *You can use the same number of beats but change the feeling of your movement.*
1. How many ways can you jump? How high? How low? Can you jump forward? Backward?
2. Jump as high as you can. What will help you jump higher? (Teacher accompanies as before.)
3 Now jump high for the first measure, low on the next, medium on the next. How many measures did you jump?
4. This time walk the first measure with the drum; on the next measure change your level and walk without the drum. When the drum begins again, rest on that measure. How many measures did you walk?

C. *Different members of your family move in different ways.*
1. How do fathers walk? Everyone take space on the floor and let's hear the sound of your feet as well as see them. (After observing, teacher establishes 4/4 tempo on the drum, plays half-note value for each step.)

2. How do mothers or grandmothers walk? How do they walk if they are wearing high heels? (Teacher plays quarter notes which are twice as fast as fathers' rhythm, using tone gourd, tone block, or tambourine.)

3. How do babies walk? (Teacher plays eighth notes or triplets on triangle, bells, claves.)

4. Divide into three groups—fathers, mothers, babies—and sit in different parts of the room; move only when you hear your rhythm; sit down quickly when another group moves. (Teacher alternates among the three groups, playing four measures of 4/4 time for each.)

5. This time you'll all move together, so listen carefully for your own rhythm and come in on beat; move in different directions and watch the space around you.

6. Let's have five or six people playing instruments—one for the fathers, two or three for mothers and grandmothers, and two or three for babies; let's have the drum set the steady tempo.

7. Now divide into smaller groups; a few of you from each group come out on the floor and establish your own rhythm; when the people with instruments feel your beat, they'll pick it up. (Alternate movers and players; smaller groups make it easier for children to observe relationship between rhythm and sound.)

UNDERSTANDINGS FOR TEACHERS—PROBLEM I

Although children are responding to measurable, counted time, in the process of moving they are sensing the number of beats kinesthetically, without mechanically counting them. They are asked to count them verbally only after they have experienced them rhythmically.

For younger children the teacher controls the groupings of beats so that there is no confusion among the children as to the pattern being presented. Older children, when given time to experiment with instruments, can more readily establish a steady, consistent beat.

The association of sound *and* rhythm *again strengthens a "listening ear" and a consciousness of the relationship of both elements to* movement. *In part C, a "listening ear" is required of both movers and players, because they are actively involved in all three elements.*

Problem II: To explore how groupings of beats form measures.

A. *Let's put different groupings of beats together to make measures.*

1. Listen to the rhythm of the drum. If it walks, you walk. If it skips, you skip. When it stops, you stop. (Teacher beats 4/4 time—four walks, four skips, alternating for eight measures.)

2. How many times did you change from walks to skips? Now walk with the drum. Each time you hear a loud beat, move in a different direction. (Teacher plays four measures of eight beats, accents first beat of every measure.)

3. You can move in directions other than forward. Change very sharply and watch for people around you; stay on your own path.
4. How many beats did you walk before you changed directions? So how many beats are there in your measure?
5. Divide into small groups and move across the floor on the diagonal. Follow the beat of the drum, then come back the same way without the drum. (Teacher varies number of beats, rhythm, and tempo for each group.)
6. *(To the participants)* How many beats did you feel? *(To the observers)* Did they come back in as many beats as the drum played?

ADDITIONAL ELEMENTS *Spatial awareness of other moving bodies; direction, path; use of different locomotor movements relating to different rhythmic patterns played on drum.*

B. *Now you can make measures of four beats and each one of you will move on your own beat.*
1. Divide in groups of four in different parts of the room. Each person in the group count aloud so we can see how many 1's, 2's, 3's, 4's will be moving together.
2. When you hear your number, make a lunging movement into space using your whole body and hold it for all four beats. Then quickly stand up at the end of the measure and start again on 1.
3. Make a group shape as you come in "on beat." Don't touch each other, but work in the same space. (Each group may move for four measures of four beats to establish feeling of continuity. Each child's movement will differ in duration, depending on the number of his beat, for example, 1 is the longest, 4 is the shortest.)

ADDITIONAL ELEMENTS Space: *range, level, body shape, group shape;* force: *that required to hold duration of beat.*

UNDERSTANDINGS FOR TEACHERS—PROBLEM II

In part A, changing the rhythm at each measure helps children sense the length of the measure and helps them recognize and respond quickly to different rhythmic groupings. Initially, children may not change directions sharply, but it is part of learning to respond to their own impulse.

Percussive accompaniment while children are moving reinforces the feeling that groupings of beats fall naturally into measures; as a result, children are better able to rely on their own kinesthetic sense to repeat the same rhythmic patterns accurately.

Singing games are effective in helping very young children develop a sense of measure. An example is, "Did you ever see a Lassie?" Children alternate standing in the middle of a circle and initiate a movement in 3/4 time to correspond to the words

go / this way and / that way and /
3   1   2   3   1   2   3

Other examples are such songs as "Shoo, Fly, Don't Bother Me" * *(2/4 time) and "On, Roll On,"* † *(6/8).*

Problem III: To explore the relationship of accented beats to time and force in movement.

A. *How can you make some movements feel more important than others?*
1. Listen to the beats of the drum. They may not all be the same, so listen first so that your body will know what to do. Now jump! (Teacher first plays six beats; then eight, six even and two accented.)
2. What happens on the smaller jumps (accented beats)? What happens to your jumps when you have a longer count?

ADDITIONAL ELEMENTS   Space: *on a longer beat, movement covers more space and has greater range;* force: *difference in energy expended on long and short beats.*

3. Now take an easy walk with the drum and stop when the drum stops. (Teacher beats a steady rhythm of twelve beats in 6/8 time.)
4. This time when you hear a louder beat, make a different kind of movement; put more energy into it. (Teacher plays three measures of 6/8 time, accenting first and fourth beats.)
5. What other parts of your body can you use?

B. *Let's put some of your ideas together and combine accented and even movements.*
1. Listen to the rhythm; make a big movement on the first important beat and a smaller movement on the second accent; let your arms also move in a big and small way so that your whole body moves to the rhythm. Children experience a listing, swinging movement around the accents. (Teacher may play tambourine, striking on accents and shaking on other beats.)
2. This time the rhythm is going to change; begin with the drum but listen as you are moving so you can feel the number of beats between each accent. (Teacher plays four measures of 4/4 time; accents first beat of measure.)
3. As you are walking, clap on the first beat, hop on the second, leap on the third, and jump on the fourth; walk in a big circle around the room.
4. Are you hopping and leaping on the same foot? Let's do it again.
5. Now the accented beat is going to change in each measure. Find ways of showing it in different kinds of movement. It can be louder, softer, lighter, heavier, larger, or smaller. (Teacher plays eight measures of 4/4 time and shifts accent to first, second, third, fourth beat in each succeeding measure; then she repeats the phrase:

---

* See *Songs to Grow On*, p. 108, listed in Bibliography.
† Ibid., p. 74.

4/4 / ⌐ — — — / — ⌐ — — / — — ⌐ — /

— — — ⌐ / ⌐ — — — /

(repeat)

ADDITIONAL ELEMENTS Space: *differentiated use of body parts (arms, head, torso, legs, feet); range; direction; level;* force: *contrast between more and less energy expended on accented and unaccented beats.*

UNDERSTANDINGS FOR TEACHERS—PROBLEM III

In this problem three types of responses to accented beats are experienced: an accent in relation to a grouping of beats, accents which divide beats into different rhythmic patterns (4/4, 3/4, 6/8), and irregular accents within a metric structure (of 4/4 time).

Accent as a time–force phenomenon is expressed through different qualities of movement (light, heavy, loud, soft, large, small) and is important for further improvisations.

Problem IV: To explore phrasing in response to percussive and melodic accompaniment.

A. *Let's put measures of beats together into longer phrases.*
   1. Divide into groups of four sitting in different parts of the room. (Teacher places four instruments in the middle of the floor, for example, a tone block, a maraca, claves, and a triangle.)
   2. Count off as you did before so that you know who are the 1's, 2's, 3's, and 4's who will be moving together. (Groups alternate for each problem.)
   3. When you hear your number, each one from a group take four giant steps toward the center, pick up an instrument in four beats, beat three beats, replace it in one beat, and walk back in four beats.
   4. Listen to the tempo of the drum; run as fast as you can to an instrument; look at it and return to your place when you hear the drumbeat. (Teacher plays eight running beats in; eight running beats out.)
   5. Now run to the center without accompaniment; on the drum signal, run back in the same tempo.
   6. This time walk toward the center without the drum, count the number of walks in, play your instrument for the same number of beats, and walk back the same way.
   7. *(To the observer)* How many beats did they play? *(To the participants)* How many beats did you walk? Not everyone used the same amount of beats in their phrases.

UNDERSTANDINGS FOR TEACHERS—PROBLEM IV

Children become aware of phrasing as groupings of measures which do not necessarily have the same number of beats and which have different patterns.

By first responding to a given pattern of measures and then repeating it by sensing the groupings of beats kinesthetically, children are learning to demonstrate a combination of related movements that correspond to a musical phrase.

Explorations in Swinging Movement

Problem I: To experience swinging as an easy flow of energy initiated in different body parts.

    A. *What parts of your body can you swing?*
1. Start very small; stand with your feet slightly apart and swing your head gently from side to side; let your ears touch your shoulders.
2. Swing your shoulders; feel your weight shift from one side to the other. What happens to your arms as you swing?
3. Now let your arms carry your body in space.
4. What's the rhythm of your swing? Do it again and listen to the drum. (Teacher picks up 3/4 rhythms from those children who have established a regular pattern; as the movement continues, the rest of the group accommodates to that rhythm.)
5. So it's a "1, 2, 3" rhythm. On which beat are you using the most force?
6. Now in big, easy movements swing your head, shoulders, arms, and the whole upper part of your body.
7. Some of you are bending at the waist and your arms are almost touching the floor; let's all swing lower and lower and lower.
8. What happens to your legs as you swing lower in space?

    B. *Your whole body is a swing; you are either sitting in it or being pushed in it.*
1. Where does it take you in space?
2. What will help you swing higher when you are standing still?
3. Feel the air passing through your fingers and pass your face as you swing.
4. What parts of your body are you using now? In what directions are you moving?
5. When you swing as far as you can go, some of you almost fall out! How can you control your body and still make the swings big?

ADDITIONAL ELEMENTS   Space: *range, level, body shape;* time: *even, rhythmic pattern of groupings of threes.*

    C. *Now let your swings take you through space. Swing up, swing down, swing side to side and around.*
1. Feel the weight from the middle of your body so that your legs and arms can swing freely.

ADDITIONAL ELEMENTS   Space: *direction, level, range, body shape;* time: *steady "1, 2, 3" rhythmic pattern in varying tempos.*

Problem II: To explore contrasts in qualities of force in swinging movement.

A. *Let's explore the feeling of swinging fast and light.*
   1. Have you ever seen a grandfather's clock? What part of it swings back and forth? (Children may not know the word *pendulum*.)
   2. Begin with little swings of a small pendulum using your heads. Feel the rhythm of the "tick-tock."
   3. Keep your head moving and pick up the swing in one arm; now add your other arm and keep the rhythm going.
   4. Where does a little swing take you in space? Are you using a lot of force?
   5. Listen to the rhythm of your swings; when you feel it, continue moving with it. (Teacher picks up 3/4 time from children, who have established a moderately fast tempo; beats lightly on drum so that children relate the amount of force to the rhythm.)

B. *Now feel the difference between swinging fast and light, and swinging slow and heavy.*
   1. Your pendulum is in a much larger clock, so it takes longer to get from one side to another.
   2. Begin with small, light swings again; as your body moves, feel the pendulum become heavier and heavier and swing further and further in space. (Teacher may accompany on percussive instruments, using two different qualities of sounds to reinforce contrast in force, for example, maracas, raspa, guiro for fast and light and gong, drum, cymbals for slow and heavy.)
   3. Do the little swings take as much force as the heavy swings? Do they take as much time?
   4. Feel the weight of the pendulum flow from the top of your head, to your shoulders, to your torso, to your legs; feel it from the middle of your body out through your arms.

UNDERSTANDINGS FOR TEACHERS—PROBLEMS I–II

Exploring swinging movements in different parts of the body helps children become conscious that in each part, energy is released and controlled in different dimensions. They become aware that the force expended in small body parts exists in their own space–time relationship and that when the whole body is involved, the movements increase in range but may be of longer duration.

Coordinating body parts in swinging movement calls forth a sense of balance when the weight shifts, elevating a leg in space. In problems of this nature children experience the feeling of shifting the center of gravity.

In problem II, expressing different qualities within the same type of movement helps children build a broader vocabulary. The image of a pendulum is used to emphasize the contrast between the two qualities of force, but children may suggest other images that are equally appropriate.

Explorations in Sustained Movement

Problem I: To experience sustained movement as tension and relaxation.

A. *Some movements we make are just like breathing—big and strong, weak and little, slow and even.*
   1. Sit together on the floor. Press your hands into your chest and take a deep breath. As you let it out, push the air away from you, slowly, slowly.
   2. Pull the air back toward you as if it were really heavy; take a breath and keep the movement slow and even.
   3. When you bring it back to your chest, explode it out in all directions; let's hear your breath "swoosh" out at the same time.
   4. Now slowly lift the air in your hands over your head and drop it down fast; scoop it up again and drop it down; let your head follow the movement.
   5. This time feel the space between your arms; scoop up as much air as you can over your head; hold it there a moment and let it flow gently down to the floor. (Repeat several times for a feeling of the continuous flow of energy.)

   ADDITIONAL ELEMENTS Time: *phrasing; contrast of fast and slow expressed through tension and relaxation;* space: *increased range of arms and torso; beginning of swinging movement.*

B. *Let's explore the feeling of "slow and heavy" using your whole body.*
   1. Stand with your feet slightly apart. You're going to fold and unfold, as if each part of you were very heavy.
   2. Feel the weight from the top of your head and let it carry your body slowly downward; drop from your shoulders, your waist, your hips, until you feel folded in half.
   3. Rest! Now use different parts of your body to unfold; feel that you have strings pulling you up from your behind, your back, your shoulders, your neck, and lastly, your head. [Teacher may accompany on drum to establish slow tempo and an even grouping of beats for phrasing (for example, eight beats to fold, four to rest, eight to unfold).]
   4. This time, bounce with the drum so that each part of your body drops lower and lower; when your hands touch the floor, bounce up again in the same way. [Teacher plays three beats for each body part, including the rest (for example, six measures of three beats for each phrase).]

   ADDITIONAL ELEMENTS Time: *responding to beat, phrasing;* space: *levels, body shape.*

Problem II: To explore qualities of force using different body parts.

A. *Feel the difference between bending and stretching in other parts of your body.*

1. Sit on the floor; open your legs as wide as you can and let your energy flow right out of your toes. (Teacher sitting on floor with children may demonstrate the difference in the stretch between flexed and pointed toes.)
2. Sit as straight as you can and push your arms out from your shoulders; feel a long stretch from the middle of your body to your fingertips.
3. Can you reach over and touch the foot on the same side as your hand? What is your other arm doing? Is your body bending or stretching?
4. Can you touch your toes with both hands at the same time? Feel the difference in the stretch when your toes are up and when they are pointed down. Where do you feel the stretch?
5. Bounce with the drum, then come back to a sitting position very slowly. (Teacher plays a given number of measures of bounces and one measure for rising.)

B. *You can also stretch the same part of your body in different ways.*
1. Have you seen a cat stretch its back? Find a position so that you can stretch just your back and feel it in your muscles. Move slowly and evenly.
2. That's only one shape and you can even make that stretch feel stronger. Where do the muscles in your stomach go when you curve your back?
3. Change the shape smoothly from a curve to an arch. Where do you feel the change in your muscles?

UNDERSTANDINGS FOR TEACHERS—PROBLEMS I–II

By exploring such natural movements as pushing, pulling, bending, and stretching, children begin to identify sustained movement as a continuous flow of impulses marked by contrast in tension and relaxation. Associating such qualities with breathing helps reinforce the organic relationship between the strength of a movement and the ability to release and control energy.

Because force only exists in space–time, exerting effort in different body parts produces an awareness that each part uses a larger or smaller range of space and creates a different body shape, and that a slow, even tempo produces a special kind of rhythmic pattern.

Problem III: To explore different elements of sustained movement using imagery.

A. *How many ways can you push a doorbell without using your hands?*
1. It's a small doorbell. What parts would you use to push it?
2. It's a heavy doorbell. What parts of you can push it?
3. Ring your doorbell more than once with the same part of your body. Ring it in the same rhythm three times.

ADDITIONAL ELEMENTS   *Rhythm is added as another dimension of force; that is, ringing three beats is a measure; if repeated several times it becomes a phrase.*

4. Now push a doorbell with two parts of your body, using light and heavy rings.

B. *Can you stretch different parts of your body just like a rubber band?*
   1. Sit on the floor; imagine that you have a rubber band between your hands; stretch it as long as you can and make it small again.
   2. If you pull it too fast it will snap, so move very slowly; feel the pull in your hands and bring it back the same way.*

C. *When you look in a mirror, the "other you" seems to move exactly as you do.*
   1. Take a partner and face each other; one of you be the person; the other be the image in the mirror.
   2. The mirror is only up to your waist, so use only the upper part of your body.
   3. Use as much space as you wish but keep looking in the mirror, so that you are watching each other.
   4. The "person" will begin the movement; keep it even in space and time so that your image will feel what you are doing and can follow.
   5. After you've explored each other's movements, we will look at each couple; we should be able to tell which person is leading the movement. (Group observes and makes suggestions as to which child is initiating the movement; then children change roles.)

[Movements require isolation of upper torso and use of upper body parts (head, shoulders, arms, hands); lower torso remains still. All elements of movement are involved—*time:* establishing a tempo that partner can follow (slower tempo requires more control of energy); *spatial patterns:* range, body shape, focus; *laterality:* (right and left sidedness) response to a reversed "mirror image."]
   6. What qualities of movement did you use to stay together—fast, slow, big, small, light, heavy?
   7. Some of you made very small gestures; feel that you are moving in slow motion because you want your image to know what you are doing.
   8. Now the mirror is from your head to the floor; use full body movement and focus on your partner all the time so that you don't lose each other.

UNDERSTANDINGS FOR TEACHERS—PROBLEM III

Pushing a door bell and stretching a rubber band are images which are used to express simple, conventional gestures in movement terms.

In part A, for example, how does a child control his energy in different parts of his body when he changes from heavy to light movements? How does he become aware that large and small body parts can move in different rhythms which reflect the amount of force he uses? In both A and B, how does he control body weight when he is coordinating the force in two body parts?

Part C also derives from a conventional image but the response is not pantomime (that is, literal gestures such as brushing teeth, combing hair, washing face, or making faces). If such gestures are used initially, the qualities of movement need to be exaggerated and abstracted. Essentially, children are responding

---

* Solutions to this problem may be seen in the film "Children Dance," produced and co-directed by the author and Naima Prevots.

to each other kinesthetically, through movement cues using the basic elements of time and space as well as force.

Problem IV: To experience sustained movement in relation to balance and body weight.

 A. *Feel how much energy it takes to lift one part of your body.*
  1. Sit on the floor and lift one leg very slowly as high as you can.
  2. Can you keep your knee straight? What is your other leg doing?
  3. How are you supporting your body?

 B. *Feel the difference when you lift two parts together.*
  1. Can you lift both legs in the air?
  2. Feel the weight in the middle of your body as you move as slowly and evenly as you can.
  3. Some of you are sitting and some of you are lying on your backs; this time begin from a sitting position. Are your movements lighter or heavier? Faster or slower?

 C. *Find your sense of balance when you lift three parts of your body.*
  1. Stand up and shake out your legs. As you are moving, feel the weight in the middle of your body.
  2. Move slowly, but use your own tempo to keep your balance.
  3. Are you using more space than when you moved two parts of your body?

Problem V: To experience sustained movement through tension and resistance.

 A. *Let's explore the feeling of pushing space.*
  1. Stand in a big circle without touching each other. Push the air away from you on one side of your body in a steady, even movement.
  2. Now use the weight of your whole body to push the air as far as you can.
  3. What parts of you will help you push further into space?
  4. You've put more space between your legs and that helps you push into space. Where do you feel the stretch in your muscles?

  ADDITIONAL ELEMENTS Space: *range, level, body shape;* time: *slow tempo with even rhythm.*

 B. *Now feel the difference between pushing space and pushing something solid.*
  1. Take an easy walk around the room in all directions. When you pass someone, nudge them gently with your shoulder and continue walking.
  2. Now walk again, and as you pass someone in front, on the side, or behind you, nudge them with a different part of your body.
  3. This time as you pass, push strongly against someone. While one is pushing, the other should try to keep your place; then move apart quickly and keep walking.

ADDITIONAL ELEMENTS   Spatial relationships: *created by contact and by moving in different directions with others*; time: *rhythmic pattern of long and short, accented or unaccented beats created by pushing and walking.*

4. Now work in partners; one of you push and the other resist; move together slowly and control your bodies so that you don't collapse.
5. There are other parts of you that are strong besides your arms and hands; feel the "push" in another part of your body.

ADDITIONAL ELEMENTS   Space: *direction, level, range, body shape.*

C. *What is the opposite feeling of push? Explore the difference between pushing and pulling.*

1. Take your partners again or choose new ones; one of you will pull, the other will be pulled; then change.
2. Feel the weight come from the middle of your body so that you don't lose your balance by pulling too hard.
3. What parts of your body are you using when you pull? What parts of you are being pulled?

ADDITIONAL ELEMENTS   Spatial relationships: *range, level, body shape.*

UNDERSTANDINGS FOR TEACHERS—PROBLEMS IV–V
In problem IV, children must control different groups of muscles against the pull of gravity by finding ways of sustaining and balancing their body weight. By elevating two or three parts of the body at the same time, whether from a stand-

233

ing or sitting position, children sense that different parts exert different amounts of force, move at different rates of speed, and cover a greater or lesser range of space.

In problem V, children are experiencing different qualities of sustained movement first by creating tension within their own muscles (for example, pushing air), and then by responding to the resistance of a real object (for example, pushing and pulling each other). In working with partners in a push-pull relationship, children learn to adjust their output of energy through a balance of resistance and acquiescence.

Explorations in Percussive Movement

Problem I: To explore qualities of percussive movement in relation to sounds of percussive instruments.

    A. *What do we mean by percussive instruments? What kinds of movements do we use to make them produce sounds? (Children's responses: Shaking, striking, hitting, beating.)*

        1. There is a special family of instruments that just makes shaking sounds. What are those instruments? (Children's responses: Bells, maracas, tambourines, rattles, gourds.)

        2. How am I playing this tambourine? (Shaking may elicit both striking and twisting movements. Beating may elicit sharp, staccato movements.)

        3. When the tambourine is shaking, some of you are twisting different parts of your body. Let's explore that feeling together.

        4. What parts of you can you twist when you are sitting down? Kneeling? Standing?

        5. Now what parts of you can you shake? Can you start with one part, then two, then three, and finally shake your whole self?

ADDITIONAL ELEMENTS Space: *use of different body parts, increased range of torso and arms from sitting to standing position;* time: *different rhythmic patterns for different body parts, different tempos among children in standing positions.*

        6. Let's give your movements a rhythm, just like the instrument. I'll shake and strike the tambourine in different ways and you follow; then you work out your own rhythms. (Teacher establishes definite rhythmic groupings in phrases of four or five measures.)

        7. Divide in small groups and choose an instrument that you must shake to make a sound; play it first and listen to it; then pick up the feeling in your movement and let it take you through space. (Children may be divided into alternating groups of "players" and "movers.")

        8. Some of you are playing maracas and some are playing bells. How do

you move when you shake the bells? Fast? Slow? Are your movements big or little?

9. Make the bells dance with light, fast, shaking movements.
10. Explore movements with the maracas in the same way. Can you shake them high–medium–low? Can you turn while you are shaking different parts? Make a shaking dance as if there were maracas attached to every part of your body.
11. Let's have some people accompany with tambourines, bells, and maracas; the rest move in small groups to any instrument you wish; feel that the force of your movement is the same that produces the sound. (Each group moves separately with its own accompaniment.)

B. *There's another family of instruments that produces sounds by hitting or beating. What are those instruments? (Children's responses: Drum, claves, tone gourd, tone block, triangle.)*
   1. Let's listen to the different qualities of sound made by these instruments; we'll have a small group play at a time; then we'll take turns.
   2. Experiment with as many different ways of making sounds as you can. What kinds of movements are you making—heavy, light, even, uneven, loud, soft?
   3. The rest of you move in twos and threes to the different sounds and rhythms that you hear. We will watch and see if we can tell what instrument you are moving with. (Children with instruments need to establish a consistent rhythmic pattern of long and short, accented or unaccented beats so that children moving will not be confused.)
   4. *(To the players)* Do you use the same amount of force when you beat a drum as when you hit a triangle? *(To the movers)* Are your movements the same with the drum as with the triangle?

UNDERSTANDINGS FOR TEACHERS—PROBLEM I

Using instruments to reinforce percussive qualities lends another dimension to children's awareness that the energy which produces sounds also produces movement. Both "players" and "movers" need guided exploration in understanding this relationship and in being able to coordinate both elements. Emphasizing the difference between the drum and the triangle points to the contrast between fast and heavy (drum) and fast and light (triangle), as well as the gradations in between supplied by the other instruments.

Working in terms of "families" of instruments helps children understand that in relation to different sounds and varying degrees of force, the body responds with different types of movements. Twisting is an excellent example of the effect of force on a movement, that is, twisting percussively to maracas or a tambourine produces one quality, whereas twisting in sustained movement would completely change its expressive character.

Problem II: To experience percussive qualities in terms of heavy and light movement.

A. *Let's explore the feeling of moving fast and strong.*
1. Sit all tucked in or kneel on the floor; each time the drum beats, thrust a part of your body in space, as if you were poking a hole in the air; then quickly pull it back again. (Teacher plays heavy beats of relatively long duration with short pauses in between so that movements have a more thrusting than striking quality.)
2. You can use other parts of you besides your arms and hands; your legs, backs, and shoulders are strong, too. (Repeat previous rhythmic pattern.)
3. This time on every drum beat let each part of your body rise higher and higher until you are standing; then move back the same way, poking holes in the air as you go.

ADDITIONAL ELEMENTS   Space: *levels, range of body parts, body shape;* time: *responding to rhythmic patterns, feeling the duration of fast, heavy beats.*

B. *Now feel the difference when you move fast and light.*
1. Take space on the floor; feel that you have strings attached to each part of your body, like a marionette.
2. Hang loosely for a moment, but don't collapse. Feel the string at each point so that you'll know where the pull will come from.
3. Move one arm quickly and sharply; each time you move it change its position in space; now move the other arm; move them together or in opposition.
4. Add your shoulders so that your movements become bigger; now move your head, arms, and shoulders as if the strings of your marionette are being jerked. (Teacher may accompany on drum, claves, tone blocks, and so on, to reinforce sharp, percussive quality.)
5. Let the strings drop and hang from your waist; relax the whole upper part of your body. Rest.
6. This time feel the strings pull from your hips, stomach, back, chest, knees, legs, and feet; start from your hips and move each part separately.

ADDITIONAL ELEMENTS   Space: *range of body parts, isolation of upper from lower torso;* time: *fast, staccato rhythm.*

7. Drop all the strings and hang over your legs, with your knees bent.
8. Now as you unfold, feel the strings pull quickly and sharply; keep your whole body moving in different directions and on different levels. (Simple percussive accompaniment may be found in *Rhythms Productions Records,* "Rhythm Instruments with Folk Music from Many Lands," Cheviot Corporation. See bibliography.)

Problem III: To explore the contrast in feeling between percussive and sustained movement.

A. *Let's explore the difference in feeling between moving slow and heavy and fast and light.*

1. Begin from any position and make a slow, heavy movement; you may lift a huge rock, or be a leaf falling, or feel like a heavy storm cloud.

2. Keep the movement going until you hear the drum signal to stop. (Teacher may play a long sustained sound on a gong or a steady series of light beats on a drum, and signal at an arbitrary point.)

3. At the signal, change the movement from whatever position you are in to fast, striking, light movements; continue until you hear the signal (maybe your rock has become a feather or your leaf is caught up in a fast wind, or your storm cloud breaks into rain). (Teacher gives exploration of percussive movement a sufficient amount of time so that child finds himself in a new and unusual position to begin the next experience.)

4. Now from where you are, feel the weight of your movements and end them as slowly and evenly as you can.

5. Let's watch each other and see if we can tell what kinds of images you were thinking about as you moved from one quality to another.

UNDERSTANDINGS FOR TEACHERS—PROBLEMS II–III

In problem II, children are exploring percussive movements as force which begins abruptly and is stopped suddenly and quickly. In part B, isolation of the upper from the lower torso and articulation of small body parts allows children to experience the ways different parts of the body exert energy in space and time.

In problem III, contrast between fast and heavy and fast and light is an expression of the two polar elements of force—strong and weak. (Weak does not imply lacking energy, but expending relatively less energy to convey a particular movement quality.)

7
POETRY

Definition and Description

Why concern ourselves with poetry in the education of young children who are just beginning to grapple with the mysteries of the written word, or with very young children who cannot read or write at all? It is not because we are interested in developing their technical proficiency or in adding more words to their vocabulary. As with painting, sculpture, and dance, poetry is a non-discursive language, and even though it speaks through words, they do not lend themselves to conventional usage. Like pigments or clay or gestures, words are simply the materials which must be put into expressive relationships and given form. When children are given an opportunity to use language freely and inventively, they use words as a poet uses his medium—not as an end in itself, but as a means of expressing thoughts and feelings. A. E. Housman offers us an apt description when he writes, "Poetry is not the thing said but a way of saying it." [1] Our concern, then, is to give children a feeling for poetry which uses words as the language of experience.

We have approached the arts for children as essentially forms coming from the "inside out." Our definition of the arts as those symbolic modes of expression

[1] A. E. Housman, *The Name and Nature of Poetry* (Cambridge, England: Cambridge University Press, 1950), p. 35.

239

that record the quality of experience now serves to include poetry as the record of experience through imagery. We view poetry as an experience which "comes out" of a poet through words and sounds which can be used to "bring out" of a child those sounds and words which are meaningful to him. In the arts, it is this "inward–outward" relationship which allows a child to grasp those aspects of experience that he feels are significant and re-create them in visual, aural, tactile, and kinesthetic forms. In poetry, it is a way of expressing images which have metaphoric, not direct, significance.

When we say that poetry is the language of experience, we need to qualify that by stating that poetry uses words not for factual, informative reporting, but as indicators of feelings toward or responses to an experience, real or imagined. Yet although poetry is not concerned with the facts of the matter, it involves "real" things, for, "is not the feel of a thing as real as the thing felt?" [2] In reflecting back to our example in the opening chapter of the two modes of knowing about a snowstorm, one, through its factual content, the other by its emotional content, we are suggesting once again that conveying the quality or value of an experience is as meaningful as an analysis of that experience in terms of physical facts or logical sequences.

As with the language of experience, the value of poetry is twofold: first, it is a mode of reflecting on one's own experience, using all the senses, to probe into the meanings of things; second, it is a way of assessing experience by discovering how one person connects with another, not merely through the recognition of shared events, but through the realization of shared feelings, both positive and negative. The very nature of poetry requires that children of all ages and backgrounds use their own thoughts and their own patterns of language to *name* experiences and feelings. If they are to name what they uniquely want and feel, they must be encouraged to express as best they can the happenings in their lives and their ever-shifting responses. Because all children seek both individuality and relatedness, poetry can make them newly conscious of levels of their own being as well as make them sympathetically aware of the innermost thoughts and feelings of others. The concern of poetry, therefore, is not the definition or classification of conventional rules of language, but the reordering and re-creating of experience through words which are self-wrought.

Because experiences are both unique and general and no two individuals necessarily respond in the same way, how do we relate to the experience of poetry? Does this imply that a poem is not "supposed" to mean anything? Perhaps we need to clarify a common misconception among teachers that the function of poetry is to draw comparisons in the sense that something is *like* something else. But it is not "likeness" that we are seeking, we are seeking the uniqueness that we are able to find within an experience. The language of poetry is personal, yet it is still a means of communicating certain emotions or states of mind which a poet expresses that we share by virtue of the poem itself. As we have suggested, a poem may awaken children to the moods and

---

[2] C. D. Lewis, *The Poet's Way of Knowing* (Cambridge, England: Cambridge University Press, 1957), p. 5.

subtle feelings of each other, and although they may differ on the intent of a particular phrase, there is usually agreement as to its general tone. At the same time, we must accept ambiguity, for uniformity of response is not a condition for understanding its meaning. Even if there is disagreement, children share a common response—the common experience of the poem which enables them to perceive something they did not perceive before.

We begin to see that a poem does not merely encompass an experience; that is, it does not frame it in words, but forms it in its own image. What kind of meaning, then, can we find in a poem? To understand the nature of the poetic experience we borrow from John Ciardi, who asks, "How does a poem mean?" [3] In a literal, grammatical sense, the question is improperly stated, but in a figurative, nonliteral sense, it is well worth pondering, for it illuminates the very essence of poetry. What is particularly striking is that it runs counter to the traditional "what does a poem mean?" and leads to further exploration, such as: "How do meanings in poetry differ from those in spoken language or prose?" "How are images created?" "How is a poem formed out of rhythm, rhyme, imagery?" "How do these elements support and sustain the meaning?"

As with other art forms discussed here, we have for too long limited children's curiosity to "what is it?" In poetry such an approach tends to confine their imaginations to describing or "explaining" a poem rather than experiencing it through the senses and molding it with the mind. Inevitably, it becomes reduced to a prose statement, with both teacher and children forgetting in the process that it was originally a poem. For the most part, what has been euphemistically called the language arts program has singularly neglected the art of language.

To broaden the question of "What does a poem mean?" is to reflect on what poetry essentially is about. Stated simply, a poem is something that has to do with what happens in an individual's life, shaped by words as expressions of feelings, emotions, thoughts, or actions. Perhaps this simple description helps us understand that poetry can open up to children their own special qualities of intelligence, sensitivity, and wit as a way of knowing and feeling. But the poetic experience is not one of teachers reading and children passively listening to poems written by adults who attempt to simulate children's experiences. It rests largely with a teacher's ability to reveal the connections between the content and children's own experiences and to guide them toward discovering those connections. Above all, it is our willingness to listen to what children have to say and to encourage them to express ideas without concern for "is that true?" or "did that really happen?" What is forthcoming is not the meaning we would get from a case history which systematically records a child's mental events and happenings. What emerges is perhaps best expressed through the imagery of a contemporary poet who says, "Speaking as a poet, it is a paying of continual homage to that other self you live with that rarely ever gets a chance to stick his head out of your eyes, your nose, or your mouth to say hello to the world. Part of writing poetry is allowing this inner self to say its piece." [4]

[3] John Ciardi, *How Does a Poem Mean?* (Boston: Houghton Mifflin, 1959).
[4] Mark Strand (comments made at the 7th National Conference on the Arts in Education, Sarah Lawrence College, Bronxville, N.Y. September 1968).

Distinguishing Characteristics

Painting, sculpture, and dance strike us directly as tangible, physical forms to which we respond with a kind of immediacy. In painting we look at color as a shape, and in sculpture we see volume as a shape; this is exactly what they are. Even in dance, movements may have significance in themselves. But poetry deals with words almost totally as symbols and is therefore an abstraction of what is actually there. The shape of a word does not give us the shape of a meaning. On the contrary, we have to interpret the meanings to arrive at an entirely new meaning, for in the poetic image, words are never what they seem to be.

What is there that we can see in a word? Nothing of itself tells us anything about it. Painting, sculpture, and dance exist as physical entities both in the making and in the way we are going to perceive them. But a word or a poem have no physicality themselves (other than the arrangement of words on a page), and thus there is no directness either in the making or in the reading. Each art form functions as a total image yet we can look at a painting and get a visual experience of color, or a tactile experience of a plane in sculpture, or a kinesthetic response to a movement in dance. In poetry there is no such direct experience either in the making or responding. It is not its physical dimension that gives it quality; it is only the subjective character ascribed to it by the poet or listener that gives it its essence. Whether the original print is enlarged to cover the page or reduced to one tenth of its size, the subject matter and content remain unchanged. But in painting, dance, or sculpture, size and shape have everything to do with the expressive quality. Thus, poetry has no "body" in the sense that these other forms do. As we hear words, we are hearing, seeing, touching, feeling something once again removed, by evoking images which we as writer, reader, or listener bring to bear.

We have maintained throughout that every art form has its own way of happening. That is, each one works within its own limitations and conventions and yet pushes our perceptions toward the edges of the unknown. Thus, unless we perceive poetry in relation to its inner qualities, a poem is never revealed to us in terms of its own uniqueness. It is in keeping with this distinction and the kind of sensibility which it commands that we treat it somewhat differently within the framework of space–time–force. However, although space is a consideration, it is of lesser import and involves more sophisticated formal problems than are necessary or desirable in working with children.

A more meaningful characteristic is one which we raised in the preceding section of how meanings in poetry differ from those in spoken language. And because poetry begins with the word, we pose the question of how words express meanings. As an art form, poetry is distinguished from everyday language in the sense that it searches for and elicits responses to the qualitative aspects of experience. But the difference lies not only in the ends it seeks, but in the means toward achieving those ends. As such, there must be something unique in the nature of the words and the way they are presented that makes it possible for the poet (and we include the child poet) to formulate language in such a way that the essential quality speaks not only to him, but to us.

Herbert Read [5] projects an interesting theory about the way language may have developed. He suggests that language originally evolved very much like children's beginning speech patterns—first, to express feelings and to name things, then to associate between a vocal sound and a bodily sensation, then to use these sounds in communication. Although there are no scientific "proofs" to this theory (although the problem of how children in all cultures learn language is of major concern to linguists), we observe this happening as children begin to connect thoughts with words and to give meanings to things.

But in poetry, as in primordial language, naming is not merely giving a name to something known. Rather, we might entertain the notion that a thing becomes known only by naming. That is, in poetry, it is not a question of "learning" the appropriate name for what is already there, or of naming things that are already a part of one's consciousness or experience. As we discussed in painting, it is a question of the emotional content—of expressing an emotional attitude or value toward something deeply felt. Thus, it is not merely naming for the purpose of identifying objects or events; it is naming by way of identifying "inside" feelings toward "outside" phenomena. Yet it is exactly a child's level of experience and consciousness, reflective of his age and cultural background, that becomes his most immediate source. For it is children's own lives which often provide the richest material for discussion and response (oral or written), ranging from the realism of "here and now" to the fantasy of "there and then."

One of the ways in which we begin to open children up to their own powers of poetry making is by having them associate their feelings with familiar objects or events. For example, in an experimental literature program, composed of poets and teachers in the Washington, D.C., metropolitan area, second graders in predominately black, inner-city schools were introduced to poetry with the supportive comment, "There are a lot of ways of saying things, some of the ways are called poems." Children listened first to staff-created poems, shared ideas, and were encouraged to observe how differently words are arranged on a page. In order to release them from preconceived notions of what a poem "should" look like, it was suggested that poetry can be "anyway thisaway." [6] Children's responses were taped and typed so that they could see their "poetry-talk" in tangible form. Each poem, no matter how brief, occupied a single page, so that it assumed importance. They looked like this: [7]

```
                          rain:
                                trees
                          bend

old shoes:                                          spring:
   my feet                                                 when
  on the                                             the
     ground                                                 leaves
                                                    come
                                                         back
```

---

[5] *Forms of Things Unknown* (New York: World, 1963), p. 109.
[6] Jeanette Amidon, Lucille Clifton, Sam Cornish, *Anyway Thisaway* (Washington, D.C.: Central Atlantic Regional Educational Laboratory, n.d.).
[7] Ibid.

rain:
                  a hole
        in the
                     ceiling

After several months, each child was presented with a booklet of the poems read in the classroom entitled "Anyway Thisaway." It was a book to read or write in, but most of all, a book to own—something for each child about himself. The comment originally made to the children appears on the opening page as follows:

There are
a lot
of ways
of saying
things.
Some
of the ways
are
called
poems.

And as a kind of conceptual and poetic summation, we find on the last page:

Poems:
ways
of putting
down reasons
for things.[8]

Some of these poems were read several years later to fifth-grade children in a predominantly white, suburban school (in another part of the country) as an inspiration of how children create poetry. Examples of these fifth-grade poems are reproduced exactly as they were written:

sky
anowhere* place

toes
a family of five

Dreaming
Your own movie theater

* a nowhere.

Blindness:
The sight of immagination

Deafness:
The sound of immagination

Blindness:
a
   world
        of
             your
                  own

Flower:
Bee's resedence

Dreaming
Losing yourself

Grin
Sorrow's disguise

[8] Lucille Clifton (poet).

apples:
a house for worms

Thus, we come to realize that poetry is a way of using words that forms something into being, rather than being formed by meanings which already exist. In the forming of new, unpredictable meanings, words take on an intensity unlike any other kind of discourse. It is perhaps for this reason that it has been said that poets speak the "essential" word. While children do not have the same command of words in terms of diversity of vocabulary or sophistication of usage, they also seek a special way to speak of something special.

Ciardi's observation that "poetry is simply more than 'something to say' or simply an elaborate way of saying something or nothing" [9] is particularly fitting here. The implication is that the use of words in poetry is not the use of a ready-made language. Because we are dealing with another language, which speaks through its own images, we need to turn to other means for understanding the "hows" of poetry. Therefore, whatever significance we give words in speech or stories becomes intensified in the poetic qualities of their sounds, the images they convey, and most important, the unexpected associations they carry with them.

But we cannot look upon poetry as an embellishment or intensification of conventional communication in the sense of a "fancy" use of words, or as a factual statement which is merely "versified." Neither can we regard it as a substitute for what we have come to accept as "regular" language. It is a particular kind of symbolic language whose elements are not linguistic but perceptual, in the same way that we regard color, shape, line, and volume in painting, sculpture, and dance. It is the subjective, subtle shades of meaning which give words their symbolic importance and present us with new perceptions which emerge only from the particular use of words themselves. We see this in two examples written by fifth-grade children:

OCEAN TIDE
The sea crashes upon the sand
    slashes, foams, and twirls the
    sand out to sea again
Just to return time after time

SUN
ruler of the world
mean when he shines
but soft when he cries
driving people out of their
minds
            by

            changing
            changing
            changing

A poem need not be "profound," in the sense of dealing with complex relationships; it may be quite simple and direct, as in the "one-liners" cited earlier. But

[9] Ciardi, op. cit., p. 667.

whether a poem is long or short, simple or complicated, the way words are selected and ordered creates their own inner meaning which reflects an emotional attitude or value toward something or someone. Thus, it is the selection and use of words which constitute the fundamental difference between poetry and discursive language.

The very fact that words are the materials of both forms of communication tends to complicate our understanding. Essentially, what is presented in normal discourse are statements based on the proper, literal use of words to convey explicit meanings. To this end, words are selected for the accuracy of what they *tell*. Poetry uses words which suggest and describe one thing in terms of another in a way that allows us to enter the poet's private world of analogy. In this sense, poetic statements are no more factual than the objects in a painting or the gestures in dance. Thus, words are selected for the way they *feel*.

It is interesting that when a group of ten- and eleven-year-olds was first confronted with the question, "What do you think a poem is?" they began to reach toward the following distinctions:

- They're sort of like stories, but mixed-up stories.
- Telling about something you're feeling.
- They don't always have to make sense, they [poets] write whatever they feel like writing.
- If you have something you really want to get out, and you can't get it out in words, you can write it down.
- It's sort of like explaining something in different words.

What these random responses reflect is a kind of intuitive knowing, because they were not based on a studied approach to poetry. The notion of "explaining something in different words" or that "they don't always have to make sense" points to a central question. Because poetry communicates largely by suggestion rather than direct statement, how are we able to respond to it? Primarily, it is because poetry plays upon our image-making powers to create word pictures in our mind. What we respond to is the way poetic statements use words to create images from abstract ideas or feelings. But we need to reiterate that they are not pictures of what is actually "out there" or "inside" merely presented in words. Rather, a poem is an interpretative word picture in that it does not record all aspects of a child's reality nor all facets of his imagination. We can look to these poems produced in this group of children:

SHADOWS OF QUIET
A room so small and yet so big
A room so full of nothing
I wander in
Into its depths
Into its shadows of quiet

ALONE
Darkness
      scared
silence pounding

```
           pouring in
           reaching  reaching
           stop. a beam of
           light. a friend.
```

Thus, meaning here is revealed through a child's own attitudes toward his experience, which is reflected in his selection of a few effective details out of many.
The process of selection is an ordering experience (both inner and outer) and
even an invention of facts. It is for this reason that we suggest that a poem is an
interpretative word picture, for even a child's fantasy is not an escape from reality
but an interpretation of how a child perceives that reality. And it is the subtle
shades of meaning to which we referred that give words their literal and symbolic
significance.

```
       Blindness      you can
                    not see
             only
                      your hands and ears
       darkness all around you
       and the fear of falling down
       Down. Blindness you can not
           see      only your
                    hand and
           ears
                    only the
       sound of trees waving and
           rain falling
                    and the sounds
       of life crashing-bashing
                    you can not
           help you.
                    Blindness you can not
           see.                                    (fifth grade)
```

This brings us to a consideration of how a word becomes a symbol. Actually,
words in poetry function as both signs and symbols. A sign is easily recognized,
because it has a conventionally understood meaning and is universally accepted.
There can be no ambiguity, for everyone must respond in the same way, according to the conventions under which we live. For example, when we see a red,
hexagonal sign on a street corner, the outline of the shape is sufficient to tell us
that it means "stop." In this case, the word is not even necessary, for like all
signs, we can still translate its meaning in verbal terms. The result of this kind
of knowing is that we become aware of a fact.

A poetic symbol is not one "thing" with a generalized meaning. Rather, it
assumes the existence of two things tied together in a very special relationship,
and it is this relationship which becomes the symbol. A sign is designed for a
general purpose; a symbol is created for its own sake but points to a meaning
outside itself. But the presence of two ideas, events, or qualities does not imply
that one thing is substituted for another or that we are dealing with a simple

comparison of one thing with another. A symbol does not "stand" for something else; it is itself, the expressive focus of a relationship. Because it is an invented meaning, it makes sense only within the poetic form to which it is bound. Thus, the meaning which it produces is not a fact, but a feeling value. Unlike the sign which we name as "stop sign," a symbol is untranslatable outside of itself. Not only is it a mode of language that is not literally true, but it cannot be explained in a language that is literally true. This poem by a ten-year-old boy reflects how a word moves from sign to symbol and takes on deeper and deeper meanings:

> Falling
>   falling
> getting nowhere
> coulors flashing by
> getting nowhere
> Scarey, awful
> feelings
> creeping throuwh you
> everything blurred
> falling
> getting nowhere

In a literal sense, we tend to think of the physical action of falling down from somewhere to somewhere. But the poet moves us beyond the common circumstance by the words "getting nowhere." When, discussing this poem, the children in this class were asked, "What's the feeling of 'getting nowhere'?" they responded by searching for the symbolic meanings:

- You sort of feel that you don't have a surface underneath you, like when you dream you're falling down.
- Like it never ends.
- You don't know what's going to happen to you.

In a symbolic sense, then, the feeling of falling is much more "scarey" than actually falling, for it leaves us with the apprehension of "nowhere." Thus, we come to realize that although meanings in poetry are always open to ambiguity, they affect us because they communicate feelings and values beyond the scope of language. The difference in these two modes of language is most clearly illuminated by Langer, who draws the distinction between the symbol "which lets us *conceive* its object" and the sign "which causes us to *deal with* what it means." [10]

Words as Symbols

When we say that words "work" in a poem, we are drawing a parallel with colors that "work" in painting, volumes that "work" in sculpture, or movements that "work" in dance. If words feel "right" in poetry, it is because they do more than point to an object or idea "out there" merely by describing things to which

[10] Suzanne K. Langer, *Philosophy in a New Key* (Cambridge, Mass.: Harvard University Press, 1951), p. 223.

they refer. As we have indicated, a word not only takes on an agreed-upon or denotative meaning, but calls forth our subjective responses so that it also takes on a symbolic or feeling quality. This is characteristic not only of poetry, but of children who, in dictating or writing a poem or even a fragment, use language for its connotative or feeling value rather than for identification. Following the inherent nature of poetry, they are less concerned with identifying an object or phenomenon than with expressing a feeling toward it.

How, then, do words function as symbols? Considering this question in visual terms, we conceive of three concentric circles which act as ever-widening shades of meaning. In the center we have the word which is itself the object, just as the word *music* conjures up an image of sounds as combinations of melody and rhythm. As with every word, music has a central meaning in the sense of its literal or denotative intent. Beyond this very small circle, a main shadow, or *umbra,* is cast, made up of our associations such as, "it's lovely to hear," "the music of the wind," "the music of a voice speaking," and so forth.

Shading off from this is an even larger circle of secondary meanings or associations, which we call the *penumbra.* It is this cloudy region which contains shades of meaning that we can scarcely grasp. In this case, for example, we relate to music as sounds that are either rhythmic, harmonious, or dissonant, but we also associate music with experiences that are "good" or "bad," pleasant or unpleasant. It is this circle which adds associations that create the most tenuous relationships to the central meaning. As they move farther and farther away from the original object, words take on wider and wider meanings and what began as one thing becomes transformed and exists in another context. We may think of it as a kind of expanding consciousness, because that is the essence of the symbolizing process. In this poetic statement of a sixth-grade girl, we can begin to explore the nature of this relationship:

> windows
> You can see
> but you cannot touch
> the sun

A window is something that we can see through as well as something that brings what is outside into our view. Therefore, we recognize its central meaning. But we also realize that the poem was not written to define the word *window,* because the meaning does not lie in its definition. It is the shading off from the central meaning (umbra) into the secondary meaning (penumbra) that offers us the special insight expressed in a particular vision of space and separation. That is, what is presented here is not a factual truth of physical distance which informs us that although a window allows us to see the sun, we cannot touch it because it is millions of miles away. Rather, it presents a metaphoric truth that the very thing that separates us from something (in this case the sun) also brings it closer. Or, put another way, a window lets us out because we see through it but it also keeps us in and makes us realize our separateness from things. Finally, there is a shadow imbued with an even deeper emotional quality. We sense in the consciousness of this child poet an aura of yearning and isolation.

Returning to the question raised earlier, we are able to respond because each of us builds up associations through our own experiences in daily life. It becomes apparent, therefore, that the widest shadows are cast by the word *I*. As the most personal point of reference, it governs an individual's entire experience and is the very essence of his poetic statement. We see this exemplified in this brief poem:

> ME PLUS ME
> The mummering* all around
> me
> Plus the quietness that
> comes so sudden

Thus, through subtle shades of meaning, words in poetry serve to abbreviate, condense, and enclose a thought or emotion, and as such, function as a feeling. But it is not the direct outcome of a feeling in the same way that crying is an outward manifestation of sadness or happiness. A poem may express an emotion or attitude, yet it may not mention a specific attitude even though it is implied.

Although children tend to be more direct and straightforward in expressing a feeling state, once it is transformed into a poem, we find that it is not simply describable in conventional language. The reason is best offered by Langer, who states, "A poem always creates the symbol of a feeling, not by recalling objects which would elicit the feeling itself, but by weaving a pattern of words—words charged with meaning and colored by literary associations. . . ." [11]

Words as Feelings

This concept of words "charged with meaning" (which has also been advanced by poets) helps us to understand how words function as feelings. In its broadest terms, it implies that words within a poem are charged with a deeper kind of meaning than they are outside it. Specifically, it is a meaning which goes directly to the emotions and is sifted by the mind. When we say that words are given a deeper significance, it is not through making abstract analyses, but in feeling— in the same way that we have considered dance, painting, and sculpture as a "felt" experience. We suggest, therefore, that in being so charged with meaning, words in poetry take on an *emotional weight*.

Thus, if words assume this weight only as they exist in a poem, how do we invest them with emotional charges or with new emotions or meanings? And once we achieve this understanding, how do we communicate this to children? We might examine the approach of a fifth-grade teacher in a school in California. When the children met again in the "poetry circle" (on the floor) after several weeks of writing, listening, and evaluating each other's poems, she began by saying, "Let's talk about the difference between *describing* something and *feeling* something—how poets use words to get you to feel certain ways." To focus on the feeling qualities, she reads some poems of first- and second-grade children from *Anyway Thisaway:*

---

* murmuring.
[11] Suzanne K. Langer, *Feeling and Form* (New York: Scribner, 1953), p. 230.

```
sometimes
death
                is
between
growing
            things


Death:
something
calls
            you
               down.
```

After a discussion of the "heaviness" of the ideas, she selects some of the poetry of her own class written at school or at home over a period of time.

```
life
the life of
someone who
does not live. silently he
                    lies there.
He does
not speak,
He does
not move        His life
            over.
```

The teacher's question, "What would be another name for this poem?" elicits the response, "death." Subsequently, much of the discussion concerns the conditions of death projected by this poet.

• I think . . . instead of saying "death—your life's over, it's finished," it's more like, "life—you don't have enough so it's over."

How do I tell
them my DREAMS
ARE all cRaMPed
up inside my mind
tRying to BReack
out with cRePY
wePY tears How
Do I tell them,

- . . . he's not really mentioning death, maybe he's afraid of it or something.
- It's like saying life is sort of like death . . . if you don't really live it.

Shifting the focus to "What does the poet do to give you those feelings?" brings attention to the way words are used. For example,

- Because in the beginning he says "life" and at the end he says "life over."
- The way at the end where he says "his life—over" without using the "is"; it sort of gives more feeling.

Such comments open the way for the teacher to observe that "there isn't an 'is' in the entire poem" and that just leaving out a word creates a more powerful feeling. She also makes the point that poets are very economical in leaving out words that are unnecessary. Thus, children by their own examples begin to relate the feeling of emotional weight through the form of a compressed image.

> How do I tell them
> my dreams
> are   cramped
>   inside my mind
> trying to break out
> with crepy, wepy * tears
> How do I tell them

Reflecting upon the previous discussion, it is interesting to note that this child had originally included the words

> are *all* cramped
> *up* inside my mind

which are erased but visible on the paper he placed in the "poetry drawer." Thus, we see the self-selected economy of the poetic statement. The poem was variously interpreted by members of the class as follows:

- Like, he has a dream and even if he tries to tell somebody, he can't tell it exactly how he has it in his mind 'cause it's in your head and things that happen to you, you might have that in your dream.
- Tears—it could be something sad.

Again, in raising the question, "How does the poet make you feel sad?" children respond,

- The way he used "creepy, weepy tears"—sort of crying, but it's hard to get out.
- He goes, "How do I tell them, how do I tell them."
- It doesn't have to be just dreams that you have at night; it could be dreams of something else—like dreams of wanting something.

Out of this searching, it becomes possible for the teacher to point out subtle

* creepy, weepy.

shades of meaning, that the word *dream* might also mean daydream, for example. And in repeating "how do I tell them" at the opening and closing of the poem, the poet is not asking for an answer, but is expressing the feeling "this is what is happening to me" in terms of "how do I get these feelings out?"

A teacher with a similar age group in a New Jersey school uses a more direct approach in making children aware of the emotional charge of words by posing the problem, "How do you feel when you're lonely, happy, frustrated, angry, afraid?" Some of the poems produced in class or at home are presented here:

SOLITARY
Sitting in solitary
Watching the years burn by
Heart beating
Head booming
die.

LONLINESS
Lonliness is when it is foggy
and the mist creeps up the
abandoned walls
The rain trickles down the hair
of a lost child.
An empty house with
creeky floors
And a clock ticking among the long
and aching sounds.

LEFT OUT
I feel left out   discouraged
I feel as if I were sealed
and left alone
And as if I were in a
different categorie

FRUSTRATION
Frustration is
untangling fishing string
Frustration is
looking into a psychodelic picture
Your stomach is like shattering glass
Frustration has a mind.

ANGER
When you are angry the
whole world turns black
everything is frustrating
its a world of your own
no one can get in your world
it is all silent
silent, silent.

FEAR
Fear is cold and still
Every sound rumbles
in your ear.

Force–Time

In painting, sculpture, and dance, we have described force as energy or forces in opposition which create an inner tension. In poetry, force does not necessarily lie in opposition but in the relationship between images. Yet poetry does affect us and the effect is of some powerful energy within us that is screened through our senses and shaped by our mind. Thus, the tension is between two images that are evoked in our mind. They do not exist on the page, for the words in a poem are used symbolically to create these images. How then does this energy force us to respond? Does it have any similarity to the way force exists in other art forms? It does if we consider that we are creating and responding to a series of images as word pictures (which may be visual, auditory, tactile, or even conceptual) which move in a certain direction. Tension is created by the very nature in which one image follows another in a certain relationship. It is this tension which we sense as suspense or anticipation which is the force of a poem.

Thus, we conceive of force in terms of the way the energy is directed. Unlike painting and sculpture, which can be read from any point in any direction, poetry has only one direction. If we read it backward or sideward (which we can do in a painting or a sculpture) it makes no sense. It is more akin to dance because both forms share the inherent ingredient of time. Each poem, no matter how simple, has a momentum of its own which forces us forward and carries us along with it. Unlike painting and sculpture, but similar to dance, poetry unfolds in a sequence of a beginning, middle, and end.

We say, then, that force is a phenomenon of direction in the sense of where a poet takes us. But it is not merely in the sequence itself which produces the tension. To use a visual image, we suggest that a poem is like an arrow. And while the poet fashions the shaft in a certain direction, the whole arrow is aimed at striking at the heart of the matter. The strength with which the poet pulls back the bow and lets the arrow go affects the force. Even if the poem is very brief and simple, there is a kind of built-in suspense, because we really don't know where it is going to lead us. In terms of our own response, there is an element of suspense toward where the direction is going, and it is this suspense which creates the tension. Thus, it functions as a condition of force and time.

In terms of a poem itself, what are the sources of tension? The simplest kind of tension exists between two contrasting images which have no apparent symbolic meaning in that they cannot be explained beyond themselves. Placed in another way, they are like two sharply focused images in a photograph with no blending of edges and therefore no blurring of meaning. They are so direct that they appear almost "tensionless." It is because the energy does not lie in their opposition, in their fighting each other, but in overlapping one another or in being placed side by side. And the placing of two images together creates still another image.

Children need to be encouraged to use the language they possess as an effective means of coping with their own realities. In listening to poems about people in ordinary situations they may be stimulated to look for poetry possibilities in their own lives. An attempt to look at someone familiar in new ways is reflected in this description.

> My grandmother
> has
> one gray
> eye.

Of one of the teacher poets with a deep, sonorous voice, a child said,

yr
voice
comes
out
of
a giant
house

The observation that another poet consistently wore shoes with no socks prompted this poetic question,

do
yr
feet
catch
cold
in
such
small
houses?

But force is not merely the tension between two things. Usually, such simple tension between images is not expressive enough for children because it is so simplified and purified. More frequently, their poems consist of one image placed against another in a sequence that winds up the tension. Therefore, what emerges at the end of a poem is an emotional or symbolic image, rather than one which is concrete. An example of the relationship of image against image is revealed in this fifth-grade poem previously cited:

Fear is cold and still
Every sound rumbles
in your ear.

"Fear is cold and still" is the first image which gives us a feeling of being frozen or even immobilized. Our body is involved but the poet does not have to say "your body" because we already respond in this way. The condensation of language, as one of the powers of poetry, also directs the energy right to the mark. Whether we read it or hear it, we feel a pause or breath between this phrase and the next. Even without punctuation we shift to the next image because the order is simple and grammatical and relates to the way children speak. So we come to the second image, "every sound rumbles in your ear." In essence, the poet is saying that even the smallest tick of a clock is enormously magnified because we are paying such attention to it. We might note that in using *you* the poet describes his sensation or feeling and transfers it to you, the reader. It is in these terms that we have referred to poetry as a communicative language.

What we have here are two relatively simple images but there is tension between them because one is a development of the other. That is, this cold, still person that *you* are is the one who magnifies the sound. To recall our figurative image of a poem, we may say that the development between two images implies some sort of direction which is the thrust of the arrow.

Leaves

slowley slowley they
wave
with
thet wind
they get tierd
and old and Brown
athey cannot hold on.

they fall
slowley slowley
They drift
in the
air down   down

until they touch the
fresh
sorcel

lifelessly they ~~lie~~ lie there

Dead

joey

There are, however, different ways of creating tension. We have contrast when one image abruptly shifts and changes to another which we feel as an opposition. We may look again at this poem:

ME PLUS ME
The mummering all around
me
Plus the quietness that
comes so sudden

"Mummering all around me" is the first image, and we may note parenthetically that *mummering* works as well as *murmuring* in creating word sounds. "That comes so sudden" is the second. If the poet had just said,

The mummering all around me
plus the quietness

the poem would not be as effective. However, in saying, "that comes so sudden" he has shut out the mummering, which implies an action. The sudden quiet means that the mummering has been abruptly cut off, so we have the action of one image overlapping another.

We also have contrast in the shifting of images in the following poem by a fifth-grade child:

Leaves
   slowly slowly
   they wave with the wind
   they get tired and old
   and brown
   they can not hold on
   they fall
   slowly, slowly
   they drift in the air
   down
      down
         down
   until they touch the fresh soil
   they lie there
      dead.

The opposition lies in the images of life and death. The first image is of leaves, who like people, "tired and old" lose hold. The repetition of "slowly, slowly" and "down, down, down" (reinforced by the placement of these latter words on the page) gives us the feeling that they are dying throughout the duration of the poem. There is also a built-in rhythm which supports the image of slowly floating downward; to read it quickly would move against this emotional intent. In the second image, the use of the word *fresh* implies that the soil never really dies and is still living. Thus, we have the opposition that what is dead comes down to the fresh soil which enables it to live, perhaps in another form.

Finally, the source of tension in every poem is the tension of suspense in terms of "where is it going?" At the beginning of this section we envisioned the direction of a poem as an arrow. Now we liken the suspense within it to the action of a spring. That is, we consider the forming of a poem as a spring being wound up which at the end of the final phrase goes "zing" like an arrow.

We might clarify here by saying that a phrase represents a feeling or idea and has nothing to do with the actual length of a line. In dealing with children's poetry, we become aware that children tend to compose short poems because they are unable to keep an involved idea in their head. Consequently, they do not deal with anything more than the tension of where the sequence is going to end.

> running
> my apple
> fell
> down
> twice

The suspense is in the "running," for we do not know what is going to happen. If it had simply said, "Running with my apple and it fell down," there would be no suspense and no poem. The spring winds up with "running" and lets go with the word "twice." We really don't know who fell down—the child or the apple. But we know that it is the suspenseful use of "twice" that makes it a poem.

Aside from such simple statements, every phrase in a poem is an event in the sense that something is happening—an object or idea is being created. The suspense is similar to that in a detective story. For example, in every paragraph of the first chapter something is happening; someone is saying or doing something and we as readers wonder where it is going to lead. If the suspense is sufficient, we keep reading until we come to the final chapter and it is resolved. The spring is unwound.

A similar tension occurs in poetry but an event is not the same as in a detective story. Suspense in a poem lies in the order in which images are presented. For example, we wind up a spring in turns of 1, 2, 3, 4, 5, wherein 5 is added to 4, 4 to 3, 3 to 2, and so forth; thus the tension is built up progressively. The reason we read a poem from beginning to end is because a spring is wound in only one direction. Thus, we view tension as an arrow being pulled taut against a bowstring or as a spring being wound up. It is interesting that without being informed of "springs" or tension as such, children feel it intuitively, for it is reflected in their poetry. Perhaps they "know" it because, as mentioned earlier, it is part of the way we talk. We listen to someone speaking a sentence and presumably we do not know how it is going to end. In poetry, that "someone" is a poet telling a story. It may be an emotional story, but we still want to know how it is going to come out.

In turning again to the poem "Windows," we begin to see how the relationships within a poem create tension.

> WINDOWS
> You can see
>   but you you cannot touch
> the sun

We are presented with four images. First, the title is an image of the word itself, for we get a visual image of a window that we look through. (As often happens, the title is an essential image, for without it we would not know what the poem is about.) In the first line, "you can see" gives us a visual image of someone seeing or trying to see. (Again, the use of *you* immediately transfers the image to yourself.) "But you cannot touch" offers a third image of hands that are not touching the object they want to touch. We don't know what that is, so the suspense is generated by the title and the first two images. How is it that you can see but you cannot touch? Then the whole poem unwinds and ends with "the sun" as a surprising image.

This poem illustrates the point made earlier that the way words are combined and the direction of the images can change its meaning. It is perhaps of added interest that in writing the poem in this way, the child put each image on a different line, thus separating the images in her own head. Perhaps this comes in response to the teacher's encouragement that each line be the shape of a thought. It is the combination of child–window–sun, in that order, which gives the poem its power. If, for example, we were to rearrange the words and put the child outside the window, the relationship would not be the same.

Thus, tension is not within the image itself; it is in the relationship between images. We need to understand that just listing images in order does not make a poem. We might think of it as similar to music, which is itself a form of suspense in time. We have harmonious and melodic relationships that are unresolved as measure follows measure until the end brings resolution, even though it may be a dischord. And so in poetry, tension lies in the relationship not only of one image to another, but of the last one with all of those preceding. We have a building up of images and therefore a building up of tension in terms of the underlying feeling or emotional tone that is being generated. This propelling force is not a condition of the image as such. Rather, we can imagine that the image is like a wheel which is rolling, and we push it. Each push makes it roll further, and all along we are asking, "Where is it going to end?"

Experiential Approach

We have explored the question of "How does a poem mean?"; now we turn to the problem of "How is a poem made?" We have investigated the process of painting, sculpture, and dance, and we also want to know what is unique about the experience of poetry making. A beginning lies in the response of a ten-year-old child to the question, "What do you think poetry is?" She replies, "Sometimes poems are like part of your imagination. When you read them they blend with your imagination." It would seem that imagination is necessary both to create and to relate to a poem. Therefore, we certainly want to encourage children to be imaginative. But what exactly do we mean? When a child's imagination grows, what changes take place?

Our initial description of the art experience as an "inward–outward" process applies equally to poetry. A developing imagination allows a child to make real to himself his innermost feelings and the feelings and experiences of others. At the same time, he reflects upon his own external world as well as the one in which somebody else finds himself. If, as this child states, poems are "part of your imagination" and "blend with your imagination," they can be a means of deeper insight and greater sympathy toward oneself and others. But if we accord praise to being imaginative, we must take children seriously as poets in the same way that we have approached them as painters, sculptors, and dancers. As teachers, then, we are concerned with giving children a belief in their expressive powers of language by nurturing their imagination.

As in all of the arts, imagination is a kind of feeling–knowing phenomenon which eludes precise definition. In a general sense, it is a process of forming a conscious idea or mental image of something we have never wholly perceived before, which comes into being as a synthesis of memories or sensory experiences. In poetry, it is the relationship of these ideas or images presented through words which give it form. The communication is twofold: A child raises the remembered feeling or sensation to his own consciousness, and brings it to us so that we become intensely aware of his moods, feelings, or ideas. Because poetry communicates largely by suggestion rather than by direct statement, such statements are formed to create relationships of words which give concreteness to abstract ideas, to clarify thoughts or moods only dimly perceived, and to evoke in others a compassionate response.

The imagination draws from both conscious and unconscious sources; thus the subject matter of poetry is unrestricted and unpredictable. What is produced are images of things once known but absent (memories), of things never seen or actually nonexistent (fantasy), or of things created in new relationships from old elements (analogies). When we refer to mental rather than visual images, we are dealing not with the picture-taking faculty of the eye, but with the picture-forming quality of the mind. Thus, although the products of a child's imagination may sometimes appear obscure or "freaky," it may actually be his way of perceiving something more deeply or of creating a singularly new vision. Although it may not be representative of something "real," imagination is not an illusion. It is for this reason that we remarked in the previous section that it is neither opposed to reality nor an escape from reality. Therefore, what we are seeking in children is an unself-conscious expression of thoughts about themselves and the world around them as they perceive it.

In the following poem by a fifth-grade child, we have an example of an emotion couched in imaginative terms:

```
             devil
                 lurking in cracks
                 in a deep dark
                 cave sneaking around
                 in white
                          tennis
                                     shoes
                 spitting
                          spatting
                 skipping
```

                    hopping
            keeping one eye
                    on the
                                witch
                                 in
                                the
                                corner
        keeping one eye
                    on the
                                witch
                                 in
                                the
                                corner

On the surface, what seems to be evoked is merely a humorous image of a witch. But there is ambiguity in every poem, and whether it is the poet or the witch "sneaking around in white tennis shoes," is not clear. But in looking more deeply, we are given the feeling that what lurks in cracks and corners is not the witch but the poet's fear. While "spitting" and "spatting" to ward off bad things, she is all the while "keeping one eye on the witch in the corner." The poet's expressed fear is defined by the presence of the witch.

The purpose of composing a poem, be it child or adult, is not to tell what everyone knows or thinks he knows, in a conventional way of recording fact or feeling. It is a way of telling by which we come to know it through feeling it, facing it, or experiencing it. What, then, prompts a child to tell something through his feelings? Although he may be attracted by a particular idea, ultimately he is motivated by emotions. That is, a poem usually does not come into being until an inner emotional force moves a child to put his thoughts and feelings into words. An image or conception is not passively formed by the mind, but by an active, receptive imagination. It is this action which leads us to distinguish between *general consciousness* and *poetic imagination*.

When we speak of poetic imagination, we are referring to one kind of sensibility which is potential to all children but which, through the poetic process, becomes concentrated and intensified. Thus, developing a poetic imagination is not a passive function wherein a poem becomes the simple transcribing or reciting of a child's sensations or experiences. Poetic imagination is revealed in the relationship or order of images which may initially arise from unconscious activity. Eventually, however, it emerges as a child consciously identifies with objects or events in his inner and outer world. Stated simply, a poem must be about "something," it must have concrete things that are visible, tangible, "smellable," and so forth. It cannot be a series of loose images or words anymore than a dance can be composed of unrelated movements. Nor can it be merely random outpouring of the emotions. Rather, it is the combination of the specific and the emotion that creates the magic.

We can describe the difference between general consciousness and poetic imagination in this commonplace situation. An eleven-year-old child walks through a park every day and sees the same tree along the way. Although she walked under this tree hundreds of times, she has paid no attention. One day, something about this particular tree strikes her and she views it in a different way, perhaps because she is more responsive. Up to this moment the tree was just another neutral element in the landscape and was merely a part of her general consciousness. Now, however, walking under the tree has an emotional effect upon her and she wants to express it. She can do this in any art form (because this is the nature of the art process), but in this case she has a verbal response to this experience. She draws upon her poetic imagination by focusing this vague feeling down into something precise in a phrase expressed as,

> the giants
> with their many arms
> and fingers
> landscaped the park

In so condensing her feelings and forming them into words she gives them new meaning.

We see the same kind of intense, condensed feeling in this image written by another child in the same class,

> A day
> as cold as ice
> slides over the world.
> Now I wait
> and sit alone.

The transformation from general consciousness to poetic imagination is a search for an affective relationship to bridge the gap between a child and the objects and phenomena which surround him. He establishes a relationship when he brings to them an emotion or feeling. As a result, he begins to perceive more clearly or in a new way the nature of his own feelings. Examples of this kind of observation are found in these poems by second-graders.

> one
> day
> I
> saw
> a
> wasp
> he flew
> into
> my house
> and bumped
> his head

> frogs
> big old worts *
> jumping

* worts—warts

on the field
at night
peeing
on your hand
   alot.

When we say a child is imaginative, we mean that he brings a penetrating eye to bear on something important to him and through his personally expressed feelings, sends out emotional vibrations to which we can respond. We make no judgments as to what he selects, for any subject is appropriate for poetry if it is relevant to a child. It does not have to be beautiful or happy, nor conform to what we think is "acceptable." When inner-city children write of rats and riots it is just as real and valid as suburban children who write of sunsets and separations. Our main criterion is that a child feels deeply enough to express it. However, as we have said, simply to focus on that "something" is not going to give us its essential meaning. But subject matter is not unimportant; it has to relate in some measure to something concrete or else nothing is communicated.

Obviously, each child brings his own depth of experiences to a poem, and these experiences will color whatever he observes. Therefore, subject matter is important to the extent that he has found something in his general consciousness that brings out his feelings which are defined by the poem itself. As a piece of art work, a poem is *what* it is because of *how* it is. It is not novelty that we look for; it is the individuality of a piece that makes it interesting. A subject need not be new or startling, for even familiar experiences can be handled in many ways. Where a theme comes from does not matter; what does matter is the excitement it evokes and the importance it has for the poet.

Thus, our approach to poetry stresses the education of the imagination through the power of language, wherein children not only read and listen to poems but "talk out" and write poetry. At the outset, we must thoughtfully consider the materials we use to "open up" children to poetry. Unless poems are carefully selected to reflect contemporary language and experience, children "turn off" and produce work which is stilted and derivative. Teachers who have engaged children in poetry making find that poems concerned with everyday experiences of twentieth-century children are the most popular. Conversely, they find that it is difficult to involve such children in "nature" poems unless a storm happens to be raging at the moment that the poem is being read.

In presenting subject matter that is direct, we are suggesting that the world we live in is a rich source of material. Children then begin to see that their experience and the form of poetry is not something remote, but is something they can deal with. Although they think of ghosts and goblins and Santa, using their experiences helps them to look into their own world to see how they fit into a larger pattern. By encouraging children to understand as well as create the details of their lives, we make poetry a means of bringing them deeper into their own experience. The process is one of listening to poetry as a springboard for the expression of a child's responses, and then writing in ways to put that expression in forms which they can see and appreciate.

Making poetry is more complex than listening. Just as we need to be concerned with what we present, so must we be sensitive to what we receive. We need only to listen to children's spontaneous language to begin to recognize the poetry possibilities within it. Even "made-up" words or phrases regarded as colloquial may be poetic images which speak of a child's time and culture. For example, such slang phrases as, "I'm hung up," "I'm uptight," "Don't bug me," are poetic in themselves. It is curious that forty years ago Mearnes implored teachers to listen to children's language nonjudgmentally. Speaking of his encounter with an eighth-grade class, he wrote, "Power of language they undoubtedly had, I mused, terrific power; but no one had apprised them of that gift, I suspected, for it is not the sort that would pass as creditable among teachers generally. It was the clipped, colloquial idiom of youth, hot, prejudiced, rebellious; ungrammatical, and impolite; highly absurd from an adult standard; but beautifully fitting as an instrument to convey genuine feeling." [12] The description could apply equally well to younger children today. His point, sadly neglected throughout these years, is that children must reflect their own language and that we as teachers must accept it.

At whatever age, we want to communicate with children in terms of their secret, "explorable" selves. Through "poetry talk" or poetry sessions, we can encourage children to listen to the way they and others put words together. As they find words for their ideas and feelings, they find another way of discovering those feelings. For example, in eliciting poetry talk with four-year-olds, a teacher asked, "How do you feel when you feel sick?"

- Bumble bees in my tummy.
- I think sumbudy tied me up.

After reaching out to the challenges of poetry, a teacher expresses her observations in this way, "It came as quite a revelation that my 'untampered' second graders who are six and seven years old write prose that is poetry. That is, their creative writing is poetic but the form is prose. I think it is important to encourage them to write in a form that is natural to them."

Developing feelings forces language into concentrated forms which is in itself productive of poetry. When children feel strongly about something, it changes their language to some extent. As we have seen in the poetry presented here, it produces a kind of force or tension because each child tries to express something that has deep roots inside of him. Thus, the language of "felt" poetry is not casual. We need to be sensitively aware that poems by children may not be "successful" in adult terms, but that they are not meant to be. What we must begin to realize is that children's poetry speaks a language of knowing and feeling—of discovering their imagination.

Elements

We want to involve children in becoming consciously aware of the emotional content of poetry—that is, of the underlying mood or feeling or tone from which

[12] Hughes Mearnes, *Creative Power* (New York: Dover, 1958), pp. 17–18.

it has developed. Our emphasis has been not only on what a poet is saying, but on how he says it, and the feeling it conveys. As we have stated, words "live" by the way they are invested with emotional charges. However, our responses are not only to the emotive meanings but to the overtones of the words themselves— their sounds, accents, and rhythms. Once recognizing the dominant emotional thread, we can examine the ways feelings are expressed through the elements of *sound, rhythm,* and *imagery.*

Because the language we are dealing with is figurative rather than literal, the impact of poetry comes not through *representing* real objects or phenomena, but in *presenting* them in new and different relationships. What, then, does a poet do to make these elements work? It was with this kind of question in mind that a fifth-grade teacher asked, "What does a poem look like?" The children responded randomly, stimulated by each other's comments:

- It has small sentences.
- Sometimes people just put writing marks down like semicolons and stuff and shape it like what the poem is about.
- A lot of times they rhyme; they have sentences that rhyme, too.
- The funny ones rhyme mostly.
- Most poems that have to do with a person's feelings don't rhyme—it's just that when you read them they blend together; it sort of sounds like it rhymes sometimes when it really doesn't.
- A poem has to have some kind of beat or some kind of rhythm or else it would probably be a story.
- The way I picture a poem is better than I picture a story; in a story I just read it but in a poem you sort of give something to it; you sort of sing it.

From these intuitive ideas, the teacher was able to probe more deeply by punctuating the discussion with such questions as, "Does a poem have to look a certain way? Does it have to sound a certain way? Do all poems have the same rhythm?" Negative answers supported by more opinions led one child to conclude, "A poem can be anything," to which the teacher reaffirmed an earlier concept that a poem can be "anyway thisaway." But this was not meant to imply that a poem has no structure, for even in this open-ended discussion, the children alluded to the fundamental elements of *sound, rhythm,* and *imagery.*

It is interesting that some of these statements find their sources in the critical writing of some of our contemporary poets. The comment that "you sing it" is reminiscent of T. S. Eliot writing in "The Music of Poetry," "while poetry attempts to convey something beyond what can be conveyed in prose rhythms, it remains, all the same, *one person talking to another:* and this is just as true as if you sing it, for singing is another way of talking." [13] Yet he also asserts that although some poetry is meant to be sung, most poetry is meant to be spoken. For example, there are other ways of speaking besides the "fuzzy, buzzy bees" or the "fluttery butterflies in the filtered blue sky." It also informs us that sound does not exist apart from meaning, otherwise we might have poetry of considerable musical quality that made no sense.

[13] Glasgow, Scotland: Jackson, Son & Co., 1942, p. 16.

This is particularly relevant today, for the music or sounds of poetry reside in the common speech of a child in his time and place. And this applies as much to a child in Harlem or Appalachia as to a child in Grosse Point or Bel Air, where we must expect and respect cultural and ethnic differences. Language is changing, partly through cultural infusion, partly because certain elements die and others are born. As new words come into being, so do new ways of speaking. In any case, it is not the exact conversational idiom of a child, his friends, or his family; it is out of the sounds he hears that he makes his poetry.

In encouraging children to begin from the language they know, Larry Neal, a visiting New York poet, evoked this "sound poem" from a kindergarten class in Washington, D.C. It is reproduced here exactly as it was recorded.

NEAL: Now I want you to do something for me. I want you to make some sounds. What can we sound like? What would it be nice to sound like?

CHILDREN: Dogs, a doll, birds.

NEAL: Let's sound like little birds. *(Children begin making whistling and blowing sounds.)* Let's all try to whistle. You whistle and I'll talk and you listen to me while you whistle. Can you listen to me and whistle at the same time? Make those bird sounds and try a bird that you all like—any kind of bird. Start—everybody together. *(Chirping, whistling, cooing sounds from all over the room. Neal walks around chanting above the children's sounds.)*
Bluebirds, bluebirds
flying through the sky.
A gray sky,
sunny skies
are singing to the
little children.
Birds are singing
to all the children:
to Heloise and Bobby
and all the names.
Tell me your names.

CHILD: Marie.

NEAL: Marie, c'mon names;
tell me your names,
names and bird sounds.
Say your names
over and over again.

CHILDREN: *(All speak their names.)*

NEAL: *(Speaking over their names)*
Your names, your names
over and over again.
Your name is a pretty name
your name is a pretty name
your name is yourself,
keep saying your names.

Beautiful sounds and words
poetry is words and sounds.
You are making poetry
as you go . . . *(picking up the rhythm of the children).*
And round and round
and round and round   *(Children join in.)*
and round and round
and round and round
and down and down
and down and down
and up and up
and up and up
Sky birds.
Say it with me.
Sky birds, sky birds   *(Children join in.)*
words, words, words, words
sky birds, sky birds.
Now real soft:
Sky birds, sky birds, sky birds   *(Children whisper in unison.)*
words, words, words, words   *(diminishing in sound)*
Green things, green things,
green things, green things.   *(increasing in sound)*
Magic, magic, magic, magic,   *(All chant together.)*
word magic, word magic,
word magic, word magic.
Play games, play games,
play games, play games,
softly, softly, softly, softly.   *(Voices lower.)*
Children, children, children, children,
children, children, children, children;
love, love, love, love
love, love, love, love,
mommy, daddy, mommy, daddy;
poetry, poetry, poetry, poetry
poetry, poetry, poetry, poetry.   *(Voices decrease to almost silence.)*
(Whistles, as in beginning.)
CHILDREN: *(Whistles as before, but in more modulated tones.)*
NEAL: Green day, green day,
green day, green day.   *(Children chant along.)*
Love way, love way
love way, love way.
Day, day, day, day.
Hey, day, day, day.   *(Voice drops with each "day.")*
Hey, day, day, day.   *(Voice moves up and down.)*
Love me, children;
love me, children.

Peace, peace, and love me.
And love and peace
and love, love,
and peace and peace.
This
   is
      the
         poem.

This is a very simple but fundamental experience in that the sensations he is eliciting from children are those of sounds, rhythm, word color. All of these function as sensuous elements which make children "turn on" to poetry. Each child, it is hoped, will perceive some kind of quality as a result of responding to these elements.

As we have noted throughout, children are moving less toward formal, poetic language and more toward their natural speech patterns. We find that instead of rhyming, children frequently use assonance, which is the resemblance of sounds in words or syllables by repeating the vowels without repeating the consonants. This is perhaps the formal explanation of the child's comment that, "it sort of sounds like it rhymes when it really doesn't." In this humorous poem, for example, there is a similarity in the sounds of "feasts" and "teeths."

PICNIC
Marching ants come
over the hill   coming   coming
hungry ants dreaming of
feasts
Sharpening their teeths
coming   coming

As evidenced here, children may make up their own words ("teeths") to continue the rhythmic feeling.

If we take our cues from children, we must also be watchful of the structure of the poems read to them. Rhyming, for example, is difficult to avoid, because it is so pervasive and children tend to work for it in their own poems. The result is that they develop a stereotyped approach to poetry in the same way that they approach sculpture from a limited, frontal view. In a sense, both emerge as a kind of perceptual limitation that is consciously or unconsciously fostered by the learning experiences we offer. Hearing only rhymed poetry subtly imposes a structure upon children and they neglect their own language and its possibilities. Inevitably, certain rhymes are paired with a familiar sense of dull predictability. Perhaps one possible way of diverting such an approach and avoiding clichés is by encouraging children not to rhyme. This does not mean that rhyme should be forever discarded, but that there are other ways available.

For example, in reading their own poetic lines or those of others (children or adults), they may be made aware of different rhythms and how a rhythmic structure works with or against the expression of a feeling. This poem by a fifth-grade child was read (anonymously) by the teacher as one of many poems produced in the class:

> The last cry of the dying dog
> left the valley
> echoing with fear

In discussing the differences in the sound between a "dog who is dying" and a "dying dog," a child commented that in using the latter, "It creates a feeling— kind of a lonely feeling." The teacher was then able to point out that it is the way words sound that contributes to the overall rhythm. Thus, children begin to realize that every poem has its own rhythm, depending on what it is trying to say. Although this is merely a fragment, we observe that children, freed from conventions, do not work from rules, but by ear and feelings. But we can help them to become "consciously rhythmical" in poetry just as we can in dance. By making them aware of the rhythmic qualities of words, they come to understand that a poetic line is not simply a quantity of language composed of so many syllables, so many accents, and so forth. We might refer once again to a child's comment, "A poem has to have some kind of beat or some kind of rhythm or else it would probably be a story." This is an important distinction between prose and poetry and we are suggesting further that there is no set rhythm for a poem. There must be accents or beats, but they create a kind of music which should correspond naturally to the emotional emphases in a poem.

In formal terms, rhythm is a sound pattern of stresses caused by accented syllables which are repeated at regular intervals. For example, words may have one syllable or several syllables, each of which are accented within themselves. If there are three syllables in a word, one is accented over the others, just as with three words in a phrase, one is stressed over the others. It is these stresses which create the rhythm. Although they generally occur at regular intervals, we have seen that the freer the poem, the less regular the rhythm. In poetic terms, then, rhythm is a sensuous element which is determined by the need to find some verbal expression for a feeling state or idea which is not necessarily logical or consistent.

Thus, rhythm is not rhyming. Children need to grasp the concept that the words of poetry are word pictures of feelings and not mechanically wrought intonations. Our position toward opening poetic alternatives echoes Mearnes, who states, "Experience has made me suspicious of all the rhymed verse by children. Rhyming is not their language; at best it is an imitation of an adult form of writing." [14]

Like words, images are denotative because they appeal to certain senses which we can identify, such as the visual, auditory, olfactory, tactile, kinesthetic. In this sense, we "feel" them in a physical way. But images move beyond this and become connotative because they create an emotional aura. Thus we also "feel" them in an emotional way. This poem, by a fifth-grade child, combines both feelings.

> I carry the stillness
> And feel the hot
> And smell the purple
> Those are things I cannot

[14] Hughes Mearnes, *Creative Power* (New York: Dover Publications, Inc., 1958), p. 13.

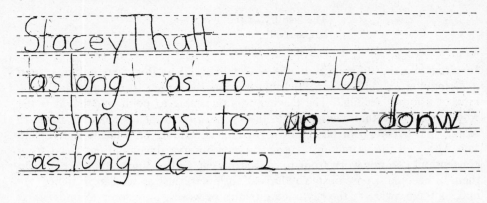

Stacey Thall
as long as to t—too
as long as to up— donw
as long as 1—2

Jeffrey White
As long as.
As long as a centuy.
As long as a trip to
Los anges to the daseart.
As long as a snael carl
across the sanfransiscobrig.
As long as a patatobug to go
arond the world.

An image is an element which is shared with prose and even more with painting and sculpture. In the latter, it has an essential function in that it is a physical presence and exists in its own right. In poetry, images combine by way of analogy or metaphor and take on a life of their own. A poetic image may be identical with or symbolic of a feeling value. We say *identical* because children tend to express images directly which evoke in us direct word pictures. We see (and hear) an example in another poem from this group of children.

WATERFALL
A waterfall crashes into
the big body of water

It sizzles past
the rocks

It bubbles when it is
standing still
It roars with
laughter

It becomes apparent that this poem is rather lavish with images, yet they do not make it especially effective. We need to reconsider the conventional expectations that a poem must contain certain images formed by metaphors, similes, personification, or alliteration. On the other hand, children enjoy "word play," and it may be used as a part of a beginning exploration. For example, a second-grade teacher in a Los Angeles public school presented the open-ended simile "as long as . . ." and asked the children to finish the phrase by conjuring up an image. The responses of two children follow:

as long as to 1–100
as long as to up–down
as long as 1–2

As long as.
As long as a century.
As long as a trip to
Los anges to the daseart.
As long as a snael carl
across the sanfransisco brig.
As long as a potatobug to go
arond the world.

On a somewhat more sophisticated level, a discussion of the difference between similes and metaphors produced these poems from a fifth-grade class.
Simile:

Fog lands like a bird
waits a while, then silently
Flies far, far away

Sadness comes to chill
the heart.
It thaws like winter

The clouds like soft
pillows in the sky, awaken
in the morning and sleep
in the night

Metaphors (loosely based on Haikus):

The sea has crashed
Beyond that
I do not know

A leaf falls to the ground

And all animals
Bow their heads in grief

Falling one by one
And pushed by the wind
winter descends

A raindrop sounds like nothing
very simple
But oh, how deceiving

Joyous songs reach everyone
but in the night
the owl cries alone

A white horse thunders by
with speed of light in the
cold starry night

Wind blows the dust,
Dust hits my face;
I can not see my friends

Our reason for introducing these types of images to children is that they will find them in poetry and can recognize them as ways in which language is used. At the same time, we need to convey that such images alone do not make a poem a poem.

There are no poems without images, but as we have observed throughout this chapter, an image does not have to consist of these grammatical devices. Because they are so commonly associated with poetry, it becomes more difficult by past standards to judge the "poemness" of a poem without them. However, we need to reconsider our preconceptions of what a poem "should be" and regard it in terms of what "is." We limit our own sensibilities as well as children's if in looking at a poem we make the judgment, "It has no metaphors, no similes, and so forth, so it is not a poem."

But this does not imply that we have no standards. Rather, we are suggesting that a poem, as is true of any piece of art work, is a unified form composed of expressive elements. Therefore, we cannot separate image from image, image from idea, or either from the language in which they are expressed. Poetry is an organization of elements through a form which communicates experience. The words of poetry are the raw materials which are shaped to make visible to our own eye what is visible to the inner eye of the poet. Thus, what we are dealing with is what Langer calls the *image of a feeling,* rather than a technical relationship of words. Yet, as we have said, feelings are neither random nor uncontrolled, but are evoked or directed toward something. Therefore, the image of a feeling must include that which the feeling is about. Such an association is an experience, and thus we have come full circle from our opening definition of poetry as the language of experience.

The image that a particular child chooses to evoke is intensely personal and it is this individuality that we are seeking. It is not important that we understand it immediately, for it is the child who must be familiar with it through his own experience. It is his "poetic right" to create relationships that are subjective and not instantly recognizable to others. Yet in exploring his own state of mind within the poetic experience, he is able to form connections with which we can relate.

An awareness of this intense, individual vitality helps us to understand that a poem defies precise, rational explanation. Read speaks to us when he writes, "We can count syllables, mark rhythm, observe alliteration and paraphrase metaphors, but it is like taking a clock to pieces to discover the nature of time." [15]

PROBLEM: To explore the difference between the way words are used in poetry and prose

TEACHER: First thing I want to ask you, what do you think a poem is?

CHILD: Telling about something, your feelings.

CHILD: Sometimes when my sister gets discouraged she goes upstairs and writes something down; it's funny.

TEACHER: What kind of things does she write? What's funny about it?

CHILD: Not exactly funny. It's not necessarily stuff that rhymes.

TEACHER: Okay, poems don't have to rhyme.

CHILD: They're sort of like stories, but mixed-up stories.

TEACHER: How do you mean "mixed-up"?

CHILD: Like fairy tales, stories like a poem.

CHILD: A lot of poems sort of describe something.

TEACHER: What kind of things do they describe?

CHILD: Flowers, people, anything.

CHILD: They don't always have to make sense, they (poets) write whatever they feel like writing. . . .

CHILD: If it makes sense to them. . . .

CHILD: Sometimes when I talk to my friend she makes rhymes by mistake.

TEACHER: By mistake?

CHILD: She says things like, "Oh, I hurt my toe!"

CHILD: Sometimes they write it in funny ways.

TEACHER: How do you mean?

CHILD: Like sometimes they use numbers to make letters, like you can have t-e-n and then use a number for the word.

CHILD: Sometimes when I write poems it's about little things, like my poem about the feather. Most people ignore little things like that.

TEACHER: So you like to write poems about little things?

CHILD: Yeah.

---

[15] Herbert Read, *The Forms of Things Unknown* (New York: World, 1963), p. 122.

TEACHER: *(To class)* Do you know what a poem is yet? I'm not so sure.

CHILD: Maybe when you like something you can write about it.

CHILD: It's like expressing your feelings.

CHILD: Sometimes you write a poem and you're saying how *you* feel except people just can't see it by looking at it; they've got to understand what the poem means and try to understand how you feel.

TEACHER: True.

CHILD: If you have something that you really want to get out that's in your mind and you can't get it out in words, you can write it down.

CHILD: Sometimes when you write down your thoughts you can get everything together.

TEACHER: What do poems look like?

CHILD: Small sentences.

TEACHER: Are they?

CHILD: No, they're lines, like.

TEACHER: Sometimes. All poems are not small sentences.

CHILD: A lot of times they rhyme; they have sentences that rhyme together.

CHILD: Most poems that have something to do with the person's feelings don't rhyme.

TEACHER: The ones you've seen don't rhyme?

CHILD: The funny ones rhyme mostly.

CHILD: Joey's right but lots of times serious ones rhyme, like one line would say something but three other lines down it would rhyme.

CHILD: Sometimes people put writing marks like semicolons and stuff and shape it like what the poem is about.

CHILD: If you want your poem to rhyme do you have to write about the same thing?

TEACHER: That's what I was going to ask. What are poems about? Do they have to be about a certain thing?

CHILDREN: No, they can be about anything.

TEACHER: Do they have to *look a certain way*?

CHILD: No.

TEACHER: Do they have to *sound a certain way*? Do they all have to rhyme?

CHILDREN: No.

TEACHER: So what would you say about poems from all that?

CHILD: A poem can be anything.

TEACHER: So we can say that a poem is "Anyway Thisaway" [16] or thisaway–thataway. It's really up to the person who is writing it.

CHILD: I don't understand 'cause I thought all poems had to rhyme.

TEACHER: You found out something today, didn't you?

CHILD: They have *rhythm*.

TEACHER: That's true. What do you mean by that?

CHILD: They have a *pace,* like.

---

[16] Sam Cornish, Lucille Clifton, Jeanette Amidon, *Anyway Thisaway* (Washington, D.C.: Central Atlantic Regional Educational Laboratory, 1969).

TEACHER: Good. How does that differ from writing regular sentences?

CHILD: Poems have more of a rhythm.

CHILD: They don't have to rhyme. It's just that when you read them the words all blend together; it sort of sounds like it rhymes sometimes when it really doesn't.

TEACHER: What does it do?

CHILD: A poem has to have some kind of *beat* or some kind of *rhyme* somehow, or else it would probably be some kind of story.

TEACHER: So a poem has a special kind of rhythm. Do all poems have the same rhythm?

CHILD: No.

CHILD: The difference in the *sentences* is that in a *story* they have to make some kind of sense, they got to be *in a certain order; sentences* in *poems* can be *in any order* the writer wants to put them in.

CHILD: The poems that don't rhyme can be like a sentence but when you read a poem, it sort of gives it a pace, a rhythm; I don't know how it does that, how the words go. . . .

TEACHER: Okay. There's a special arrangement of the words.

CHILD: Usually if I read a poem I get more of a picture in my mind than in a story.

TEACHER: What do you mean by picture?

CHILD: It doesn't explain more to you, you just get a feeling.

CHILD: You get a mellow feeling.

TEACHER: I want to stay with picture. I want to know what you mean by that.

CHILD: Sometimes if the writer is really in a sad mood when he writes a poem you can feel that same feeling and also picture what the poem is about.

CHILD: Sometimes poems are like part of your imagination; when you read them they blend with your imagination.

CHILD: Sometimes if I read a poem I get a completely different picture in my head than what it says.

TEACHER: Let's stay with that.

CHILD: Say I read a poem about a balloon and it's floating up in the air or something like that, then I start to see a balloon floating around.

TEACHER: So you can actually see a picture of what's happening.

CHILD: You don't get the same feeling when it's a story.

TEACHER: What's different about it?

CHILD: I don't know.

TEACHER: Maybe that's something you'll find out.

CHILD: Two people wouldn't think of the same picture in their heads.

TEACHER: That's very true.

CHILD: My sister wrote a poem and I didn't get a picture about it, I got a feeling.

TEACHER: How does the poet help you get a picture?

CHILD: When some poets are writing, they don't put a title on it; they let somebody read it and then if you try to get the picture that the writer gets it's not going to be exactly the same.

CHILD: Sometimes the writer, to give you a good picture of how he feels, will use somebody in the story as himself and the rest of the people as friends of his or enemies.

TEACHER: Are you talking about stories, poems, or both?

CHILD: It could be both.

CHILD: The way I picture a poem is better than I picture a story. In a story I just read it, but in a poem you sort of give something to it, you sort of *sing the poem.*

CHILD: Sense it. . . .

CHILD: When a poet writes a poem you get an eye-picture in your mind; he usually describes it the way Celia wrote her feather poem; I forgot it but she describes it.

CHILD: Sometimes I have a dream and I describe the dream on a piece of paper . . . and if it's good, I dream the dream again.

TEACHER: It's the difference between "what is" and what you "feel it to be." Is that it?

CHILD: Yeah.

TEACHER: If I were a poet and I had a feeling that I wanted to put in a poem, what kinds of things could I do to make you know how I was feeling?

CHILD: You do like Chris said, a character in your poem not like you. Maybe an animal, but the same kind of character so that the reader knows it's you.

TEACHER: How does a poet make the pictures that you see?

CHILD: In words.

TEACHER: So we can say that poetry is *word pictures.*

CHILD: Sometimes people make up things in poems, like they'll take a poem and change it to a different thing, like in some nursery rhymes the poets are sort of telling their feelings but they change characters and things like Humpty Dumpty.

CHILD: Well, I think books with pictures sort of wreck it.

TEACHER: Why?

CHILD: Because it takes away your imagination. It's sort of good to imagine it by yourself.

TEACHER: So you get your own picture. You said something interesting; you said sometimes the poet gives you a picture and it reminds you of something else.

CHILD: I haven't read any poems but I like what Angela said because when I read *The Yearling* there wasn't one picture in it and I still had a good idea of what everything looked like.

TEACHER: How did you know how everything looked?

CHILD: The way the author described it.

CHILD: Nobody's ideas could be the same; like he says he got a picture of what he thought it was, but if somebody read a poem exactly the way he read it it wouldn't be the same thing, it would be a completely different picture.

CHILD: If you're reading a book and it doesn't have a picture on that page and you turn the page and you see the picture you saw in your mind.

TEACHER: Do you see the picture you saw in your mind?

CHILD: Sometimes.

CHILD: The writer is more real in a poem. Sometimes he can put a lot more feeling in a poem than he can in a story, like in a poem you don't have to put in chapters or stuff that sometimes stop the feeling.

CHILD: Well, you know they say in stories that the author has a picture in his mind and that's why he writes it down.

PROBLEM: To explore the way words are used to name experiences

TEACHER: We can make poetry about things or colors that we see everyday. Let's think about how colors make things feel to us. What is gold?

CHILD: Gold is gold.

CHILD: Gold is honey.

CHILD: Gold is a ring.

CHILD: Gold is paint.

CHILD: Gold is grass.

TEACHER: What time of the year is gold grass?

CHILD: Autumn.

CHILD: I said brass!

CHILD: Andrew's pants are gold.

TEACHER: Look around the room, what is gold?

CHILD: The door knob.

TEACHER: Look outside the window.

CHILD: The trees.

TEACHER: What makes them gold?

CHILD: The sun.

TEACHER: Look beyond the trees, what is gold?

CHILD: The sunshine.

TEACHER: Look at the people around us, what else is gold?

CHILD: Your belt.

CHILD: Corn can be gold.

TEACHER: You know what? The colors that interest you are the ones you should write about. I'll read you a poem that this grown-up wrote about "What Is Red"? [17] but just the last part because it's more interesting.

> Fire-cracker, fire-engine
> Fire-flicker red—
> And when you're angry
> Red runs through your head.
> Red is an Indian,
> A Valentine heart,

[17] Mary O'Neill, *Hailstones and Halibut Bones* (Garden City, N.Y.: Doubleday, 1961), p. 44.

> The trimming on
> A circus cart.
> Red is a lipstick,
> Red is a shout,
> Red is a signal
> That says: "Watch out!"
> Red is a great big
> Rubber ball.
> Red is the giant-est
> Color of all.
> Red is a show-off
> No doubt about it—
> But can you imagine
> Living without it?

TEACHER: Is there such a word as giant-est?

CHILDREN: No-oooooo!

TEACHER: But does it work?

CHILD: Yes.

TEACHER: Which means that poetry is making up your own words to express a feeling.

CHILD: Red keeps you alive.

CHILD: Blood-red.

CHILD: Blood is red and heart is red.

TEACHER: That's a really good beginning line, "red is a color that keeps you alive." That's talking poetry. Let me read you some very simple poems written in the fifth grade, which give different meaning to things you are familiar with.

> cats:
> funny
>   freaky
>   fat
>   and weary
> that have
> machines
>   in there
> stomach

>   Eyes
> little colorful round
>   marbles
> seeing life   all
>   around
> us
> looking up, down, and
>   sideways
> seeing the world
>   alone.

We have twenty minutes in which to write. See if you can "feel" color.

You don't have to write about a color, but just for fun, see if you can put colors into words that make us feel your feeling.

Separate when you write; don't sit next to each other because poetry is a very private thing.

DISCUSSION

TEACHER: Here are some of the poems you have written.

> Hord * is the moon with rokss † and
> The sun with a happy face

> grean is a Metol in
> The sping is a flour stem
> blowing in The breez.
> grean is sumones t shrut
> saying big bear. grean
> is filling you get in The
> air.

Translation: green is a metal in
the spring
is a flower stem
blowing in the breeze.
green is someone's T-shirt
saying "Big Bear"
green is (the) feeling you get
in the air.

I'm not going to tell you what this poem is about; see if you can feel what this is:

> Dimetrodon
> long tale,
> fan on his back,
> sharp teeth,
> meat-eater.

CHILD: Dinosaur.

TEACHER: How did you know?

CHILD: Because it has a fan on his back.

TEACHER: That really makes him very special. I was talking to Bridget yesterday about what is the most special thing about him. Is there another animal that has a fan on its back?

CHILDREN: Yes, no.

CHILD: A peacock.

TEACHER: But there are very special things about this poem that let you know it's a dinosaur. What else?

CHILD: A meat eater with sharp teeth.

---

* hard.
† rocks.

CHILD: Dimetrodon

TEACHER: A dimetrodon is something you've studied about.

CHILD: If it's a meat eater it must be a dimetrodon.

TEACHER: You see how few words that are put together give you the feeling of this animal? Here's another one:

BOB CAT
Running! hiding!
crawling about
Be on the lookout!
don't shout!

What kind of feeling do you get from that? Who's the poet talking about?

CHILD: A bobcat.

TEACHER: Is he just talking about the person who is around the bobcat? What's he talking about?

CHILD: Bobcat?

TEACHER: Is he talking just about the person, or is he also describing the quality of the bobcat? How?

CHILD: Running, hiding.

TEACHER: How?

CHILD: Crawling about.

TEACHER: Do you get a feeling you know where he is all the time, this bobcat?

green is a Metol in The spring. it is a flour stem blowing in The brezy. green is someones t shurt saying big bear. green is filling you get in The air.

CHILD: No.

TEACHER: No, and it's just the words that tell you that. Who is he saying should be on the lookout—to whom?

CHILD: To the person that sees the bobcat.

TEACHER: Yes, then she's not talking to the bobcat anymore. Who's she talking to when she says, "Be on the lookout, don't shout"?

CHILD: You!

CHILD: He can spring from behind the bushes.

TEACHER: That's right. She's talking to you, the listeners. So in four little lines she's telling you about how the bobcat moves and what to do if he moves toward you. That's a poem.

CHILD: That's my first true poem.

TEACHER: That's really a fine poem.

PROBLEM: To explore the elements of poetry in relation to rhythm, sound, and imagery

TEACHER: Let's think about how does a poem feel, how does it look, what does it sound like? Here's a poem that one of you put in the "tiger's mouth" of your poetry box.

> A dinosaur dinns* on a vine
> at half past 9
> a very good time
> is half past 9
> he began at 10 to 5
> do you like to dinn on a vine
> hm?

CHILD: That's a story.

TEACHER: Is it?

CHILDREN: Yes. . . . No.

TEACHER: You're shaking your head. Why do you think it's not a story?

CHILD: 'Cause it doesn't have to be short to be a rhyme, I mean a poem.

TEACHER: That's right, poems can be long or short, depending on how much you want to say. What else do you notice about this poem?

CHILD: It rhymes.

TEACHER: What rhymes?

CHILD: *Nine* and *dine*.

CHILD: Vine.

CHILD: Nine, dine, time.

TEACHER: But it's not the kind of poetry that has a rhyme like,

> duh-duh, duh-duh, duh-duh, duh-duh

* dines.

a dinosaur dinns, on
a vine at haff past 9
a verry Good Time is haff
past 9 he began at 10 To
5 do you like To dinn
on a vine hm?

duh-duh, duh-duh, duh-duh, duh-duh
(Sounds like a doggerel rhythm.)

The rhyme is built into the rhythm. Listen to it again. *(She repeats poem.)*

CHILD: Who wrote that?

CHILD: I did.

CHILD: That's good!

TEACHER: I didn't read it the way she wrote it. Let me show you what it looks like on the page. I'll read it again and see if you can hear the difference:

> a dinosaur dinns on
> a vine at half past 9
> a very Good Time is half
> past 9 he began at 10 To
> 5 do you like to dine
> on a vine hm?

What's the difference in the way I read it the second time?

CHILD: You acted as if you weren't as interested in it as much as the other time.

TEACHER: Well, I really am interested in it both ways. It could be the way the lines are run together that takes away some of the interest.

CHILD: Well, one word on each line is not enough.

TEACHER: Oh yes, you wouldn't want to put one word on each line in a poem like this.

Here's a poem written by someone in the fifth grade:

> DOUGHNUT
> Squeeze   squish
> pull   the dough
> Shape it in a circle
> and cut out the hole

CHILDREN: *(Laughter.)*

TEACHER: You're laughing, so what kind of poem is this?

CHILDREN: A funny one.

TEACHER: A funny one; it has humor. . . .

CHILD: It has rhymes in it too.

TEACHER: Not exactly rhymes, but they sound the same. What are the two words that rhyme?

CHILD: *Dough* and *hole.*

TEACHER: Shall I read it again? (*As teacher reads children shout, "dough" and "hole."*) *Dough* and *hole* aren't spelled the same but they sound the same and that's rhyming in poetry. Here's another poem from *Anyway This-away:*

```
          if
            a
          wasp
              sting
                you
                  & he
                      die
          you  might
                  say
                    a
                  wasp
                    is  not
                        very
                            wise
```

CHILD: A wasp stings a boy and he wouldn't be wise becauses he loses his stinger.

TEACHER: What happens to a wasp when he stings somebody?

CHILD: He dies.

TEACHER: So what does the poet say to the wasp?

CHILD: You're not wise because you stung someone.

TEACHER: Yes. Can you talk to an animal or an insect if you want to?

CHILD: Yes.

CHILD: No. Just a parrot, a dog and a cat.

TEACHER: In a poem you can talk to anybody or to yourself. If you want to say to a wasp, "if you sting me you're not very wise," you can say that because a poem doesn't have to be real.

CHILD: A poem doesn't have to be true.

PROBLEM: To discover how words are used to express feelings

TEACHER: This is another poem that was put in the "poetry drawer." I want you to think about what gives you the feeling of this poem.

```
              waters
                   running
                         free
            free
                 to
                      rome *
            clear waters
                          running
                                free
```

I would like to know what feeling you got and how you think you got it.

CHILD: Some water is like in a swimming pool or a sink, that's all closed in, but this is sort of like streams in a country; they're free and they don't have anything to keep them in—they belong to everyone.

TEACHER: It seems like the key word you picked up is *free*. Let's read it again and see how the use of that word gives you that feeling. *(She repeats the poem.)*

CHILD: At the end he says, "clear water." He could mean the pollution of the clear water, and how they're knocking down all the trees and things, and building houses where rivers used to be.

TEACHER: So *clear* for you means used to be clear but isn't anymore.

CHILD: Yeah.

CHILD: I get the feeling that people are polluting and there are streams and places where they're free of all the pollution and all the things people dump into them.

CHILD: I feel a lot different. I feel like it's a river in the country and it's roaming down a really peaceful place; I don't feel anything about pollution or anything.

TEACHER: What is the poet talking about? What is the main idea about the water?

CHILD: It can just go, it's free, it's not like a street or anything.

TEACHER: Listen to where the *free's* are in the poem. *(She repeats the poem.)* How do you get the impression that *free* is important in this poem?

CHILD: He repeats it.

TEACHER: Yes. He has got two *free's* together and *free* is the last word in the poem.

CHILD: He wants to get that impression into your mind.

TEACHER: And he really does. What do we call the movement of a poem?

CHILD: The *rhythm* or *beat* of it.

TEACHER: Listen to this one:

LEAVES

slowly, slowly
they move with the wind
they get tired and old
and brown

* roam.

```
they cannot hold on
they fall
slowly, slowly
they drift in the air
down
        down
                down
until they touch the fresh soil
lifelessly
they lie there
                dead
```

CHILD: It's sort of like they're going through the life of leaves.

TEACHER: Who's going through the life of leaves?

CHILD: The poet.

TEACHER: The poet has become a leaf; that's why this is a strong poem. Do you understand the difference between *looking* at a leaf and saying "it's green and it's got veins and it's hanging there," and *being* that leaf? This poem is a leaf. That's what I mean about writing a poem from the inside out instead of from the outside in.

CHILD: The poem is about a leaf—the leaves that fall and lie on the ground, but to me it represents someone.

CHILD: That's what I mean when I say the poet is the leaf.

CHILD: Not necessarily the poet, it could be a person.

CHILD: In a way it's like a person, it could have started as a leaf but it could be a person. People just wave in the wind and then when they start getting old and start falling down and then they lie on the ground dead.

CHILD: Seems like the leaf is straining to hold on to its life.

CHILDREN: Yeah, yeah.

TEACHER: How do you get that impression? Let me read the first part again. *(She repeats it.)*

CHILD: Because they are getting tired of holding on.

TEACHER: Tired and old and brown; that's really nice.

CHILD: It's sort of like a person's life is the life of a leaf. And they're sort of living like they feel their life is a leaf.

TEACHER: Okay, I think that has been said in about three different ways and I agree with you. There's something interesting in the last part of the poem that gives you the feeling of this poem.

```
they drift in the air
down
        down
                down
until they touch the fresh soil
lifelessly
they lie there
                dead
```

There are opposites here.

CHILD: Like when they drift down slowly but they hit the *fresh* soil. The soil is still living cause it never really died.

TEACHER: Right. That's really a nice opposition. Because what is dead comes down to the fresh soil and enables it to live. What kinds of things does the poet do to make it work?

CHILD: The way the poet uses the words and the way some words are used over again.

TEACHER: Be specific. What word is used over again?

CHILD: In the end, *down* is used over again and in the beginning. . . .

CHILD: The way he explains that it's really slowly, slowly dying and all of a sudden he just goes "dead."

TEACHER: Right, it's been dying all this time and then it's dead. Now how does he do that?

CHILD: He says "slowly, slowly down," and then "lifelessly," which is still life, and then we get "dead."

TEACHER: We get "slowly, slowly" and then "down, down" and we have a feeling that it is "dying, dying" and then "lifelessly."

CHILD: In a way it's the same word as *dead*—he falls down lifelessly, then he's dead completely.

TEACHER: How does the poet do this? With pictures? With rhythm? How does he get the feeling of "dying" and then "dead"?

CHILD: I guess he does it with *rhythm*.

CHILD: You start floating down.

TEACHER: It would really be hard to read this fast; you'd have to follow the feeling of the words and go "slow-ly, slow-ly."

Here's another poem that has a similar kind of feeling:

> Falling,
>   falling
> getting nowhere
> colors flashing
> by
> getting nowhere
> scary, awful
> feelings
> creeping through you
> everything blurred
> falling
> getting nowhere

CHILD: It's like when you're falling you're really getting no place in particular.

TEACHER: How does this person feel about getting nowhere? What's it like, and how do you know?

CHILD: When you're falling down you sort of feel like you don't have a surface underneath you, like when you dream you're falling down. . . .

CHILD: . . . like it never ends.

TEACHER: What kind of feeling is that? Is it, "Oh great, I'm falling"?

CHILD: Scary.

TEACHER: Okay. *(She repeats the poem.)* How do we know it's scary aside from the fact that he says *scary?* Is this really happening? Is this person really falling, like from a plane or something?

CHILD: No.

CHILD: It starts like falling that never ends.

TEACHER: What do you mean by falling?

CHILD: It's like a dream.

TEACHER: It's dreamlike, for you. Angela, you said "not having a surface to land on."

CHILD: You don't know what is going to happen to you.

TEACHER: Okay. When you don't know what's going to happen it feels like falling. Do you see that? It doesn't mean this person is falling off a cliff or plane or whatever. He wants to give you a picture of how he feels. He feels like he's falling; he's not necessarily falling. Let's try this one:

> How do I tell them
> my dreams
> are   cramped
>   inside my mind
> trying to break out
> with crepy, wepy * tears
> How do I tell them

CHILD: It's like you've got something to say and you have to get it out and you can't get it out.

CHILD: You'd get it out in dreams but only to yourself; you want to get it out but it just sort of stays there.

TEACHER: Why?

CHILD: It's like with the cramped part, he's sort of saying it's in there and there is so much sort of wedged in but it can't come out.

TEACHER: Listen once again, okay? *(She repeats the poem.)*

CHILD: Like he had a dream that even if he tries to tell somebody, he can't tell it exactly how he has it in his mind.

TEACHER: So it's hard to say what you have in your dreams; it's hard to tell people how you feel. I feel that this is a very strong poem and I want to see if you can tell what things make it strong. *(She repeats the poem.)*

CHILD: Tears—it could be something sad.

TEACHER: Does this poem make you sad?

CHILD: Well, yes.

CHILD: Yeah, it does.

TEACHER: What does the poet do?

CHILD: The way he uses "creepy, weepy tears," sort of crying, but it's hard to get out.

TEACHER: Right, it's all locked inside. How does the poet do this?

CHILD: He goes, "how do I tell them, how do I tell them?"

* creepy, weepy.

TEACHER: Yes, that's the way the poem begins and ends. And that's what is so
painful: "How do I get this out?"

CHILD: Tell him!

TEACHER: The poet isn't asking you for an answer; the poet is saying, "This is
what's happening to me." There is really a strong *image* in here; see if
you can find it. *(She reads the first four lines.)* What's the picture that you
get that's so strong?

CHILD: All these different things cramped up in his head and he can't tell them.

TEACHER: Yes, these dreams are cramped up in his head trying to break out.
You don't usually think of dreams that way. I get the feeling that this
poet's head is just about to explode.

CHILD: It doesn't have to be just dreams you have at night; it could be dreams of
something else—like dreams of wanting something. . . .

CHILD: . . . like daydreams.

TEACHER: Beautiful. I've got some more poetry that I think I'm going to save
for next time. I think you've had enough for one day. I'd like you to spend
the next forty minutes writing.

PROBLEM: To explore ways words are used in forming a poetic sentence

TEACHER: We're going to do something a little different today. I want to talk
about sentences in poetry. How do we know what word should go where,
or if anything should go anywhere? Maybe anything can go anywhere.
What do you think a line of poetry represents?

CHILD: I don't understand.

TEACHER: Is there any way you could space a poem differently so that it would
read better or make better sense to express what's inside the poem? Look
at this one that I've put up on the board:

> waters running free, free to rome *
> clear waters running free

CHILD: If I really want to separate things to make a different feeling, then I
write, "rivers running free," then "free to roam," and on a different line
"clear waters running free."

TEACHER: How does that change things? What does that do?

CHILD: You don't read them together.

TEACHER: Yes, it separates what?

CHILD: Feelings.

TEACHER: Okay, feelings or thoughts. Brian, your hand was up.

CHILD: Yeah. I got a different way of writing it. On the first line I would have it
diagonal, like down.

* roam.

TEACHER: (*Writing on board*) What do you want to be diagonal?
CHILD: "Waters running free."
TEACHER: Like this?

> waters
>   running
>   free

The diagonal starts here with *waters* and goes down to *free*.
What would be the difference if we put them on two horizontal lines or on the diagonal?
CHILD: Brian's idea would read more like a rhythm.
TEACHER: Give me an example; read it.
CHILD: Well, like the way you put it,

> "waters,
>   running
>   free"

it's like a waterfall.
TEACHER: So that changes the rhythm for you. That's the way I would read it. Anyone else have a suggestion as to how this could be written? Okay, so those were two ideas. Chris said that the new line has its own feeling and I said that each new line had its own feeling or its own thought. The point is that the *line takes the shape of the thought*. That means, *each line might have a different shape*. We might not choose two diagonals. We could have one diagonal and one something else, but the line should be in the shape of the thought. Does everybody understand that? That's sort of complicated. I noticed that people are writing some really fine poems and they're all sort of bunched together. Now I'm reading them to you the way I would space them because they make better sense to me. What would I do with this one I've put up here?

> SKIN BOARDING
> gliding on wet sand
> flying on a bouncy carpet
> down
>   down
> fishes looking at you
> right in the
>   eye

CHILDREN: (*Laughter.*)
TEACHER: Anyone want to say something about this?
CHILD: It sounds like the person has a thing about fish.
TEACHER: This poem's called "Charley." This is the way the poet wrote it:

> Keep going Charlie
> your not as smart
> as everyone else
> but keep your mind

> going, with all your
> fantasy and imagination
> that's all you have
> keep going Charlie
> you might make it
> some day, keep going

CHILD: Sounds like the person who wrote the poem is not as smart as everybody, but has something that is as smart as everybody—like it's their imagination.

TEACHER: Fantasy and imagination. I think we understand what it's all about. What makes it strong, if you think it's strong?

CHILD: It sort of sounds like, "Don't say anything but keep going."

TEACHER: Keep going! Okay, let me read it again. *(She repeats the poem.)*

CHILD: The person who says it's Charley is sort of mean but nice and sort of teases him.

TEACHER: What gives you the idea of teasing? I'm just curious about that.

CHILD: "That's all you have."

TEACHER: It might be the way I read it. I don't think that necessarily has to sound that way—let me read it again. Let's see if it does have to sound that way. *(She repeats the poem.)*

CHILD: I think the fact that he says fantasy and imagination is good, not teasing him, but good.

CHILD: They're saying, "You know like fantasy and imagination is all you have, but you might be able to make something out of that."

CHILD: It depends on the way the reader reads it. Because the first time, you sounded like you were teasing.

TEACHER: Right, it has a lot to do with the way it is read. That is why the poet has to do as much as he can to make sure it is going to be read the way he wants it to be understood; that is why we were talking about lines and things. That is one of the problems with this poem. It could be reorganized as far as lines go and it would read better.

CHILD: It doesn't sound like someone else is saying it to him; it is like he is sort of thinking it.

TEACHER: About himself? Or someone else?

CHILD: About himself.

TEACHER: So if that is the way you feel about it the poet is speaking from the "inside out."

CHILD: The thing that makes it sound so strong is the poet says "keep going." He says it about five times in sentences. . . .

CHILD: The reason it sounds so sarcastic is because it says, "keep going—maybe you'll make it."

TEACHER: Or you could read it that way. Actually it says, you "might" make it. I can read it "you *might* make it" or "you might make it"; it depends on how it is read. The emphasis on words is important, too. That's why it is so wonderful when poets record themselves reading their own poetry, because it is easier to tell how they meant it. If I can find my Dylan

Thomas records and find something that would be good for you to listen to, I'll bring them in and you'll hear a great poet reading his own poetry greatly and you'll see what I mean.

CHILD: I sort of go along with Joey's idea; that he's describing himself as someone who's not really as smart as anyone else because he may have some problems.

CHILD: He thinks he has an imagination, like he has dreams of doing some things he has never done before, and he wants to keep up with other people, so he says he might make it. I think Charley is the person who wrote it.

TEACHER: That's a possibility. Here's another feeling entirely:

> CLOWN
> In a car
> crash, bang
> pants fall
> down
> running, running
> down
> crack a joke
> honk my nose
> That's the way it goes!

CHILDREN: *(Laughter.)*

TEACHER: Is it fun to be a clown?

CHILDREN: No.

CHILD: I think it's an act. I saw a couple of acts of clowns in cars that crash up.

TEACHER: It's interesting how this is written because the *downs* are written on angles going down. Is there anything more you want to talk about? I think it would be great if this week end if you could spend half an hour doing some writing. Try to get yourself alone or in whatever circumstances are best for you to write in. Just something over the week end so we'll have materials to use for Monday.

PROBLEM: To explore the way words in poetry are used to create images

TEACHER: It's hard to sit down and write a long poem so I want us to start with something really simple. Choose something, maybe a concrete thing, and let your imagination go and see what you feel about that thing and what it reminds you of.

CHILD: Can we go outside and do it?

TEACHER: If you think that will help you you certainly can. I'm suggesting that you take one idea at a time. You can write as many of these as you want.

CHILD: When you talk about a poem, different parts of it make you get different feelings.

CHILD: Do we have to have things like commas and everything?

TEACHER: No. I won't even correct your spelling. Do what you want to do and the other stuff doesn't matter; the important thing is getting your ideas down. Just as examples, let me read you some poems from something called *Anyway Thisaway;* it's a collection of poetry: [18]

Bird
  is a dark
place
    for singing
safe
   from
     rain

CHILD: It's beautiful.

TEACHER: What's beautiful about that? *(She repeats the poem.)*

CHILD: They wrote down what they thought, not what they thought other people would think about the poem.

CHILD: It's like it's raining, it's dark out, and when he's in his nest it's dark, so it's a dark place for him to sing.

CHILD: It reminds me of a bird in the wintertime but he wants to be someplace where he's warm.

TEACHER: Where is this bird?

CHILD: In some dark place, in a cave probably; it's like he's not free.

TEACHER: Let me read it again. *(She repeats the poem.)*
Notice it didn't say *in* a dark place. It says, "Bird *is* a dark place for singing. . . ."

CHILD: Maybe they put themselves in the bird's place.

TEACHER: To feel how it would be to be a bird?

CHILD: You can't really talk except to other birds, sort of like dark. . . .

TEACHER: Where, where is the dark place?

CHILD: Inside of himself.

TEACHER: So the bird *is* the place, not *like* a dark place. He is a dark place for singing. Who got that "safe from rain" part?

CHILD: Inside himself; he can't wait because he's got fur on the outside.

CHILD: Fur?

CHILD: Feathers.

TEACHER: I haven't seen too many furry birds lately! What do you think this poem is about:

yr
voice
comes
out
of
a giant
house

<hr>

[18] Sam Cornish, Lucille Clifton, Jeanette Amidon, *Anyway-Thisaway* (Washington, D.C., Central Atlantic Regional Educational Laboratory, 1969).

CHILD: Like your mouth is really big, your voice is just coming out.

TEACHER: So what's the house?

CHILD: The mouth.

TEACHER: What about a "giant house"? Your voice doesn't just come from here (*points to mouth*). Where does it come from?

CHILD: Your whole body.

TEACHER: Do you get the feeling it is a deep-down voice? Now do you see what I mean by picking something concrete—birds, voice, anything that gives you a certain feeling about something?

DISCUSSION

TEACHER: I want to start by reading one called "Tunnel" that is exactly what we were talking about yesterday:

<pre>
                    Tunnel
          darkscary   anethere *
                    world
          I feel
                    alone
</pre>

How do you react to that?

CHILD: I like that.

TEACHER: What do you like about it?

CHILD: It gave me the impression I was in a tunnel and it's just black. . . .

CHILDREN: Yeah, yeaah.

CHILD: . . . and all I see is black all around me.

TEACHER: What did the poet do to give you that feeling?

CHILD: "Dark and scary," like. . . .

CHILD: . . . there's no one else.

TEACHER: So the poet describes not only what the tunnel is like but how he felt about it.

<pre>
          Death:
          sad, empty
               cries
</pre>

CHILD: Someone in our class?

TEACHER: These are all from this class. This one I would like to see put into a longer poem, but it's very nice standing alone too:

<pre>
          the lust * cry of the dieing
          dog
               left the valley
          echoing with fear
</pre>

* another.
* last.

Does anyone have a reaction to that? *(She repeats the poem.)* What two things are coming together?

CHILD: Fear.

CHILD: Echo.

CHILD: Valley.

TEACHER: We could go through every word of the poem but it's the way echoing and fear are connected.

CHILD: He says, like "dying dog."

TEACHER: Yes, that's nice. What's that called by the way?

CHILD: Alliteration.

TEACHER: You like the way that sounded. What does that create? "The last cry of the dying dog." Notice it didn't say, "the last cry of the dog who is dying."

CHILD: It stands out.

TEACHER: Okay, it stands out and it creates a special what?

CHILD: It creates a feeling.

TEACHER: How?

CHILD: Because it says of the "dying dog."

TEACHER: Yes, it has its own rhythm, that's exactly what I mean, and the rhythm would change if I said, "the dog who is dying."

CHILD: You really kind of feel you know the dog, you know? I feel like it's alive because the last cry kind of opens and nobody's there.

TEACHER: Kind of a lonely feeling.

CHILD: It sort of sounds something like the person is sad about it, like "echoing fear."

TEACHER: Let me read it again, because the way it is stated is stronger than the way a lot of people are remembering it. *(She repeats the poem.)*

How do you feel at the end of this thing?

CHILD: It's sort of like animals that have lived in an area and die; it still sort of echoes the spirit.

TEACHER: How does it make *you* feel? Mark, how do you feel?

CHILD: It's sort of a mellow feeling at the end.

TEACHER: For me it's an empty feeling.

Do you know what mellow means? Mellow is actually used to mean kind of calm and smooth. I don't really feel mellow; empty is more how I feel. Like empty and helpless. I get the feeling of this enormous valley and this one cry and the echo of this cry makes me feel empty.

EYES
little colorful round marbles
seeing life all around us
looking   up
                down
and sideways
seeing the world alone

CHILD: Would you read it again? *(The teacher repeats the poem.)* Sounds like the person is seeing everything alone, to me it comes stronger than the other parts.

CHILD: It's like the poet is seeing eyes through marbles and looking sideways.

TEACHER: The *sideways* kind of got to me, too.

CHILD: They're sort of really wandering, looking for something.

TEACHER: What do you think looking for something has to do with the last part, "seeing the world alone"?

CHILD: The rest of your body can't see.

TEACHER: Okay.

CHILD: It seems like the eyes are looking for somebody. Looking around and seeing the world alone. Looking for somebody or something to keep them company.

TEACHER: Does anyone have anything else to say about the poem? Okay, I want everyone to write some poetry and this will be the last writing you do, at least for this class. Then we'll go on next week . . . so I'd like everybody to work now.

PROBLEM: To distinguish between describing something and feeling something through the language of poetry

TEACHER: Let's talk about the difference between *describing* something and *feeling* something—how poets use certain words to get you to feel certain things. You've got the idea of how they use pictures to make you feel certain ways; let's think about sound, or the way words work together. I want to read you a few things from *Anyway Thisaway* and then I want to read you some of your own things.

These poems from *Anyway Thisaway* were written by second-grade children:

> sometime
>
> death
>
> is
>
> between
>
> growing
>
> things

Does that do anything to anybody?

CHILD: It's sort of like saying that nature keeps its balance—like lions and animals eat other animals, and other animals eat plants.

TEACHER: That's a good start. Does anyone else get anything from that? Do you want me to read it again?

CHILDREN: Yes.

TEACHER: *(She repeats the poem; there is no response from children.)* If nobody wants to say anything about that one we can go on to another one. Here's another one on death. I don't mean to be hitting you with death this early in the morning; it just happens to be on that subject.

> death:
> something
> calls
> you down

CHILD: It's like when you die, someone wants you to, not because they don't like you, it's just your time, like it's pulling you down into your grave.

CHILD: It's like when you're dying you're sort of helpless and you can't save yourself and you're being pulled down.

CHILD: When you're going down, down, down, it's like you're dying a painless death.

TEACHER: Okay, let's read some of your own things and we'll see your reaction to them.

> Waiting
> Waiting
> Waiting
> For something that is
> not there
> They *will* come

CHILD: Will you read that again? *(The teacher repeats the poem.)* It's like saying if it's not there it will come sometime.

TEACHER: What will come sometime?

CHILD: Something that you're waiting for that isn't really there.

TEACHER: That's a good start.

CHILD: When you're really waiting for something badly and you want it real badly—like Christmas to come—you keep waiting for it and it seems like it takes forever.

TEACHER: Do you enjoy waiting?

CHILDREN: No.

TEACHER: It's not a joyful thing.

CHILD: Sometimes it is.

CHILD: If you had everything you really wanted and you didn't wait for it, you just got it, you wouldn't be very happy because you got everything, and what are your hopes for now?

TEACHER: A poem is like talking to yourself. Listen to the last line—that poet is telling himself something: "they will come."

CHILD: Well, I don't think it's anything like Christmas, because it says, "they" will come.

TEACHER: Right. What is the person who wrote this poem really saying? What is "waiting" for him?

CHILD: For somebody?

TEACHER: So how is he when he is waiting for somebody?

CHILD: Lonesome.

TEACHER: He's all alone, sure. Does anyone want to say anything else about

Waiting

, Waiting.

Waiting for
somthing that is not
there,

They will come

life
the life of
smone who
does not live, silenty He
lies There.

He does
not speek,
He does
not move His life

over

Joey

it? Okay, then let me ask you some questions. How do we get the feeling that waiting isn't such a terrific thing for this poet?

CHILD: He says, "waiting, waiting, waiting."

TEACHER: So you can see how the repetition of the word can give you a certain feeling. How do we know that it's a person this poet is waiting for?

CHILD: " 'Cause he says 'they.' "

TEACHER: So you see the word tells you what's going on. It's just one little word, so you have to be alert. Here's another one:

> LIFE
> The life of someone
> Who does not live
> Silently, he lies there
> He does not speak
> He does not move
> His life
> over.

What would be another word for that poem?

CHILD: Death.

CHILD: He's not saying that once you're dead you're finished.

TEACHER: What kind of death is this? Shall I read it again?

CHILDREN: Yeah.

TEACHER: *(Repeats poem.)*

CHILD: It's like saying when you're dead you're not really dead, there's still the spirit there . . . of your life.

TEACHER: I got something quite different from that; I wonder how the rest of you feel.

CHILD: I think it's sort of saying, "Death, your life's over"; it's more like, "Life, you don't have enough of it so it's over."

TEACHER: Why is it over?

CHILD: 'Cause he's lived long enough. . . .

TEACHER: I don't know if there's evidence in this poem for that. Why is it over?

CHILD: He's not really mentioning death; maybe he's afraid of it or something.

CHILD: When you think of something that's death, you think of it as a scary thing or something bad that's happening, but in this it seems really sad. But it doesn't seem a bad thing that he's dead or can't move.

TEACHER: What is there about it that makes you feel that it's not bad?

CHILD: Because he says in the beginning it's like another life.

CHILD: He's putting it in different words; it's sort of like explaining something in different words.

TEACHER: Let me read this poem once again. I want you to see what the poet does to give you a certain feeling about this. *(She repeats the poem.)* What does he or she do to make this work?

CHILD: The way at the end where he says, "his life—over," without using the "is"; it sort of gives more feeling.

TEACHER: If I say to you, "His life is over," or "his life—over," the second one is stronger. Just by leaving out a word it sometimes makes it more powerful. What I'm asking is, "How is it possible for him to make you see that story in so few words?" What I mean is, poets are very economical; they don't use any words that aren't necessary.

CHILD: It could be that he's just lonely. It doesn't necessarily mean that he's dead. He just might not be doing anything, just sitting there.

TEACHER: What does the poet do that makes you feel that way?

CHILD: There's "life is" in the beginning of the poem and it ends with "life."

TEACHER: There isn't an "is" in the entire poem, which I think is remarkable.

CHILD: Also, in the beginning he says "life"; he's not living. . . .

TEACHER: "He does not live. . . ."

CHILD: And it's like saying that life is sort of like death, too.

TEACHER: If you don't what?

CHILD: If you don't really live it.

TEACHER: So this poem is telling you a feeling about something. I think you're beginning to see that a poem has to have some kind of built-in secret to it.

A TEACHING-LEARNING ENVIRONMENT

8

TEACHER AS
EDUCATOR-ARTIST

A Qualitative Approach to the Teaching–Learning Process

Engagement in the arts offers a particular challenge to teachers, for we are not dealing with subject matter and content in a conventional sense but in an entirely different context. At the beginning of this book we defined "subject" as the individual and "matter" as the education of feelings and the development of sensibilities. In a similar vein, we now consider that the content of the learning experiences lies in the responses of the children. What is suggested is an approach to the teaching–learning process which considers the feelings and sensibilities of teachers as well as children. It is because the art experience demands a very personal and even physical relationship (to children and media) that we conceive of a teacher as an educator-artist. The conceptual approach offered here is intended to open a teacher's perceptions to the complex and fascinating ways in which children become involved, and to the meanings in the arts themselves. We envision the nature of the process as being made up of two worlds—the child's and the teacher's—and where those worlds converge, learning usually takes place.

Perception and Participation

Therefore, a teacher needs to see herself not as one who "gives" art to children (as tourists "do" the Louvre), but as one who can open up windows on the

303

world to children as well as herself. A classroom teacher need not be a practicing artist in any of the forms discussed here, although her own participation as an adult for purely pleasurable reasons will heighten her own sensibilities. Because the arts have always been the stepchild of education, there are too few resources available for teachers seeking adjunctive educational experiences. Just as we have reported the responses of children to classroom experience, so may we note the responses of teachers who have participated in workshops conducted by the author in various parts of the country. They range from nursery to elementary schools, public and private, in suburban and inner-city communities.

- At first I felt I could not do any art work. Knowing that I didn't have to make "something" for anybody, I enjoyed working with the materials and I was quite surprised at my own accomplishment. It is important to be left alone and not to create to please someone else. Through these experiences I learned that children should not be disturbed while creating nor should they ever create to please someone else.

- I have not only derived great enjoyment from activities of this kind but also realized that I could teach it. There is a professional creative dance teacher at my school and I have always thought of it as "her area," but I realize that I can contribute, too.

- At the beginning I was very authoritarian and afraid to allow much freedom. As the year wore on, I found I had more control in a free situation than I had expected.

- I am still very unsure as I need to do more teaching in the arts. Obviously, children have varying abilities and there must be different criteria as to the performance of each child. I feel all children should be required to be present yet none should be *made* to participate.

The continuing lack of in-service training is doubly ironic in the light of current experimental studies aimed at introducing the arts in the classroom. Those designed to use packaged media or curriculum guides conclude that there are no "teacher-proof" materials, and reveal the need for more workshops and classes. Our thrust is also to integrate the arts more deeply into the classroom as essential ingredients of literacy. But we cannot conceive of a significant innovation in any educational program that does not have at its center the attitudes of the teacher. Because he is constantly called upon to make educational as well as aesthetic judgments, his beliefs, feelings, and expectations make up the ambience of the classroom and determine the quality of learning within it.

One of the unknowns in education is whether we are developing new capacities for creative efforts or are simply making it possible for a child's existing capacities to flourish and deepen. The old "nature–nurture" question as to whether creativity can be taught or summoned is not the issue here. Ultimately it is within the domain of the teacher to provide an environment that stimulates either condition. We favor the position that children learn to develop an "educated eye," a "listening ear," a "consciously rhythmical sense" because they are aware of what they do, and more importantly, of what they do that is exciting. It requires the sensitive presence of a teacher to provide experiences in keeping with their unfolding capacities. If we sit idly by and wait for such capacities to emerge, why should they come to school at all?

MAKING AESTHETIC JUDGMENTS

Children produce work which is both beautiful and banal. If no one is near to suggest the difference in terms of its qualitative aspects, they are less able to develop a perceptive eye so necessary in becoming a creator–performer–critic of their own work. As a result, they tend to rely heavily on the judgment of others, to imitate someone they think is "better" or even worse, they copy themselves. The delicate role of a teacher is to help children reach a balance (realizing that it may be constantly shifting) between being too satisfied with their work or never satisfied enough. In the first instance, it involves moving a child beyond what he already knows away from responses which tend to be stereotyped or repetitive. In the second, it is a question of making him aware and appreciative of his creative efforts by helping him understand that we are concerned with the "how" and "why," not the "right" and "wrong." Our feeling, then, is that growth is not enough, nor is environment, unless the teacher is considered an essential part of that environment.

PROVIDING FREEDOM WITHIN STRUCTURE

Creative teaching exists and can be observed. Far from letting children follow wherever their impulses lead them, however, the teacher must take responsibility for stimulating, guiding, channeling, and discussing—all of which involves a passionate commitment. It takes an open mind to be aware of a child's way of seeing the world, but it takes a disciplined mind to design experiences geared toward increasing his comprehension of reality without sacrificing the idiom of his own perceptions and transformations. The character and diversity of art and its experience accommodate a broad range of individual differences among children. What speaks for one child may not speak for another. Our intent in presenting these diverse art forms is to make a child aware of the relationships of the varied aspects of the total art experience. In so doing, we encourage him to communicate or express these relationships through forms which best speak for him. It is the individual child, rather than the medium, who ultimately determines the significance of the art experience. We provide alternatives because we recognize that his choice of forms emerges from his needs and potentialities.

More than a decade ago, Jerome Bruner asserted that "all intellectual activity anywhere is the same, whether at the frontier of knowledge or in a third grade classroom. . . . The difference is in degree, not in kind." [1] He offers the example that, "The schoolboy learning physics *is* a physicist, and it is easier for him to learn physics behaving like a physicist than doing something else." [2] In like manner, we say that a child engaged in the arts is an artist, and it is easier for him to learn while behaving like an artist than it is while behaving like a hobbyist. A teacher who behaves like a fellow artist can help bring this about.

Because investigation in the arts involves feeling as well as knowing, there is no age level which has a monopoly on such investigations. Regardless of age, background, or depth of experience, we all possess feelings. Considering a child's emotions and his need to give them form is no less valid than the same con-

---

[1] Jerome Bruner, *The Process of Education* (New York: Random House, 1960), p. 14.
[2] Ibid.

sideration is for an adult. With this conviction, a teacher can accept the child-artist as a fellow human being searching into the fundamental problems of the art process, with its attendant subjective aspects. Because the experience of giving form to feelings is largely determined by personal variables, a teacher certainly cannot predict what the finished product will be. For this reason, teaching in the arts must encourage search and inquiry, rather than demand explicit, predetermined solutions.

USING QUALITATIVE INTELLIGENCE

Thus, the teaching of art experiences requires the same kind of qualitative intelligence as the creative process itself. And because our underlying premise is that art is both child centered and content centered, we are also concerned with the qualitative changes in children's behavior, as well as the formal, expressive elements in an art form. We anticipate and encourage in children an expectant excitement in working with media and in forming something out of their imaginations. There is a satisfaction which comes from bringing something new into being and of seeing the results of their efforts and energies in tangible form. The satisfaction may be only momentary, for we cannot make children accountable for their fluctuating feelings, saying, for example, "You liked it yesterday, why don't you like it today?" At best, his ongoing efforts may merge and evolve into forms which speak to him in a most personal way in the sense of, "This tells me something about me." What we are sharing, then, is the excitement of the discovery.

9
CREATING AN ENVIRONMENT FOR THE ARTS

Setting the Scene

Introducing the arts in the classroom demands an alternative approach not only to learning but to an environment that supports and nurtures that learning. Recent investigations by educators as to why children do not learn, or even more serious, why they have no interest in learning, point to sources within a deprived environment, either cultural or sensory or both. We wonder where the label "culturally deprived" really belongs—to the child or to the educational environment? We know that although children have potential ability, they cannot create out of nothing. There must be things and relationships in the environment which can provide the impetus. Specifically, we are referring to the emotional climate created by the teacher in her role as teacher-artist, and to the nature of the learning experiences she presents to children. Thus, in order to call forth children's natural attributes and encourage them to develop a feeling of commitment toward what they are doing, the teacher must set the scene. Because the arts are an expressive phenomenon, the relationship between that expression and the environment in which it takes form is inseparable. Therefore, "setting the scene" involves considerations of space and time.

Space

Although we usually cannot select the shape and size of a room, we can control the components of space and time. A physical environment must be especially compatible with the arts, because they have their own physical requirements. Not only is the very process of working with them a physical act to the extent that all of the senses are involved, but we must submit to the physical demands of the medium itself. In any case, the problem becomes one of rearranging the classroom so that the working space and the amount of time are given equal consideration. We need to think of space in terms of how much is required for the comfortable execution of the experience itself and how much is necessary to allow a child to put distance between himself and another, and between himself and his work.

PAINTING

In the primary grades, for example, we frequently see easels placed so that children have to stand back to back. We might ask ourselves (if we have not already observed this), "What happens if both children step back at the same time?" Or, because wielding a brush is a kinesthetic as well as a visual action, "What gets painted if a child swings his arm over his shoulder?" Such spatial limitations impose a constriction on children and involve the inevitable peace-making efforts. The result is that energies are diverted into a discipline problem instead of toward an art experience.

SCULPTURE

Sculpture is itself three-dimensional and the heart of the process is working in the round. This tells us that the space which a child occupies must also be three-dimensional, in the sense that he must be able to walk around and see the piece from all sides. Whether painting, sculpting, or writing poetry, children cannot work effectively when sitting elbow to elbow. The art experience is active but it is also contemplative. Even very young children need space to stand away from their work to reflect upon what they have done and to entertain new ideas. In the same way, they need the physical freedom to move around the room either to get materials or to observe quietly the work of others. The effect is to stretch their minds as well as their legs.

POETRY

Poetry is perhaps the most private undertaking of all, yet it begins as a group experience. There is a kind of intimacy in sharing ideas that comes from sitting in a "poetry circle" or informally on the floor, where it is easy to look at and speak directly to one another. The place and space of writing depend on the flexibility of the teacher. If children are reciting their poems because writing is difficult and unduly time-consuming, teachers can best work with small groups in quiet corners of the room. Writing, however, requires a special kind of quiet, because children are listening to the words in their own heads. In deference to this, teachers may see fit to extend the working space beyond the classroom walls to another area, either inside or out, and, we hope, to the home.

DANCE

Of the arts described here, dance makes the greatest demand for space. In some schools, a gym or cafeteria is available, but in most cases, it is up to the classroom teacher literally to "push back the desks." [1] If the area selected is in the center of the room, the effect is of a stage in the round, which is fitting, because dance is three-dimensional. This is easily done if tables or desks are placed sideways along the walls, with chairs pushed underneath (inviting children to sit on the floor). However the area is defined, it must be ample enough for children to move at least in small groups at a time, so that there is a continuous alternation of participants and observers. Watching others grapple with similar problems helps to sharpen children's perceptions and offers them alternatives which they may absorb into their own movement studies. [For more detailed discussion on the dance environment, see Geraldine Dimondstein, *Children Dance in the Classroom* (New York: Macmillan, 1970).]

Although the arts are presented within the social milieu of the classroom, ultimately, each child is searching for his own expression. For this reason we need to provide freedom of movement for the active child as well as space for the solitary child to work uninterruptedly. In general, we want to establish a physical environment that permits the entire class to engage in shared experiences, depending on the nature of the problem, and that is conducive to children working in small groups and even alone.

TIME

Although we treat time as a physical dimension, we must also recognize that in the arts, it implies the opportunity for a child to work at his own rate of speed. The time it takes for the initial encounter with the problem and the duration of its execution varies with each child. Some children attack a problem immediately and seem to be able to organize ideas in a kind of ongoing way leading to a solution; others are slower and more tentative about beginning and work in spurts; still others begin quickly with a flash of ideas and a flush of enthusiasm and find that they are slowed down in bridging the gap between intent and execution. Along with these variations we must give thought to the traditional assumption that children need to be working all the time (or else they are "playing"). It is partly for this reason that we suggested that children have space to move around.

OBJECTIVE AND SUBJECTIVE CONSIDERATIONS

Just as we need to re-examine conventional ideas of order and disorder vis-à-vis freedom of movement (of both objects and children), so do we need to reconsider preconceived ideas about children's attention spans, especially those of young children. We tend to become proscribed by developmental theories

[1] Albert Cullum, *Push Back the Desks* (New York: Citation Press, 1967).

(usually drawn from areas other than the arts) and to use them as absolutes in determining our own schedules. We only know how much time a child can sustain and what he can do by allowing him to do it. The experience of the author in sharing perceptions with teachers and working with children is that when the latter are thoroughly engaged in an exploration, regardless of age, they tend to stay with it from thirty to ninety minutes.

Yet it falls to the teacher to allow an appropriate amount of time to encompass a bit of discussion, a lot of "doing," and some group evaluation. We qualify a "bit" of discussion because although we cannot talk a piece of art work into being, we can talk it out of existence. As has been seen in each of the prototype lessons in this book, the first part of each session is devoted to a brief introduction of concepts (either verbally or through a presentation of visual materials) in an open dialogue between students and teacher as to the nature of the problem and alternative ways of searching for solutions. It should also be noted that children are not encouraged to tell specifically what they are about to do. They may experience the vicarious excitement of creating in discussion, so much so that when actually working it out, their energies are dissipated and the results are uninspired.

Because time is such a subjective element, we need to take clues from children as to how much is appropriate for each learning experience. It is up to the teacher to effect a delicate balance. Too much time does not guarantee qualitative results (yet children should be given the option to take a break or even leave the scene), just as too little time may inhibit their ability to focus on or develop ideas. We are not interested in superficial exposure but in involvement. Thus, our consideration of the physical environment is in terms of how it looks and how it feels.

Concern as to how it looks raises a deeper question of, "Whose environment is it?" It is immediately evident upon entering a classroom as to whether it reflects the efforts of the children or the teacher. In the latter case, bulletin boards are decorated with carefully cut stencilled drawings of topical objects, depending upon the time of year—for example, the inevitable black cats on halloween, turkeys at Thanksgiving, Santa Claus at Christmas, bunnies at Easter, and so forth. Beyond this, they are usually replete with carefully lettered charts and schedules as moral and literal reminders of expected behavior.

If, on the other hand, the classroom reflects the creative efforts of children, space is not only given to bulletin boards but is extended throughout the room. For example, an ever-changing exhibition of paintings, sculpture, or poetry serves not only for group evaluations but for viewing by other classes. What is especially important is that whatever space is available, it include not only "good" work but all work. This is particularly valuable for those children who feel the need of some tangible evidence of success. But for all children, it sets up a world for children to observe based on their own production and their own perceptions.

10
VALUING CREATIVE EFFORTS

Expectations and Values

How do we evaluate in the arts? As teachers, we can only do so in relation to our own expectations and values. But before we can speak of evaluation, we need to reflect upon the goal stated at the beginning of this book. Within an educational context, we defined the purpose of the arts as the education of feelings and the development of sensibility. Because the subject of art is the individual, we expect that children, as individuals, will become more perceptive and more sensible through an involvement which engages both their minds and their senses—specifically, that they will become visually literate in painting and sculpture, become consciously rhythmical in dance, and develop expressive powers with language that will help them feel in words. We conceive of sensibility as the imaginative transformation of the qualitative elements of an art form leading to an awareness which is aesthetic.

Evaluation is the expectation of change. Therefore, we need to ask, "What shall be the nature of this change?" We anticipate a change that is more than a general awareness of experience. Rather, a child who charges his senses with the visual and tactile excitement of painting and sculpture, the expressive movements of dance, or the mind's-eye images of poetry is going far beyond the normal bounds of experience. We are suggesting that in a very practical as well as symbolic sense, he is extending the boundaries of his knowledge and his capacity for aesthetic experience.

311

WHAT IS SUCCESS?

Any evaluation requires that we make judgments as to what should be taught and what we deem are relevant learning experiences. Having taken the position that the arts are essential in the education of children, and having selected concepts and explorations that we feel are appropriate for children of all ages, we now turn to the question of what we are asking for in terms of children's artistic production. We know that we neither want nor expect every child to produce the same thing, for within our frame of reference, this would constitute "failure." How, then, do we regard "success"? In its broadest sense, success involves considerations of a child's own expectations and values toward his own production, what he produces, and how he does it. Such an assessment is much more difficult to make than in subject-matter areas of math, science, or history, because it is not a question of measuring his performance against conventional standards. Rather, the methods he uses and the knowledge he derives evolve out of very sensitive perceptions which he needs at a particular moment in space-time. Therefore, our evaluation is based on outcomes which are unpredictable.

Our purpose in teaching the arts is to open a child's sensibilities as well as his abilities. We function on the premise that all children can achieve some degree of success. We are not dealing with quantifiable, replicable data, nor are we training children to become professional artists, so what can we look to as the agent of change? Our expectations are based on the value judgment that it is better for children to become involved in the arts than not to become involved. Therefore, one of the things we are evaluating is the extent and depth of that involvement. Our criteria fall within two broad categories: a child's general participation in the various arts and the quality of his creative problem solving. In both cases, we view participation in terms of engagement and commitment.

QUALITY OF CHILDREN'S PARTICIPATION

The extent to which children participate is always a concern of the teacher, but it must be a concern for individuals, not for a show of numbers. The very nature of the creative process demands voluntary participation, because more is involved than responding to established patterns. This places greater responsibility upon a teacher, because she must establish a delicate balance in terms of her participation and judgments. Within a conceptual framework which offers a structure for ideas and feelings, the teacher's role is one of reducing constraints and expanding choices. At best, judgments are made in an atmosphere which stimulates free inquiry, individuality, and diversity. In an open area like the arts, we must be able to encourage the unanticipated and deal with it. Creative efforts are revealed most freely in a nonjudgmental atmosphere. However, "nonjudgmental" does not imply that we do not make judgments, but that anything is possible. That means that we encourage children to experiment, improvise, and even pursue unproductive avenues of exploration. It is important that the child be permitted to discover for himself those paths which prove unproductive in relation to what he is trying to express. As a child becomes aware that he has succeeded, in part, in making tangible an innermost feeling or idea, he begins to value himself as a creating, forming being.

It becomes evident that a teacher's participation is crucial. His or her commitment as teacher-artist is that he suggests directions but does not impose solutions. What we anticipate is that this kind of open-ended experience will lead children to a love of art and an appreciation of their own efforts. Therefore, we need also to bear in mind that if self-discovery is to be of value to a child, he must not rely solely upon the teacher. Even though she is available, she need not always be present to give assurance at each stage of the decision-making process. Each child must experience a certain amount of "aloneness" because of the highly personal nature of his thoughts and feelings. However, underlying this "aloneness" must be a feeling of mutual commitment between teacher and child. Children need to sustain their beliefs in their own intuitive feelings so that they are not looking to the teacher for the "right" answers, but to themselves for the pleasures of finding alternatives.

SHARED JUDGMENTS

This kind of involvement enables a child to share his judgments with his peers and, in his own way, to internalize the feelings and ideas embodied in their products. In any artistic effort, each child is creating his own work, yet he becomes aware that others are engaged in the same process. Through group evaluations and discussions, he learns the value of diversity in shared efforts. As an inevitable by-product, he comes to realize that there is no need to imitate or feel competitive about another's ideas, for no one's work is "better" than anyone else's; it is different.

This brings us back to the issue of how we determine "success." Because all paths of discovery move along uneven and sometimes inconsistent lines, teachers must realize that not all aspects of an arts program may be of interest to all children, nor that they will respond equally to different problems. As we do not recognize "failure" in the conventional sense, we judge each child according to where he is at any point in his creative growth, not from where we wish he might be. We take as an indication of this growth his ability to move beyond the forms of his most recent expression—that is, to push beyond his own boundaries. If he brings a form into being that is new to him and shows development in terms of where he was in the beginning, that is more important educationally than whether that response has ever occurred before. It is interesting for teachers to observe which children relate to what problems, with the understanding that there is more than one path to self-discovery. Familiarity with her own children is a necessary condition for the classroom teacher, for what she observes of children in other areas of the program provides insights for the arts. By the same token, a child's experiences in the arts reveal aspects of his personality which may not be reflected elsewhere. Again, the response to individual differences calls for sensitive judgments. Children who do not easily participate must be given their own time, yet they need to be encouraged by teachers as well as children to feel that they are involved, if only on a less active level.

Perhaps part of the magic of the mix of teacher and child, and child and child vis-à-vis evaluation, is that because there is no "right," there is no "wrong." Regardless of the kind of response offered or the level on which he is producing, he is never subject to the humiliation or embarrassment that comes with being judged against others. With ongoing evaluations throughout the year, children learn to evaluate what they are doing. Continuously and informally, they see themselves revealed by the objects and phenomena they produce, and the revelation is kept before their eyes at all time. Painting, sculpture, dance, and poetry become alternative modes through which the children see themselves and the world in new ways, and these become tangible sources of excitement.

We are concerned, then, with developing children's perceptions and abilities to evaluate their own work and the work of others critically. This kind of "critical perceiving" emerges out of a heightened sensibility, which relates once again to our major goal. To be effective in the education of the senses, our criteria are twofold: (1) an awareness of the *sensuous or qualitative elements* in the work—that is, the affective qualities of movement, color, line, rhythm, and so forth; and (2) the *expressive significance* of the work in terms of its emotional meaning. The effect of these criteria is to develop children's critical perceptions in the sense of understanding and appreciating aesthetic relationships not only in their own work, but in their environment.

THE CHILD AS CREATOR–PERFORMER–CRITIC

The approach suggested here is that children experience the creative thoughts and processes of an artist. What this involves is the responsiveness and perceptiveness of a creator or performer, and the critical judgments of an informed listener or observer. All of these experiences are imperative if children are to be given a depth of participation which allows for the development of sensibility. As a creator, performer, interpreter, and evaluator, a child grows from his own personal experience in judgment making within the complete spectrum of the art process. He will, we hope, become largely responsible not only for his intellectual and aesthetic growth, but also for the rate and direction of his own progress. Speaking of his experiences with elementary school children, Kenneth Koch writes, "Treating them like poets was not a case of humorous but effective diplomacy as I had first thought; it was the right way to treat them because it corresponded to the truth." [1] Thus, our assumption is that children need and want to express themselves, and must be given the right to do so.

[1] *Wishes, Lies, and Dreams* (New York: Chelsea House, 1970), p. 25.

BIBLIOGRAPHY

KNOWING AND FEELING

BRUNER, JEROME. *On Knowing: Essays for the Left Hand*. New York: Random House, 1960.

————. *The Process of Education*. Cambridge, Mass.: Harvard University Press, 1961.

DEWEY, JOHN. *Art as Experience*. New York: G. P. Putnam's Sons, 1958.

GHISELIN, BREWSTER. *The Creative Process*. New York: New American Library, 1955.

LANGER, SUZANNE K. *Feeling and Form*. New York: Charles Scribner's Sons, 1953.

————. *Problems of Art*. New York: Charles Scribner's Sons, 1957.

————. *Philosophy in a New Key*. New York: New American Library, 1964.

READ, HERBERT. *Education Through Art*. 3rd ed. London: Faber and Faber, Ltd., 1958.

TEACHING AND LEARNING

ASHTON-WARNER, SYLVIA. *Teacher*. New York: Bantam Books, 1963.

BLAND, JANE COOPER. *Art of the Young Child*. New York: Museum of Modern Art, 1968.

CULLUM, ALBERT. *Push Back the Desks*. New York: Citation Press, 1968.

EISNER, ELLIOT W. *Educating Artistic Vision.* New York: Macmillan Publishing Co., Inc., 1972.

FELDMAN, EDMUND. *Becoming Human Through Art.* Englewood Cliffs, N.J.: Prentice-Hall, Inc., 1970.

JAMESON, KENNETH. *Art and the Young Child.* New York: Viking Press, 1968.

LOWENFELD, VIKTOR. *Creative and Mental Growth,* 5th ed. New York: Macmillan Publishing Co., Inc., 1970.

MARSHALL, SYBIL. *An Experiment in Education.* Cambridge, England: Cambridge University Press, 1963.

SCHWARTZ, FRED R. *Structure and Potential in Art Education.* Waltham, Mass.: Ginn-Blaisdell, 1970.

WACHOWIAK, FRANK, and R. THEODORE. *Emphasis: Art,* 2nd ed. Scranton, Pa.: International Textbook Co., 1971.

PAINTING

ALBERS, JOSEPH. *The Interaction of Color.* New Haven, Conn.: Yale University Press, 1963.

ARNHEIM, RUDOLPH. *Art and Visual Perception.* Berkeley, Calif.: University of California Press, 1954.

GROHMANN, WILL. *Paul Klee.* New York: Harry N. Abrams, Inc., n.d.

LASSAIGNE, JACQUES. *Matisse.* New York: Skira, 1959.

——. *Miro.* New York: Skira, 1965.

SHAHN, BEN. *The Shape of Content.* Cambridge, Mass.: Harvard University Press, 1957.

SCULPTURE

American Sculpture of the Sixties. Los Angeles, Calif.: Los Angeles County Museum of Art, 1967.

KAHNWEILER, DANIEL H. *Les Sculptures de Picasso.* Paris: Les Editions du Chêne, 1948.

LIPCHITZ, JACQUES. Los Angeles, Calif.: Los Angeles County Museum of Art, 1967.

MOORE, HENRY. "Notes on Sculpture," in Brewster Ghiselin (ed.), *The Creative Process.* New York: New American Library, 1952.

READ, HERBERT. *The Art of Sculpture.* New York: Pantheon Books, 1956.

——. *Arp.* New York: Harry N. Abrams, Inc., 1968.

SCHNIER, JACQUES. *Sculpture in Modern America.* Berkeley, Calif.: University of California Press, 1948.

DANCE

DIMONDSTEIN, GERALDINE. *Children Dance in the Classroom.* New York: Macmillan Publishing Co., Inc., 1971.

FINDLAY, ELSA. *Rhythm and Movement* (Applications of Dalcroze Eurythmics). Garden City, N.Y.: Doubleday & Co., 1961.

HAWKINS, ALMA. *Creating Through Dance.* Englewood Cliffs, N.J.: Prentice-Hall, Inc., 1964.

HOOD, MARGUERITE. *Teaching Rhythm and Using Classroom Instruments.* Englewood Cliffs, N.J.: Prentice-Hall, Inc., 1970.

MURRAY, RUTH LOWELL. *Dance in Elementary Education.* New York: Harper & Row, 1963.

RUSSELL, JOAN. *Creative Dance in the Primary School.* New York: Frederick A. Praeger, 1968.

SHEETS, MAXINE. *The Phenomenology of Dance.* Madison, Wis.: University of Wisconsin Press, 1966.

CHILDREN'S SONGS AND GENERAL COLLECTIONS

BAILEY, CHARITY. *Sing a Song with Charity Bailey.* New York: Plymouth Music Co., Inc., 1955.

BONI, MARGARET B., and N. LLOYD. *Fireside Book of Folk Songs.* New York: Simon and Schuster, 1947.

————. *Favorite American Songs.* New York: Simon and Schuster, 1956.

GLAZER, TOM. *A New Treasury of Folk Songs.* New York: Bantam Books, 1961.

JENKINS, ELLA. *This Is Rhythm.* New York: Oak Publications, n.d.

————. *The Ella Jenkins Song Book for Children.* New York: Oak Publications, 1966.

KRUGMAN, LILLIAN D., and ALICE J. LUDWIG. *Little Calypsos.* New York: Carl Van Roy Co., 1955.

————. *Song Tales of the West Indies.* New York: Carl Van Roy Co., 1955.

LANDECK, BEATRICE. *Songs to Grow On.* New York: Marks-Sloane, 1950.

————. *More Songs to Grow On.* New York: Marks-Sloane, 1954.

————. *Echoes of Africa.* New York: David McKay Co., Inc., 1961.

LOMAX, JOHN, and ALAN LOMAX. *Folk Song, USA.* New York: Signet Books, 1966.

SEEGAR, RUTH CRAWFORD. *American Folk Songs for Children.* Garden City, N.Y.: Doubleday & Co., 1948.

SIEGMEISTER, ELIE. *Treasury of American Folk Songs.* New York: Alfred A. Knopf, Inc., 1943.

Weavers Song Book. New York: Harper & Row, 1960.

YURCHENCO, HENRIETTA. *A Fiesta of Folk Songs from Spain and Latin America.* New York: G. P. Putnam's Sons, 1967.

POETRY

CIARDI, JOHN. *How Does a Poem Mean?* Boston: Houghton Mifflin Co., 1959.

ELIOT, T. S. *The Music of Poetry.* Glasgow, Scotland: Jackson, Son & Co., 1942.

HOUSMAN, A. E. *The Name and Nature of Poetry*. Cambridge: Cambridge University Press, 1950.

KOCH, KENNETH. *Wishes, Lies, and Dreams*. New York: Chelsea House Publishers, 1970.

LEWIS, C. DAY. *The Poet's Way of Feeling*. Cambridge: Cambridge University Press, 1957.

————. *The Poetic Image*. London: Jonathan Cape, 1958.

MEARNES, HUGHES. *Creative Power*. New York: Dover Publications, 1958.

READ, HERBERT. *Forms of Things Unknown*. New York: World Publishing Co., 1963.

POETRY COLLECTIONS

BARNSTONE, ALIKI. *Real Tin Flower*. New York: Crowell Collier, 1968.

BEHN, HARRY (trans.). *Cricket Songs* (Haikus). New York: Harcourt Brace Jovanovich, Inc., 1964.

DUNNING, S., E. LEUDERS, H. SMITH. *Reflections on a Gift of a Watermelon Pickle*. New York: Lothrop, Lee, & Shephard, 1967.

ELIOT, T. S. *Old Possom's Book of Practical Cats*. New York: Harcourt Brace Jovanovich, Inc., 1939.

GIOVANNI, NIKKI. *Spin a Soft Black Song*. New York: Hill and Wang, 1971.

GROSVENOR, KALI. *Poems by Kali*. Garden City, N.Y.: Doubleday & Co., 1970.

HUGHES, LANGSTON. *Don't You Turn Back*. New York: Alfred A. Knopf, Inc., 1959.

KEEGAN, MARCIA K. *Only the Moon and Me*. Philadelphia: J. B. Lippincott Co., 1969.

LEWIS, CLAUDIA. *Poems of Earth and Space*. New York: E. P. Dutton & Co., 1967.

LEWIS, RICHARD. *Miracles*. New York: Simon & Schuster, 1966.

O'NEILL, MARY. *Hailstones and Halibut Bones*. Garden City, N.Y.: Doubleday & Co., 1961.

SMITH, WILLIAM JAY. *Mr. Smith and Other Nonsense*. New York: Delacorte Press, 1968.

TALBOT, TOBY. *Coplas—Folk Poems in Spanish and English*. New York: Four Winds Press, 1972.

INDEX

319